Triptych

Three Studies Of Manic Street Preachers' The Holy Bible

Rhian E. Jones
Daniel Lukes
Larissa Wodtke

16pt

Copyright Page from the Original Book

Published by Repeater Books
An imprint of Watkins Media Ltd

19–21 Cecil Court
London
WC2N 4EZ
UK
www.repeaterbooks.com
A Repeater Books paperback original 2017
1

Distributed in the United States by Random House, Inc., New York.

Copyright © Rhian E. Jones, Daniel Lukes, and Larissa Wodtke 2017

Rhian E. Jones, Daniel Lukes, and Larissa Wodtke assert the moral right to be identified as the authors of this work.

Cover design: Johnny Bull
Typography and typesetting: K.DESIGN, Winscombe, Somerset
Typefaces: Chaparral Pro & AG Old Face

ISBN: 978-1-910924-98-3
Ebook ISBN: 978-1-910924-89-1

All rights reserved. No part of this publication may be reproduced, stored in a retrieval system, or transmitted, in any form or by any means, electronic, mechanical, photocopying, recording or otherwise, without the prior permission of the publishers.

This book is sold subject to the condition that it shall not, by way of trade or otherwise, be lent, re-sold, hired out or otherwise circulated without the publisher's prior consent in any form of binding or cover other than that in which it is published and without a similar condition including this condition being imposed on the subsequent purchaser.

TABLE OF CONTENTS

PART I : Unwritten Diaries: History, Politics and Experience through The Holy Bible   1

   CHAPTER 1 : Leaving the Twentieth Century   3
   CHAPTER 2 : Prologue to History   31
   CHAPTER 3: Epilogues of Youth   69
   CHAPTER 4: New Moral Saviours   99
   CHAPTER 5: Archives of Pain   131
   CHAPTER 6: Images of Perfection   165
   CHAPTER 7 : Won't Die of Devotion   190

PART II : Fragments Against Ruin: The Books of Manic Street Preachers' The Holy Bible   219

   CHAPTER 1 : Comfort Comes   221
   CHAPTER 2 : Reading Too Much into The Holy Bible   234
   CHAPTER 3 : Against Literature: Therapy?'s "Potato Junkie"   243
   CHAPTER 4 : A Heap of Broken Images: T.S. Eliot's The Waste Land   247
   CHAPTER 5 : Holocaust Pop: The Holy Bible's Nazi Materials   256
   CHAPTER 6 : Sylvia Plath: Holocaust and Self   263
   CHAPTER 7 : The Industrial Holy Bible   276
   CHAPTER 8 : Foucault: Archives of Pain   286
   CHAPTER 9 : Spectacles of Suffering: The Third Man   301
   CHAPTER 10 : Unrequited Love in The Torture Garden   305
   CHAPTER 11 : Unmanifesto: Selby and the Christing of the Miserable Self   313
   CHAPTER 12 : What a Fantastic Death Exit 2: David Bowie's Outside   330
   CHAPTER 13 : Depressive Realism, Militant Depression: Lars Von Trier's Melancholia   338
   CHAPTER 14 : Ballads of the Sad Young Man: Richey Haunts   342
   CHAPTER 15 : Books about Richey I   353

- CHAPTER 16 : Books about Richey II   356
- CHAPTER 17 : Interview with Richard Author Ben Myers   360
- CHAPTER 18 : Dying in the Summertime: Purity's Doomed Romance   378
- CHAPTER 19 : Literal Castrations: Valerie Solanas   385
- CHAPTER 20 : Art: Site of the Body-Disaster: J.G. Ballard   392
- CHAPTER 21 : The Hokey Bible: Laughter in The Holy Bible   401
- CHAPTER 22 : If Bible America   405
- CHAPTER 23 : The Bible as Literature   409
- CHAPTER 24 : The Unbearable Whiteness of The Holy Bible   413
- CHAPTER 25 : A Portrait of the Artist as an Old Man: The Dresser   416
- CHAPTER 26 : Why I Hated the Wildhearts (and the Boo Radleys)   422
- CHAPTER 27 : "Dancing in the Moonlight"   427
- CHAPTER 28 : Hopelessness   428

PART III : Architecture of Memory: The Holy Bible and the Archive   443
- CHAPTER 1 : Past Presence, or Forever Delayed   444
- CHAPTER 2 : Archive of Pain   454
- CHAPTER 3 : Archive Fever   514
- CHAPTER 4 : Archive Retraced   553
- CHAPTER 5 : Rewind, Fast Forward, or Retro-Futurism   592

Selected Bibliography   633
Repeater Books   639
Index   641

Manic Street Preachers are an education. No other popular artist of the last quarter-century has done more to inspire academic investigation, whether as an active catalyst (the innumerable cultural, political and historical references in the Manics' lyrics and record sleeves; the much-vaunted "Richey reading list") or as passive subject matter themselves (as a case study in Trojan Horse entryism; as an example of the interplay of authenticity and artifice, and so on).

My own 1999 biography, *Everything (A Book About Manic Street Preachers)*, has itself been the topic of several theses, adding yet another layer to this sediment of meta-texts. At the time that I wrote it, I knew that mere dates and facts could never adequately convey the Manics' importance, so I interrupted the narrative with a series of essays on various aspects of the band, connecting them to broader cultural themes (an approach heavily influenced by American writer Greil Marcus).

In *Triptych,* Rhian E. Jones, Daniel Lukes and Larissa Wodtke take that process even further, zooming in on just one album—*The Holy Bible*—with a microscopic intensity that modern rock writing rarely, if ever, attains. (That's largely because this isn't "rock writing", *per se*. Not in the traditional, hack sense anyway. It is academic writing of the highest calibre. By which I mean, incidentally, that among all its other qualities, it is unfailingly *readable,* and not prone to deliberate obfuscation.)

That *The Holy Bible* is the Manics' masterpiece is beyond question (though one writer in *Triptych* does directly question that description.) It isn't only their greatest album, but one of the greatest albums ever made: I personally place it on a pedestal alongside Bowie's *Low* and Public Enemy's *It Takes A Nation Of Millions To Hold Us Back.*

The exact reasons for its greatness are illuminated with intimidating vividness here. *Triptych* (the title, of course, being a pun on *The Holy Bible*'s tripartite cover art, *South Face/Front Face/North Face* by Jenny Saville) consists of three mutually-complementary essays, each shining a searchlight onto the album from a different angle.

Rhian E. Jones, herself a product of the same South Wales mining valleys as the Manics, places the band in their correct socio-historical context, frequently (but never self-indulgently) using first-person reminiscences to illustrate her argument. As singular and jarring as *The Holy Bible* may have seemed in the post-political, carnivalesque Britain of 1994, Jones' chapter demonstrates that it did not simply drop, unannounced and fully-formed, from a clear blue sky, nor even slate-grey one.

Daniel Lukes begins from the intriguing perspective of an outsider who failed, at first, to recognise the fellow outsiders in the Manics. He then proceeds to apply lit-crit techniques to what is, lest we forget, "just" a rock record, taking the "Richey reading list" to an extreme by venturing deep into the works of Eliot, Mirbeau, Selby, Plath and a host of others. There is, he tacitly acknowledges, a danger that immersing oneself in the Manics' cultural diet is not always healthy: one section, with lovely self-awareness, is titled "Reading Too Much into *The Holy Bible*".

Larissa Wodtke's contribution, perhaps the most poetic of the three in style, makes the case that *The Holy Bible* functions as a kind of aural museum (there is, one is reminded, a reason why we call such artefacts "a record") that would come to define the band's every action in the decades since its release. Her deconstruction of the album's lyrics is forensic and fascinating.

Any intellectual analysis of popular music inevitably lays itself open to mockery from those who have yet to shake off the straitjacket of received notions of "high" and "low" culture. (Dare to take pop seriously as an art form and a cultural force, and an appearance in *Private Eye*'s Pseuds Corner column is an occupational hazard.) But such concerns should be cast aside, especially when dealing with Manic Street Preachers, who reward deep thought more than any other band of their generation.

The very best music writing offers the reader hitherto-unconsidered ways of listening, and new ways of thinking about pop. *Triptych* achieves that, in considerable style. It's an insane book, whose very existence seems improbable and odds-defying. The closest comparison is perhaps *Invisible Republic* by the aforementioned Greil Marcus, a book about just one album, *The Basement Tapes* by Bob Dylan (one of the few artists to inspire as much academic endeavour as the Manics). Then again, *The Holy Bible* is an insane, improbable, odds-defying album.

Triptych is a book I wish I'd written, while knowing, deep down, that I never could. I'm grateful that someone else has, or to be exact, that three other someone-elses have.

Simon Price, 2016

PART I

Unwritten Diaries: History, Politics and Experience through The Holy Bible

RHIAN E. JONES

To Kasper, Emily, Sara and Siân

CHAPTER 1

Leaving the Twentieth Century

"There are parts of the country where the 90s didn't happen, they just passed in a slow iron-grey drag, and though I've never been there I imagine Blackwood in South Wales might have been like that too. It's not poverty these places have in common, it's the sulkily self-sufficient feeling of not mattering: the sing-song accents, the patches on the jackets, the dead industries, the endless guesthouses that used to be farmhouses, the metal on the radio – all one side of a timeless equation of which the other is metropolitan contempt."

– Tom Ewing, *freakytrigger.co.uk*

"We've got to be understood in the context of where we've come from. We really have."

– Nicky Wire

WORKING-CLASS CLICHÉS START HERE

All unhappy provincial towns are both alike and unhappy in their own way. Richey Edwards famously claimed that if you built a museum to represent the Manics' home turf of Blackwood, "all you could put in it would be shit. Rubble and shit." In the moribund middle of the 1990s, a short enough trek from 80s Blackwood, the only place in my own town which sold records was Woolworths, which had the Top Forty on cassette and little more. In August 1994 I entered the white strip-lit aisles, tense with trepidation, and tried to preorder a copy of *The Holy Bible* by Manic Street Preachers. My enquiry was met with the same look of horror-struck uncertainty with which my mother, that same year, asked me whether I'd been in a punch-up—I hadn't, my Rimmel eyeshadow palette and I were in our ill-advised experimental period, but the mistake was understandable.

Like all such teenagers, I was ludicrous and insufferable. When I look back on my teenage years I remember wanting to escape them, and the 90s, as quickly as humanly possible. My adolescence felt like being stuck on a train station platform, bags packed, waiting in vain for my ride out to arrive. The 90s were a shapeless, watery, self-indulgent decade, still waiting to be plumbed for meaning in any notable depth. Following the fall of the Berlin Wall, history had apparently ended, which raised the question of what on earth we were meant to do from here on in. In small-town post-industrial non-Camden Britain, before mass internet access, 1994 was another world, another planet. Living through the decade as a teenager felt like being kept in a holding pattern with no hope of coming in to land—as though you were, as a Super Furry Animals song of 1996 had it, constantly "Waiting to Happen."

Both I and the Manics grew up under the shadow cast by the year-long Miners' Strike of 1984–5. There had of course been any amount of miners' strikes during the Welsh coalfield's two-hundred-year history, but the Miners' Strike usually gets those capitals, and certainly deserves them. This particular strike—the Big One—was iconic and historic, and came to symbolize some of the decade's defining themes: Thatcherism's triumph over the country's trade unions, the demise of the country's old heavy-manufacturing order, and the abandoning of much of the country to the vagaries of a post-industrial economy. James Dean Bradfield juxtaposed the experience of growing up during the strike with developing the knowledge of hatred:

> We set ourselves the rule that we would never write a love song because we just felt that everybody knew what it was like to fall in love, and everybody knew what it was like to have a broken heart, but not everybody necessarily knew what it was like to hate something or to really hate somebody. I just think we are of our environment, wherever we come from. Just when we were getting into music, at about fourteen or fifteen, the

Miner's Strike was going on right on our doorstep. That really affected our whole community and everything. Sometimes, you know, you're just part of the circumstances that surround you.

(qtd in JereC7)

The Manics were in at the death of coalmining; I grew up in the graveyard. By the time of *The Holy Bible,* ten years after the strike, a de-unionized and privatized industry had been turned into either museums, or rubble and shit:

> On Friday nights in the Welsh valleys, miners go from pub to pub hunting for their employers to claim unpaid wages. Pay cheques bounce, mining companies close and re-open under other names, men are sacked for being union members or refusing to work on Christmas Day [...] Dotted around the wreckage of the South Wales coalfield, mining heritage museums are opening up on the sites of former collieries, where visitors can go underground to see re-creations of the horrific conditions in which miners toiled in

the early years of this century. In working private pits nearby, the re-creations are for real.

(qtd in Milne)

Growing up somewhere so solidly, triumphantly bleak, made you solidly cynical. We spent the 90s being assured, by politicians, media and popular culture, that we were All Middle-Class Now. We were told the 90s were post-ideological, when what was meant was post-socialist. We were told the battles of the 80s had been won, but we were conscious that we'd been on the losing side—and that, as losers, we weren't meant to still be hanging around and getting in the winners' way. For those of us the 80s left bereft of jobs and prospects, in the 90s the listless, frustrated boredom of adolescence just kept dragging on. In 1994 my teenage world was turning with excruciating slowness. I wanted something stripped down and sped up, songs that had the sharpness of neat spirits. Something to blow away the dust I dreaded settling upon my brain and body.

PERPETUALLY STUCK IN A SEPIA FILM

Anwen Crawford: "We lived in a part of Sydney that I think we intuitively sensed was analogous to the Welsh valleys: the part of Sydney with a long and severe stigma attached to it, the part of Sydney that the rest of Sydney regards as trash ... I see the expression on people's faces, to this day, if I tell them which part of Sydney I'm from: a quick mixture of surprise and distaste. People hated us, and we hated them for hating us, for presuming that we were idiots. We got the Manics, even though we were on the other side of the world."

The music writer Steven Wells described the Manics as a speed band in an E age; for me they were also colour in an age of grey. Growing up where I did, I felt like I'd been defeated before I even began. There was, for most of us, no thought of getting out—due not to an absence of intelligence or imagination or talent or drive, but due to a lack of direction for any of it, and a lack of faith that any of it would get us anywhere. So you may imagine how it felt to discover a band, close-knit since childhood, defiantly dressing ridiculous, wrapped in fake fur and glaring at the world through thick black kohl, not so much taking refuge in the past as weaponizing it and making declarations like: "Our romance is based on where we come from and the desire to escape ... Our romance is having total power because we know we have nothing to lose. We're secure in the knowledge that we already lost a long time ago" (qtd in Forrest, "Cut"). The Manics made me aware that I—and they—had company and comrades both in history and the here and now, however out of step and out of time I felt. Other people had thought these things before, and felt this same discontent with what their world had to offer. They made me aware of a way out, a way of moving on, where otherwise I was offered only stasis and stagnation.

In 1994 I was more or less the only Manics fan I knew. Too young to be there from the start—and didn't I know it—I'd read the lyrics to "From Despair to Where" in the unlikely setting of *Smash Hits* one damp spring afternoon, and the rest was history. To relieve my teenage boredom I now had, besides alcohol, the cultural resources that came with being a Manics fan: the discussions they inspired in fanzines and exchanges in the letters pages of the music press, their stacks of recommended reading and listening. The more I expanded my horizons through reading, the more dissatisfied I grew with the surroundings I was stuck in, and the more I listened to the music of the past the more frustrated I grew with its present pale imitations. I seemed to have chosen the worst possible band to become obsessed with, and the worst possible time to become obsessed with them. Not only was the first Manics album I'd bought the critically panned and over-slick *Gold Against the Soul,* but the drama and damage surrounding the band in the summer of 1994 seemed to suggest there was no guarantee they would even manage to drag themselves on after a third album that looked set to be their last.

Summer's promise was epic, immense—six weeks of school holiday, when they began, they seemed like they wouldn't, couldn't end. But before too long, summer dragged. Summer was static. Summer held you in suspension. I spent the summer of 1994 being primed to hear *The Holy Bible* by the music press, who mediated and magnified the band's internal crises. For me and others like me—small-town, provincial or suburban kids beyond the pale of London's bright lights, gazing wide-eyed on stories of the gig-circuit—the weekly music press served as a channel of cultural discovery. Every Wednesday lunchtime saw me, lower lip bitten with anticipation, heading into town to snag the latest issues of *Melody Maker* and *NME;* our newsagent stocked all of three copies, and I never found out who, if anyone, bought the others. Back then the music press existed for a constituency that the mainstream didn't cater for or even really recognize; in

April 1994, I read the death of Nirvana's Kurt Cobain reported in a few column inches on page nine of the *Daily Mirror,* as though such news had little to interest anyone who might be reading. I had to wait for the *NME* front cover with its black and white picture of Cobain—that iconic eyelinered thousand-yard-stare—which treated the death as an image to stamp on the decade, a way of ascribing meaning to a meaningless time.

Kurt was becoming a secular saint, but, for me and for much of the music press, the overriding iconography of 1994 was that of Richey Edwards: hollow-eyed and hollow-cheeked, his sharp words softly spoken, his skin scattered with scars, tattoos and cigarette burns, apparently attempting to purify his flesh through mortification like an early Christian martyr. The high drama of that summer—rumours of suicide, breakdown and breakup, hospitalization, potential collapse and implosion—saw the Manics play two festivals without their guitarist. In July it was announced that he was suffering from that time-honoured catch-all, "nervous exhaustion," and would be taking a break from the band.

Shortly afterwards, in the run-up to the album's release, the music press published its lyric sheet as a promotional double-page spread. The spread was full of blanked-out words, black bars on white, making it look like a chessboard. I thought it might be some kind of fill-in-the-blank puzzle, some kind of tease. It took me some time to realize that what was blanked out was every instance of profanity in the lyrics. On the album, presumably, all this would be unhidden, uncensored, unapologetic. I couldn't wait to hear it. Late in August, I returned to Woolworths and left this time in triumph, *The Holy Bible* clutched under my coat like a samizdat publication. The album dropped into the summer of 1994 and split it open with the force of a depth charge.

REVOLUTION REVOLUTION REVOLUTION REVOLUTION

Phil Bird: "I can remember Faster coming out, it being

dismissed on some 'Jukebox jury' type show on GLR – 'they're good – but you can't really hear the words,' I remember the video (probably from the ITV chart show) and Top of the Pops and just being blown away by it. I was only twelve and don't think I really got it completely, but there was just something about the combination of music and slogans that drew me in. It wasn't like everything else."

History, of course, has a habit of not ending, and certainly hadn't ended in the 90s. It's curious how bored I felt, given how much was going on under the end-of-history radar. The early 90s saw riots in Los Angeles, the splintering of Yugoslavia, and, closer to home, the dismantling of the Labour Party's reason for existing. As some things fell apart, other things were brought together: in August 1994, the IRA declared a unilateral ceasefire which would last until 1996. Two months before this, the summer of 1994 kicked off with a jamming of the BBC's switchboard with over 25,000 outraged calls—still a record number—following the appearance on its chart showcase *Top of the Pops* of a man in a black balaclava, which many offended viewers interpreted as a showing of paramilitary solidarity. For me, the balaclava's arguable menace was fatally undermined by the fact that someone had scrawled "JAMES" across it in white paint, as though his Mam had sought to guard against anyone else mistakenly picking it up from the school cloakroom.

James Dean Bradfield—for it is he—fronted a startling performance of the album's lead single "Faster," its outrageous impact apparently owing to the militant chic in which he chose to dress, but surely also something to do with the eruption into living rooms across the land of a song which goes on to paraphrase Goebbels, Hesse, and Orwell over Sean Moore's implacable drums and a scree of speed-metal guitar. The whole spectacle—the scything solo, the military regalia, the final *so damn easy to cave in/man kills everything* spat out in brutal staccato—was exhilarating. I felt drunk on it. I knew I had chosen to waste my time in pretentious and preposterous obsession with exactly the right band. The Manics were due to reappear on a subsequent week, but after this performance they were, as Nicky Wire recalled with characteristic archness, "overlooked, shall we say."

Mark Patience: "In the run up to the [2014] Holy Bible tour I would listen to the album on the bus both to and from work every day. I would sit with the lyrics displayed on my phone and really try to make sense of what I was listening to. I found that the album started to get under my skin and into my psyche in a way it hadn't previously. I found [the lyrics] to be bleakly depressing in tone yet somehow that didn't translate across to how I felt when I listened to the album."

Although Mark Patience became a fan of *The Holy Bible* retrospectively, my engagement with the album twenty years earlier was very like what he describes. *The Holy Bible* was its own country, with a language you needed to learn in order to cross the border. The album taught me words I didn't know, mostly in order to describe it adequately. I needed words like "scabrous" and "abrasive" to pin down its peculiar atmosphere, to express its tension and its claustrophobia, to do justice to Bradfield's furniture-chewing Rottweiler growl. The music felt frantic, jagged, viciously melodic. Guitars prowled and skittered, lashing like the tail of a cornered animal or buzzing like a trapped cloud of flies. And the lyrics! Still a Burroughsian cut-up as on previous albums, still a plethora of namechecks, allusions, politics and history illuminating a world beyond my own—but somehow concentrated and distilled here, and individually focused rather than the scattergun sloganeering they had previously spread interchangeably over several songs.

The album was, at last, not static and not stuck. It was something fast, unstable and unstoppable. It was speed metal, metal and speed. At times its pace felt breakneck, like something unravelling—the headlong slalom of "Revol," the skittering plunge of "P.C.P."—but you didn't want it to slow down. There was a thrill in hanging on for the ride, when so much of my teenage years had been spent chafing at the bit, awaiting the point at which I could pull away and see how fast this thing could go. I may have been moving only inside my head, clinging onto the music, but I was moving at a dazzling, desperate speed.

The definitive 90s troubadour Noel Gallagher, departing recession-struck Manchester via the time-honoured escape route of strapping on a guitar and playing some rock 'n' roll, wanted his band's debut album to sound "like an aeroplane taking off." *Definitely Maybe,* also released in 1994, has come to instantly define the decade, but its escapist trajectory was an optimistic and naïvely uplifting one. *The Holy Bible,* equally definitive, offered a different escape route—one whose end might be a brick wall or an unknowable void. Keeping this possibility in plain sight, I took the road out anyway.

TARNISHED GLITTER

At last, just as it seemed they never would, the 90s ended. What did it mean to leave the twentieth century? Despite the personal crisis represented by *The Holy Bible,* the band's trajectory had taken them from despair to triumph via the critical and commercial success of "A Design for Life" and their consequent establishment as a respectable, credible outfit. Accepting awards for Best Band and Best Album at the 1997 Brits before performing "A Design for Life," the band dedicated their win to "every comprehensive school in Britain which the government is trying to eradicate."

In February 1997, rock guitarist *manqué* Tony Blair was still the Leader of the Opposition, though the election which would deliver his tamed New Labour a landslide victory was only months away. Although the decade was already more than half over, in many respects what we think of as the 90s had not even begun. The Manics' critical and commercial victories—and, more significantly, their politicization of them—were a reminder of the band's particular brand of working-class identity, rooted in a tradition of escapism and aspiration through education, which had long been absent from both politics and pop culture. In the last days of John Major's frayed and decaying Conservative government, it was easy to hear this as the opening shot in a battle that would take back the country. The Manics' own attitude, as expressed in "A Design for Life," was one of typically few illusions, the white-hot irony of the chorus an epitaph for the scorned and neglected industrial working class from which the band had come. ("I don't think we're Old Labour," mused Wire at a later date. "More Classic Labour.") The Blairite 90s—only three years to Major's seven—were enough to sweep away the grey in a flood of glorious, vacuous Technicolor, but Blair went on to prove the sceptics right.

Almost three years later, New Year's Eve 1999 offered a multitude of ways to mark one's leaving of the twentieth century. The country's official Millennium celebrations were generally agreed to be a predictably embarrassing waste of money. In London on the windswept Greenwich peninsula, a white elephant of a Dome arose, its business-friendly contents marketed as an antidote to

Britain's "damaged culture, low self-esteem, shrinking pride and a diminishing position in the world" and—rather remarkably, after that litany—as a statement of "optimism for the future." Initially a Conservative project, the Dome was meant to cater to a perceived popular need for "the sense of congregation, of coming together" (Weight 692). The fact that such a collectivist need could be identified by a Conservative Home Secretary demonstrated how glaringly apparent the damage done by 80s individualism was by the end of the 90s. That longing for congregation and coming together had in fact been manifested throughout the decade in the struggles to maintain the free party scene, the rave and techno gatherings in contravention of the Criminal Justice Bill, the crowds at Oasis' mass gig at Knebworth, and the public hysteria over the death of the Princess of Wales. Ultimately though, these were popular and semi-spontaneous, largely autonomous gatherings; they could not be imposed and directed from above. We might have wanted to get loaded and have a good time, on Millennium Eve as on any other occasion, but we objected strongly to being told to do so.

The corporate cynicism and political incompetence that characterized the Millennium Dome generated apathy, mockery and hostility rather than an optimistic coming together. The kind of congregation we appeared to be seeking was more happily fulfilled, on the same night, by the Manics' sold-out and celebratory gig in Cardiff's Millennium Stadium. For me, the night proceeded as the best nights do: drinking in successively degenerating venues (City Arms, Yates' Wine Lodge, Wetherspoons, and eventually the doorway of McDonalds at dawn), reaching the stadium by following the trails of shed glitter and moulted pink boa feathers that covered the streets. Scrubbed-up and sanitized, millennial Cardiff already felt a world away from how it had in the early 90s, in a nation that, after devolution, seemed very far away from being "British." Cardiff's newfound confidence and cool did not necessarily extend to the rest of Wales, especially the still-deprived Valleys, but things felt steadier and more sorted in comparison to an England which felt increasingly confused and resentful, uncertain of its status in a way that the branding-exercise of Cool Britannia had done nothing to resolve. The Millennium Stadium was full to capacity and the gig had much in common with the rugby matches it normally hosted—except, perhaps, that while victory for the Welsh rugby team is exceptional and rarely expected, for the Manics triumph seemed assured. The gig was both communion and homecoming.

By the turn of the millennium, I had made my getaway. I was in London, at university, immersed in activism, study and the city. I no longer defined myself by my status as a Manics fan, due to their changes and my own, to divergent interests, to other bands, to a run of mediocre albums that said little to me about my life. We had drifted apart like embarrassed exes after an intense teenage fling, but returning for this gig was automatic, an irresistible reunion. I found myself happy to coast for an evening rather than restlessly waiting to speed away.

WHOLE DAYS THROWING STICKS INTO STREAMS

Berry Jordan: "Between 1996 and 1998 I listened daily/weekly and photocopied lyrics, cut them out or drew them out and plastered them on my wall. It's funny if you ask if I listen regularly, no I don't, occasional tracks by chance – they just cast me back to a time of smoking, or talking about politics and the situation a lot, of raging against the machine a bit. From that period there are albums (most actually) that I would never listen to again but I would happily listen to The Holy Bible *because it stands up like a monument. It's so strong, even if its ideas and ideals would date it now, it was still incredible at the time. Shocking, political, harsh and that was what was brilliant and refreshing about it."*

Jeremy Deller: "[The Manics' fanbase] was exactly as I expected, which is a community in itself. But now with the internet it's much easier to really feel part of something. Before it was fanzines, letters, maybe phone calls, but now of course it's something else. So maybe it's about something that has disappeared."

(qtd in Pyzik "Orgreave")

Manic Street Preachers were my first experience of fandom, although I wouldn't have called it "fandom" at the time. The 90s are a decade with little online record, and it can be difficult to reconstruct the texture of 90s fandom, particularly compared to the level of activity now possible among contemporary fans. For me at least, fandom was based around the weekly music press, fanzines, sleeve art, gigs—physical and tangible things, rather than virtual and more or less instant communication. Today bedrooms, via laptops, can contain the entire world, but in 1994 my bedroom was small, stifling and static. Then as now, being fans of a band inspired individuals to create and communicate, overcoming atomization, isolation and alienation—but everything happened in slow-motion. The time between tours could stretch to years, and the weeks or months between dispatching small change and a self-addressed envelope to some obscure provincial address and getting back a fanzine or a bootleg recording, or the point after sending in a letter to the music press, awaiting its possible publication, could hold you in unbearable suspense.

The fandom when I knew it was also based around running off and sleeping in bus stations to follow tours, spending whole days or even weeks in ritual preparation for gigs: spray-painting and stencilling charity-shop shirts, planning cross-country journeys while plastering on eyeliner, whiling away the queuing time drinking own-brand vodka from the bottle. Taping the occasional gems of the Top Forty onto blank cassette, capturing *Top of the Pops* performances for posterity on shaky VHS. *Communiqués* and bedroom manifestos. The music press, too, was a forum for debate and disagreement and for finding comradeship, whether with the bands featured, the writers of letters or the journalists themselves. You kept up with your friends and idols in staggered dispatches, through words in smudgy ink and pictures on glossy pages.

Of course, this was how the band communicated too: sending off their demo tapes to London like distress flares, plastering their record sleeves and themselves with politics and philosophy condensed to four-letter words. Many fans peppered our own communication—fanzines, letters, mixtapes, the envelopes they were sent in—with slogans and snatches of lyrics, as a ready-made argot and frame of reference. At school, I gradually identified other fans of the band, and they identified me, by the lyrical fragments written on school folders or on the sleeves of khaki jackets like a clandestine code. We all knew what we meant. Lyrics can be signs, signals and shibboleths, sometimes bridge and sometimes barricade. Throughout my part of this book, I have taken chapter headings and subtitles from *The Holy Bible* and from songs outside it, hopefully showing that Manics' lyrics, like a cut-up collage, can cross-reference and interrelate and, when juxtaposed, illuminate each other.

Emily Jones: "The Manics have arguably had a bigger influence over me in terms of culture, politics, personal appearance, etc. than anything else and I would go as far as to include my comprehensive school education in that. They encouraged me to educate myself outside of the curriculum by researching the people, events, books, films, etc. mentioned in their lyrics and interviews, and by researching the quotes they used in setlists and album booklets. They also helped me, inadvertently of course, to decide what I want to do with my life and I found inspiration (for want of a better word) in their music and interview material to pursue it."

My part of this book looks at the album in its personal and political context, in an attempt to understand why it was so important both to me and to everyone else who was moved to contribute. I write about the experience of hearing the album, rather than the experience of producing it; my perspective is that of the listener and the fan more than the musician. The album's songs are discussed individually and in the context of the album, grouped vaguely by theme rather than in tracklist order. They are also discussed in the context of the world surrounding the album and the conditions in which it was produced. I will be drawing on my own background—that of a small-town teenage girl to whom music was everything—and on the associations and connections that made sense to me against that background. I am grateful for the contributions of other fans, some quoted here and some not, some of whose experiences resonate with me and some of which don't. All these contributions have shown me that *The Holy Bible* attracted, entertained and inspired in contexts outside Britain and beyond the 1990s, and that it will continue to do so.

CHAPTER 2

Prologue to History

Scot Kaeff: "[In my record shop in Northern Kentucky] we used to stock a lot of imports and, when The Holy Bible was released, we got a copy in and I snagged it immediately. I listened in awe ... literally, just awe. The ferocity of the album, the despair and disgust matched with the melodicism. It was something new, to hear a band hold such a gut-wrenching mirror up to the world and actually capture the shock and dismay in the studio ... It's the desperation. The 360-degree view of the darkened heart of where we've let ourselves go, who we've become and wondering how to get out [...] No one wants to look there, to those stories, to those people, but they're part of all of us."

Lorna Cort: "It really should be regarded as a piece of modern art. A perfect document of a band at the top of their joint creative game, eloquent, honest and so raw ... Who ever wrote songs like that, apart from the Manics?"

The trouble is that *The Holy Bible* is hard to describe. It can seem both preposterously overblown and horrifyingly stark. It can seem relentlessly, desperately grimdark: even before you listen to the thing, you have to get past the *grand guignol* grandstanding of titles like "Archives of Pain," "Die in the Summertime" and "The Intense Humming of Evil." Sunless as a sewer and raw like an open wound, the album starts as it means to go on with the leprous "Yes" and gives no quarter. *The Holy Bible* is a pitiless record: in an era when it seemed grief had to be performative to be believed, *The Holy Bible* refuses to accept the performance of grief as sincere. Every tear is false. The album is heavy with unhappiness over the wrongs of human history, it repents and is sorry, but grief is not a get-out clause, and neither is repentance. Everyone is guilty. The entire fifty-six minutes can feel like a disapproving judgement on the listener. *The Holy Bible* is an overcast and stifling record, with even its gentlest moment, "This is Yesterday," no more than a fleeting slant of sunlight through dark clouds. Even the gleefully careering "Revol" is weighed down by the futility of faith in either love or revolution, and shot through with *détourned* fascist slogans. Richey and Nicky's lyrical shorthand, firing off historical, cultural and political shots while frequently neglecting to add definitive articles, had never been the easiest thing to follow or decipher, but on *The Holy Bible* this tendency is turned up to eleven. Listening to the album, one can feel there is too much packed into inadequate containers, with the time to adequately express anything fast running out. James Dean Bradfield slips into a personal vernacular of yelps and barks and howls, almost but never quite left without breath, drilling lines of dizzying or mystifying intricacy into the ear with merciless precision. If previous songs could seem contrived, track after track on *The Holy Bible* is compulsive. If earlier work could seem pretentious or glib, students of Meaning adopting a posture of Meaning It, this time they really meant it to a shocking and aweing degree. *The Holy Bible* is a cataclysmic, apocalyptic, *fin-de-siècle* record: gazing into the abyss of the twentieth century, it finds the abyss gazing back. Fury, horror, pity and despair pile up until we reach the album's penultimate track, a remembrance of the Holocaust woven around creepily tumbling drums and metallic, industrial screeches and shuffles, the ending agonizingly dragged out, drums stumbling to a close, a blink of breathing-space, and then it's all over bar the shouting (or, to give it its official title, "P.C.P."). *The Holy Bible,* perfect for its purposes, is a fearless, flawless record.

The Holy Bible is a hidden gem—or rather the opposite, a dark and rotten un-gem, a lump of coal fated never to turn diamond —of the late twentieth century. It exists almost entirely on its own terms. On one level it is a head-on reckoning with all the manmade atrocities and failures known to history, and on another an extraordinarily specific self-dissection by one man in particular. The album's unflinching focus on horror, dysfunction and morbidity made it a more uncomfortably personal listen than previous material, where such themes had been dealt with in abstract and general terms or outwardly directed. Besides the personal universals of sex and death, the album takes a political position on consumerism, freedom of speech, British and US imperialism, gun control and capital punishment, fascism, communism, war, genocide, white privilege, anorexia, political correctness, abortion, murder, rape, and prostitution. The personal crises documented in "Faster," "4st 7lb" or "Yes" appear almost as rational responses to the social and political horrors that surround them. Conversely, the "political" can almost feel like bright spots, moments of relief, when set against the heaviness of the personal, and it's tempting, though overly simplistic, to think of the former as Nicky's more detached lyrical contributions while any deeply personal content is Richey's. But, right from the opening of "Yes," in which economic and sexual exploitation are shown to mirror each other, the album makes its case that the personal and political are intimately intertwined and there can be no neat separation.

The album's darkness made it a strange proposition in the summer of its release, but its perspective would never have been a popular one in 1994. It ignores, or actively refuses, many of the narratives of its time, notably the twin triumphs of Britpop and Blairism and their boom-time optimism. But while it may be antithetical in style and subject matter to the rest of the 90s musical pantheon, *The Holy Bible* belongs there because of its engagement with key themes of the time, including the impact of the end of the Cold War, the crisis of working-class identity and representation, the growth in confessional art, and a rise in self-harm and eating disorders, especially among the young. The complex political views expressed on the album are grounded in the band's origins in the political traditions and social morality of post-industrial South Wales, which shaped a particular working-class and masculine identity now increasingly suppressed and marginalised in popular and political discourse. *The Holy Bible* unlocks a hidden history of the 1990s in which we may locate the origins of several present crises.

STRATEGY

Richey: "I've always got an idea in my mind of how I want to express myself and I think the first album was slightly too naïve [...] now when I write I can almost hear James' music and I know what works and what doesn't work."

(qtd in "Richey's")

James: "We lost ourselves for a short while there, but this new album was done with the realization that we needed to regain some kind of control and do this album completely outside of the record industry [...] to actually make the album sound honest. To make it sound as if we'd recaptured our own language again."

(qtd in JereC7)

The Holy Bible marked a shift in the perspective, image and perception of Manic Street Preachers. Despite its arguably adolescent outlook, the album is a more grown-up, considered and accomplished product than *Generation Terrorists,* the 1992 album with which the band attempted to secure their place in history. The plan then, in Nicky Wire's words, had been to "make one brilliant debut double LP that sells millions of copies, and as long as we've made our statement and perhaps changed something then I just want to disappear and go back to live with my mam" (qtd in Smith, "Outrage"). This was commendably but hopelessly ambitious, and the band themselves admitted as much. Acknowledging the failure of *Generation Terrorists* to change the world, Richey said: "The world had changed, perhaps more than we realised. People didn't care about such things anymore. It wasn't like 1977, when you could make a statement and get taken seriously" (qtd in Turner, 111–12). By the time of *The Holy Bible,* Wire's desire for domestic retreat was probably stronger than it had been two years earlier, but the band's ambition had been tempered to a more realistic edge, their youthful frivolities streamlined into a sharp and deadly seriousness. As a consequence *The Holy Bible,* although recorded in a third of the time of *Generation Terrorists* and with a third fewer tracks, comes far closer to achieving the definitive and enduring quality that constitutes a "statement."

In musical terms the album is also markedly different from its predecessors. While *Generation Terrorists* was endearingly messy and sprawling, 1993's *Gold Against the Soul* was a taut and polished but airless affair, with much of the debut's personality muffled. Again, the band was conscious of this: in 1997 James Dean Bradfield acknowledged that the band's live performances include only a few songs from *Gold Against the Soul* because "we just don't like much of it." According to Sean Moore, the album had suffered from the band's attempts to emulate their US influences, and their approach to writing its follow-up was to rediscover "a little bit of Britishness," drawing on their formative punk and post-punk influences including the Clash, Magazine, Wire, PiL and Gang of Four. This decision might have been made at a time when early Britpop bands like Blur and Suede were vocally opposing Britain's cultural domination by US music, but that seems wholly coincidental. In fact, *The Holy Bible* sounds less like its 60s-enthralled British peers and more like a handful of contemporary US bands—the industrial grind of Nine Inch Nails or Tool, the viscerally personal rage of Hole, the heavy melodic slabs of the Pixies or Nirvana—many of whom had, thanks to transatlantic cultural cross-pollination, been influenced by 70s and 80s British punk and post-punk in the same way as the Manics.

In the aftermath of *Gold Against the Soul,* the band also seem to have become aware of the tension between their world-conquering ambitions—associated with the larger reach and greater expectations they perceived in US artists—and the reality of what achieving these goals might mean. A year before *The Holy Bible*'s release the band had, in a vaguely surreal development, spent two nights playing support to US MOR hair-rockers Bon Jovi at Milton Keynes. Having accepted the support slot with subversive hopes of being able to "hijack" the 120,000-strong audience, the band instead found themselves too overwhelmed and uncomfortable to salvage anything from the experience. In a cautionary tale of being careful what you wish for, they were left feeling "like we'd sold out," for the first time in a career in which deliberately and spectacularly selling out had been at the top of their to-do list.

> "The enormity of it all was quite frightening," adds Richey. "You ask yourself, 'Would you really like to do this? Would you want to pander to crowds for two hours every night?'"
> Nicky: "It's the difference between living in obscurity like The Stooges or being huge. I think we try and marry the two aspects."
> (qtd in Arnopp)

The band's discomfort with their glimpse down the corridors of global success prompted Wire to declare that their next album would be motivated by artistic rather than commercial desires, "a completely artistic statement [which] will truly represent us." Whether or not the experience also prompted the band's desire to shy away from the intimidatingly ambitious associations of US rock, withdrawing into "Britishness" as a less scarily large, more secure and manageable destination, *The Holy Bible* signified a disciplined, almost puritanical renouncing of what Bradfield called "all that decadent rockstar rubbish." The band rejected Epic Records' idea of recording in Barbados, and instead retreated to the tiny confines of Sound Space Studios in Cardiff's dingy red-light district. They raced through the recording process in a brief but intense four weeks, which seems to have been a time of variable emotions: engineer and co-producer Alex Silva attributes the break-up of his relationship to the long hours involved, and Richey spent much of the time in tears, drinking the day away or sleeping on the studio's settee. This is balanced by Wire's insistence that recording the album "was a really good time, honestly" and by James and Richey's after-hours excursions to Cardiff bars and clubs—what Bradfield described as "really ordinary things"—set against the extraordinary album that was meanwhile taking shape.

The Holy Bible is able to convey its message so effectively partly because of the emphasis on clarity and directness in its production. From the densely packed lyrics to the stripped-down sound to the shoestring recording budget, everything was pared down to essentials in the interests of "honest communication." If *Gold Against the Soul* had been the Manics' most unfocused period, an album on which the band felt they had "inhabited too many personae," *The Holy Bible* is focused, like a laser beam, to what can be an uncomfortably acute degree. According to Bradfield, the album was constructed with "academic discipline," the band working to headings and structures "so each song is like an essay." This provides a further contrast with *Generation Terrorists,* which seemed to constitute not a series of essays but an essay in itself, albeit an overly ambitious one written during a speed-assisted all-nighter.

This discipline, this seriousness, gained Manic Street Preachers a new set of fans and won them wider critical acclaim. *Kerrang!* called the album "the first thing they've done that deserves to be called great." From the hostility and ridicule directed at their early efforts, and the artistic wrong-footing of *Gold Against the Soul,* with *The Holy Bible* the band were finally taken as seriously as they sometimes took themselves—although not without personal cost.

LET'S GO TO WAR

> *James Dean Bradfield: "Three words for 1994? Bag of shit."*
> (qtd in Sawyer)

Few things seemed to signify the Manics' new seriousness more than their switch away from *Gold Against the Soul*'s uncertain aesthetic, in which remnants of the old era—white jeans, eyeliner, feather boas—blended uneasily with fragments of Americana and glittery gameshow-host jackets. They exchanged this for a new uniform—literally—of military gear bought in army surplus stores while touring in early 1994, for what they described as an homage to the Clash in their *Combat Rock* incarnation. The Clash had long been a source of musical and aesthetic inspiration for the band; watching a ten-year anniversary broadcast of a Clash gig had electrified the teenage Manics and become, in suitably militaristic terms, "our unifying moment ... our absolute bullet-point – a rallying call" (qtd in Cummins 172–73). In the increasingly ominous conditions of 1994, however, putting on uniform seemed to signify an attempt at self-defence and closing ranks by a unit who felt themselves under attack, facing an unrelenting barrage of critical or prurient attention from the music press and increasingly from more mainstream media. Whether withdrawing behind conceptual "back-to-our-roots" lines, or pulling up the drawbridge of Sound Space Studios, the album's production was imbued with a sense of defensive retreat. In an *NME* interview given after the revelation of Richey's psychiatric treatment, James illustrated the band's siege mentality and the protectiveness of their bandmate with which it was bound up:

> The fact that 95 per cent of your readers say they feel an affinity with Richey or feel the need to support him, that pre-empts the fact that the last five per cent think he's a c—for it. Because they actually think he's playing up to the people who feel an affinity for him, for what he went through. They feel that it's just another little angle, that's all. (qtd in Bailie, "Traumatic")

Whether you were a fan or a casual observer, it was difficult to miss the sense of crisis surrounding the band in the run-up to the album's release. Kurt Cobain's suicide in April 1994 had made headlines worldwide and focused mainstream—often ill-informed—attention on the latest in a line of Tragic Rock Heroes. Many misguided perspectives on Richey written in the same year assumed his story was the predictable one of a star turning to drink, drugs and mental breakdown as a result of failure to cope with fame, while others simply presented him as an example of irresponsible wasterdom. Kurt's death cast a long shadow over much of the music press, but Richey's self-harm, anorexia and alcoholism were the escalation of longstanding problems and hardly an attempt to emulate Cobain.

The Manics' spring tour of Thailand, where Richey took a fan's knife to himself and went onstage bleeding from the chest, is generally agreed to be the point at which things were veering undeniably off-course. After the release of "Faster" in June, Wire "felt something wasn't right. Everything caught up with us [...] There's only so far you can go with the 'soldiering on' mentality" (qtd in "Manics"). In July, Richey was taken to the psychiatric unit of Cardiff's Whitchurch Hospital, and by August he was in the more select surrounds of the Priory clinic. The Manics played as a three-piece at July's T in the Park and August's Reading Festival. Reports of their touring and recording were littered with alarmist pull-quotes, and rumours swirled of inter-band tension, hospitalization and suicide attempts. In August, *Melody Maker* advertised their Manics interview with the lurid cover-line RICHEY'S CRACK-UP and the quote: "His self-abuse has escalated badly ... he's drinking, he's mutilating himself..."

After watching the Manics, with their full line-up, perform "the show of their lives" at Glastonbury a few weeks earlier, *Melody Maker*'s Taylor Parkes observed that "it was obvious to everyone that this was a band approaching terminal velocity" ("Manic" 12). The band themselves, at the eye of a hurricane to which all other eyes were glued, seem to have acknowledged this sense of crisis to varying degrees. Nicky spoke of the idea that the band's seemingly disastrous trajectory had been preordained, "a massive self-fulfilling prophecy" of spectacular implosion, and explained Richey's final decline as the resurgence of problems that he had been dealing with for far longer than might be assumed. Although Edwards' disappearance in February 1995 has become perhaps the best-known thing about him, before the time of *The Holy Bible* such an ending seemed neither inevitable nor predictable. His coping mechanisms seemed to indicate just that: an ongoing process of coping, not an impending terminal failure to cope. Wire, despite being conscious after the fact that songs like "Die in the Summertime" and "4st 7lbs" were "pretty obviously about Richey's state of mind," claimed not to have been able to admit this at the time, observing that "even if you're quite close to someone, you always try to deny thoughts like that." Bradfield, retrospectively reflecting on Richey's increasingly evident self-harming, said:

> I think back to those times and think "Why didn't we see the gathering storm," but we were still in thrall to the canon of visual work that Iggy Pop had done, and people like that. You know, we still felt as if we were still part of rock n roll expressionism, I suppose. (qtd in Cummins 181)

The idea of rock music and performance as artistic projection rather than strict autobiography—Picasso's notion of art as the lie that helps us understand the truth—underwent a collapse in the 90s. Authenticity became elevated as the highest form of art and the value of an artist's work began to be defined by how much "authentic" personality and life was considered to lie behind it. Throughout 1994, dissections of the Manics' internal drama seemed to take up as much space as their music did—with, especially in Richey's case, an accompanying erosion of the divide between his private and public personae. Both he and Bradfield used the term "drama queen"—in mocking and self-deprecating but indicative ways—to describe themselves, and specifically to describe their experience of 1994. Spectacles like Richey's emergence onstage in Bangkok, having cut himself with knives given to him by a fan, could be read as an act of resistance to his own objectification—he deliberately had not, for instance, acquiesced to the fan's request that he look at her while cutting himself. But in another sense, he seemed unable to resist engaging with, accepting and exacerbating the personalized drama that was increasingly characterizing his public presentation.

This, too, contributed to the sense of crisis out of which *The Holy Bible* emerged, leading Simon Price to describe the album as "the sound of a group in extremis [...] hurtling towards a private Armageddon."

BE PURE, BE VIGILANT, BEHAVE

Even without its musical nods to Bauhaus and Sisters of Mercy, *The Holy Bible* has a distinctly Gothic atmosphere. Both melodrama and psychodrama, the album is haunted by the twentieth century and its returning nightmares. It is full of impending doom, open black ruins, crumbling edifices, deadly cliff-falls, and places defined by and designed for mass incarceration, torture and death. Horrors lurk in the shadows and there are constant screams somewhere off-stage.

The Gothic tradition, its supernatural tropes also encompassing body horror, self-harm and atrocity obsession, has been a constant cultural presence throughout the nineteenth and twentieth centuries, but has been more usually associated with female artists and audiences than male. Coinciding with the rise of Romanticism, the 1790s saw the development of women's novels which blended sentimental narratives with aspects of the supernatural. Highbrow contemporaries disliked these Gothic novels and their overwhelmingly female readership, frequently mocking them as overblown and histrionic, but more recent criticism has viewed the genre as a progressive and subversive art form which explores the fractures and dark sides of capitalism, imperialism, patriarchy and the concept of Enlightenment itself. *The Holy Bible* can be seen as part of a continuum of attempts by those without social, cultural or political power to use Gothic tropes and imagery to express pain, assert opposition or exert control.

Ellen Moers coined the term "Female Gothic" to describe narratives which provide a way of "articulating women's dissatisfactions with patriarchal structures and offering a coded expression of their fears of entrapment within the domestic and the female body" (90–92). Centuries before

Burroughs and the Beats, or Salinger's takedown of "phonies," the Gothic novel provided an art form through which

> women writers could first accuse the 'real world' of falsehood and deep disorder. Or perhaps, they rather asked whether masculine control is not just another delusion in the nightmare of absurd historical reality in which we are all involved. (Doody 111)

The Holy Bible accuses and asks in similar fashion, with its male author sometimes adopting a female voice—the sex worker in "Yes," the teenage girl in "4st 7lb"—in order to do so. In place of the brassy, bolshy and brightly-lit women in, for instance, the promo video for 1992'S "Little Baby Nothing," *The Holy Bible*'s protagonists, like pursued and persecuted Gothic heroines, stand in shadow, in suffering, and largely in silence. The album's fictional female voices, whose confessional register would risk being derided or dismissed if the product of actual women, are paradoxically strengthened through being written and sung by men.

Richey was rarely compared to female artists and *The Holy Bible* is rarely compared to works by women, despite the perception of confessional art and literature as a female preserve and despite the band's referencing of its earlier practitioners—notably Sylvia Plath, a longtime Manics icon whose namecheck lends a lone drop of oestrogen to the chorus of "Faster." (This failure of association may be explained by that artistic double standard which holds that when women write about their personal crises, it's "confessional writing," but when men do the same it's just literature.) At the time of *The Holy Bible,* Richey was endlessly compared—and courted such comparisons—to other fragile, heroically tragic young men: Rimbaud, Van Gogh, Ian Curtis, the "lamb-like youths" of Allen Ginsberg's "Howl" who were "falling apart under the conformist, corporate systems—dying on train lines, burning their arms with cigarettes, hacking at their limbs, jumping off the Brooklyn Bridge" (Bailie, "Traumatic"). After 1994, as *The Holy Bible* took on the same posthumous significance as *In*

Utero, Edwards and Kurt Cobain became lauded as twin transatlantic tragedies.

Rather than Kurt, however, Richey's most under-acknowledged counterpart is Courtney Love. *The Holy Bible* is his definitive statement just as Hole's second album *Live Through This,* released four months earlier in 1994, is hers. For me, tracing the steps of many teenage girls before me, the summer of that year was a summer of desultory sex, self-hatred, and the thousand mortal shocks that teenage female flesh is heir to. *The Holy Bible* and *Live Through This* allowed me different ways of getting through it. Love's messy, confessional raging was at odds with Edward's cerebral psyche-dissection, but both seemed to take aim at the same targets: body horror, emotional isolation, alienation from one's own being and mind. Both seemed determined to peel away the decorative superficial to get to the ugly but authentic heart of the matter.

Richey, through his visibility and articulacy—and the fact that he was taken seriously by the press and his peers—acted as a channel and a catalyst for fans of the band to admit the existence of problems about which they might otherwise have felt obliged to keep silent. The airing of his problems in the press occasioned a flood of letters, mostly from teenage girls, expressing identification with him. An uncomfortable consequence of this, though, was the frequent extolling of Richey above female artists who dealt with such themes. In a retrospective on the band, Stuart Bailie reflected that:

> The letters that have reached the NME since Richey's disappearance suggest that there's another huge constituency of fans out there – the cutters, anorexics and bulimics ... Many of these people plainly felt that they were sharing a "secret" with Richey. He made them feel better, less like freaks. ("Traumatic")

Bailie then makes the more dubious claim that, before Richey, there had been "no-one to represent these individuals in popular culture." In fact, references to eating disorders, anxiety, depression and self-harm were a staple concern for women in punk and post-punk, and for their 90s inheritors in the Riot Grrl movement. But, mirroring the neglect of women writers of the Gothic before Walter Scott made the genre "respectable," it seemed as though a male artist—first Cobain, then Edwards—was required to lend 90s neurosis and its artistic expression some critical credibility. Princess Diana's unprecedented soul-baring on primetime TV, her discussion of bulimia and cutting, might have brought female neurosis into the 90s mainstream, but it was Richey's soul-baring along similar lines that the alternative press found 4-Real enough to applaud.

Courtney Love in her 90s heyday did not appear to employ self-harm or anorexia as methods of control or self-expression, although she addressed both in her lyrics. Instead, she was constantly reviled or ridiculed for behaviour and attitudes which got, and still get, her male contemporaries praised and indulged. The respect accorded a contemporary like Richey, the mourning for his lost genius, was something for which I could not at the time imagine a female equivalent;

self-harm and self-destruction in a male rock star was proof of tortured sensibility, too delicate for this world, while in a female rock star it was just a lurid spectacle. Women overwhelmed by circumstance—addiction, abuse, mental breakdown—are seen as victims and tragedies rather than heroes. If on the other hand they do not self-destruct, if they outlive and overcome their circumstances, as Courtney did, then they are seen as monstrous, villainous, or a joke. Courtney is a survivor where Richey was not, and yet Courtney survives as demonized and notorious while Richey has transcended his existence with his legend mostly spotless—still an immaculate Madonna next to Courtney's tarnished whore.

While many Gothic novels contrive to reach a happy ending, smoothing over and soothing the horrors experienced in reaching their conclusion, Female Gothic narratives often complete their depiction of the transgression of social taboos by resisting closure. *The Holy Bible* follows this tradition in its refusal to repent, its denial of peaceful resolution to the conflict and horror it describes, and its commitment to self-destruction (rather than healing or moral improvement) through suffering. On darkly compelling songs like "Yes," "Faster" and "4st 7lb," *The Holy Bible* exhibits the same kind of survival without redemption, the same defiance of one's circumstances without ever quite overcoming or transcending them, that leads the critic Anwen Crawford to classify Hole's *Live Through This* as

> a rare example of feminist rock music. But the feminism it articulates is not affirmative or celebratory. It's full of anger and shame; it revels in psychic and physical wounds ... There's a gothic quality to it: nothing is healed, nothing is overcome.
> (qtd in "The 331/3")

Far from offering closure, *The Holy Bible*'s final line is the jabbered coda of "P.C.P."—a last stand against the overwhelming forces of unreason that comes across as equally hysterical—and its last word is the hectic dismembering, over ten frenzied notes, of "amnesiac."

IMPOSSIBLE TARGETS

After the media storm around Richey Edwards' disappearance in February 1995, and the band's commercial success with "A Design for Life" the following year, the reputation and sales of *The Holy Bible* grew steadily. As of 2014, it had sold more than 600,000 copies worldwide, and has consistently been placed in the top ten or twenty best albums of all time in surveys from *Q* to *Kerrang!*. But in 1994, although *The Holy Bible* reached number six on the UK album charts on its release, it sold less than the band's critically-derided previous albums. Its three singles all performed worse than expected, and critical praise failed to translate into chart placings in either the US or mainland Europe. Wire described the album as a commercial disaster, after which "there was nothing to build on and nothing to lose." At the time, Richey connected the band's ongoing history of failed idealism and implausible ambition to the "beautiful dream" of Soviet communism invoked by the album's artwork and iconography:

> We're on our third album now – we're only supposed to have made one that sold 20 million – the biggest debut the world has ever seen. Stupid, naïve, impossible targets. Everything I've liked has always failed in some way. That semi-logo we've got, the Soviet veteran of war medal, CCCP. The reason I liked that was just because it did fail, that it was a beautiful dream. But it's completely disproved; not the ideology of it, but the way people put it into practice [...] When people talk about us, they've still got this idea that the music can actually like, Change The World, or Smash The System. That's nonsense; I've never thought a band could ever do anything that important. It can change individuals, it can create a common ground for important issues, but in terms of actually doing something, changing the economic infrastructure, it's not gonna do that, it never has done.

That's what needs to be changed if anything's to happen.

(qtd in Bailie, "Interview")

Richey's notes for "Of Walking Abortion" included the sharply incisive line "Modern life makes thought an embarrassment." The 90s saw a noticeable backlash against the earnestness, seriousness and unapologetic political engagement which had marked much of the previous decade, especially in independent and alternative subcultures. The 90s were instead fuelled by the release of tension, by the insistence that we no longer needed to think so hard about it all. Thatcherism and Reaganism were about to segue under Blair and Clinton into a softer politics, one more suited to getting our breath back after the brutal, high-stakes bouts of the 80s. But, despite Britpop's invoking of totemic Sixties imagery, the 90s were a kind of 60s in reverse. In place of the coming together of mass social movements, there was growing isolation and individualism; in place of expanding social mobility, there was the pushing out of the working-class from politics and culture; and, under the 60s-liberal veneer of Blair and Clinton, there was a sharp turn to the right with resurgent nationalism, the capitalist co-option of feminism, and middle-class appropriation of working-class culture under cover of "irony," which went along with a wilful anti-intellectualism (Jones). The Manics had always raged against deliberate stupidity and advocated immersion in the literature, history, art and philosophy that had sustained them when growing up. They continued to do so even as the pop-cultural IQ-level plummeted all around them:

> Nicky Wire: "I did a lot of my reading young. Now I'm just amazed that so many people in bands don't even read a book till they're like 28, and then it's like, 'I've just discovered Ken Kesey!' Or Bono's just discovered Dadaism and Situationism. It's very sad that at 30 or whatever he is, he feels he's suddenly seen the light."
>
> (qtd in "Waxing")

At a distance of thirty years, the 90s appear as a lull, a relatively stable and content intermission, between the end of the Cold War and the onset of a post-9/11 future. But, beneath the decade's blandly buoyant surface, something darker was stirring. In April 1995, one year after the death of Kurt Cobain and two months after Richey's disappearance, *Melody Maker* pictured both men on its cover to advertise a panel discussion between artists and readers on "a year of suicide and breakdown." The coverage reflected a more general media panic over "what is happening to our young people?", which pulled in everything from a rise in teenage binge-drinking to a supposed self-harm epidemic, with Kurt and Richey sensationalized as exemplars and instigators of this malaise. Cobain's death had inspired copycat suicides by teenagers around the world, we were told, while Richey's more select number of acolytes were apparently cutting their arms, starving themselves and shaving their heads in spellbound imitation of their idol.

The "discovery" of widespread and intense unhappiness in the 90s, particularly amongst the young, was regarded as something shocking and inexplicable. Why weren't we happy? Why, with apparently all battles over and liberal utopia at hand, were we nonetheless enacting disaffection and destruction on ourselves, directing against our bodies and our futures the hatred and violence we were told had dissipated along with the fear of nuclear annihilation? It was almost as though we were expected to believe what we'd been told, rather than the socio-economic evidence of our own eyes. The idea that unhappiness could have a structural or political cause was regarded as hopelessly outmoded. If you were unhappy, you needed to fix yourself—there could be no question of the system needing fixing, for it had proved its worth simply by outlasting all others. So on we lurched, still punch-drunk and reeling from the 80s but denied the means to articulate the fact that the fight was still on. In a context that encouraged papering over the structural cracks, whether political or personal, the refusal to do so became a fault-line which ran throughout the decade. We were told throughout politics and pop culture in the 90s that this was the best of all possible worlds, while *The Holy Bible*'s fatalism, pessimism and nihilism stood in stark contradiction to this. Which side were you on?

Anxiety could be expressed in the 90s, and damage acknowledged, but only if it was framed in terms of emotion and not economics. Much of *The Holy Bible*'s power is derived from the tension between this confessional, solipsistic tendency—the personalized expression of unhappiness through self-harm, mental illness or disordered eating—and the band's recognition of the systemic roots of much of this unhappiness in political neglect and economic inequality. Still socialist at heart, they focus on the material basis of oppression and the conditions, not simply the people, to be fixed. *The Holy Bible* attempts to give a voice to the unheard and the silenced—the victims of murder, war, purges, the prison-industrial complex, institutional abuse and exploitation, addiction, their own minds and bodies, or simply their awareness of the unbearable shiteness of being. However, it makes this attempt with no hope of redemption or improvement, and with little faith in the potential ameliorating power of the collective, of strength in numbers. Their early Clash-inspired Last Gang in Town ideal, the use of "us" and "we" as done to great effect in "You Love Us" and as resurgent in "A Design for Life," is notable by its absence. In fact, collectives in *The Holy Bible* are almost always destructive, used as examples of totalitarian horror or the madness and passive complicity of crowds. The album's insistence that the terrors of the outside world are mirrored in an interior world of self-hatred, degradation and the wish for death, further limits the possibility of resistance. The present state of things is condemned, but no alternative is offered since no alternative is plausible. *The Holy Bible* is an angry, angry record, but for much of the time its rage is directed inward. In this it reflects the primary lesson of the 90s: rather than attempting to change the world, we were reduced to attempting to understand life through staring blankly at our navel.

CHAPTER 3

Epilogues of Youth

Faster – Die in the Summertime – This is Yesterday

> Living within a world run by elders, youth clearly sees all that is wrong, but is powerless to affect change ... The frustration spills out into polarizing rhetoric that admits no grey, just black and white.
> – Jon Savage, *Teenage* (14, 135)

> Chucking her under the chin, he said, "What are you doing here, honey? You're not even old enough to know how bad life gets." And it was then Cecilia gave orally what was to be her only form of suicide note, and a useless one at that, because she was going to live: "Obviously, Doctor," she said, "you've never been a thirteen-year-old girl."
> –Jeffrey Eugenides, *The Virgin Suicides*

TEENAGE 20/20

Manic Street Preachers, with a career currently spanning three decades and a combined age of 139, still tend to be associated with a particular form of adolescent intensity. The artist Jeremy Deller, who compiled an exhibition on Manics fan culture in 1997, described the typical fan as

> quite easy to guess. Not surprisingly, it was a sixteen-year-old girl who lived in the countryside or at least not in London, and who didn't have many friends. The classic pop fan, who was very intelligent, and read a lot. Not necessarily [working class] but definitely not wealthy.
> (qtd in Pyzik, "Orgreave")

The young Manics' attitude to their adolescent fanbase was invariably generous, informed by empathy with music-obsessive teenagers and perhaps by a recognition of how adolescent the band's own outlook was. In early 1994, Richey claimed that they

"never minded doing teenage magazines like *Smash Hits* which some bands refuse to do. I just find that incredibly patronising. I know when I was 14, music was the only thing I cared about"
(qtd in Forrest, "Preaching").

The Manics were a band—and *The Holy Bible* is certainly an album—that only a teenager could properly love. Suffused with self-pity and self-disgust, lacerated by doubt and despair, boiling over with melodrama and self-mythologizing, the album is full of lines and images of bodily dissatisfaction or dysphoria ("can't seem to stay a fixed ideal"; "the first time you see yourself naked you cry") that mean the world to a mind and body encountering the unstable territory of adolescence. The album deals with themes—loss of innocence, realization of mortality, the search for social and political alternatives—which inform much of adolescent psychology and many coming-of-age narratives. This tendency is further expressed in invocations of stalled growth and self-destructive resistance to the adult world, whether the morbid nostalgia of "Die in the Summertime" or the *anorexia nervosa* epic "4st 7lb."

The Holy Bible is marked by an insistence on polarized extremes and absolutes. It draws dividing lines using the blazingly judgmental language of moralism and puritanism: one is either pure or lost, things are either purity or perversion. It articulates moral certainties of its own while criticizing their application. This idealist absolutism, too, is adolescent, informed by the rejection of an adult world whose willingness to compromise implies weakness, corruption or surrender. But the album simultaneously suggests how unsustainable this idealism is, both personally and politically. Political idealism becomes either the broken, impossible dream of Soviet communism or the nightmare of fascism, while on a personal level, staying a fixed ideal is acknowledged as impossible too: one must either live with change and compromise or remain pure and unsullied by opting out of the world entirely. In physical and metaphysical terms, the impossible struggle to stay a fixed ideal is juxtaposed with the external urging to accept an unsatisfactory adult world, to give up on striving for perfection—"That's the way you're built my father said"—all of which is antithetical to a certain adolescent mentality.

The young Manics found themselves inspired by punk's ten-year anniversary, despite experiencing the movement at a decade's distance. *The Holy Bible*'s adolescent qualities give it a similar ongoing appeal to contemporary listeners. In part this is due to the timeless nature of the teenage angst captured on the album, but it also reflects that peculiar millennial dislocation whereby many more young people currently seem unable to fully extricate themselves from adolescence. The rules of the twentieth-century intergenerational social contract held that hard work in school would pay off with sustained and rewarding employment. This promise—if it ever actually held true—conclusively broke down in post-industrial Britain, but there has been no consequent re-evaluation of the emphasis placed on work as an overarching life goal and source of personal purpose and validation. When younger citizens increasingly cannot obtain the traditional signifiers of adulthood—earning a secure wage, buying a house, starting a family—then teenage angst, including that articulated on *The Holy Bible,* is no longer confined to one's teenage years.

The emotional intensity of adolescence can be difficult to fully recollect in the relative tranquillity of age. At best the attempt inspires affectionate nostalgia, at worst a self-abasing cringe. I recall one fanzine writer in' 93 or' 94 expressing her anxiety that, "one day"—we could of course never imagine this day would come, but still its possibility loomed with Gothic dread—she would be middle-aged and boring and unable to do anything but laugh at the idea that she had ever once loved a band called Manic Street Preachers. It was a common and recurring fear (and I remember being convinced it would never happen to me, but of course that was before I heard *Know Your Enemy).* The Manics, particularly on *The Holy Bible,* excel at capturing the aspects of idealistic, absolutist, restless and reckless adolescence that can make us embarrassed to recall ourselves at that age; we are embarrassed by them *now* because they remind us of being embarrassingly *then.* But to sneer at the band—and, implicitly, at their fans—for the adolescent qualities of much of their best work is to miss the point, just as to sneer at their early "Clash in a school play" image is to overlook or ignore the fact that they were genuine, unapologetic fanboys. The Manics worshipped, learned and emulated. They needed their stars, just as their fans did.

I AM NOTHING AND SHOULD BE EVERYTHING

Political and personal development collide in adolescence, as teenagers form ideas about the political domain and the social contract—rules and obligations through which the state, civil society and the people live in harmony—and how they as individuals fit within that order. This also means that adolescence can be a time when, attempting to apply to one's world as it practically exists the rules one has absorbed from the institutions of an earlier generation—parents, schools, political or religious establishments—one finds that world severely lacking. The absence during one's teenage years of distracting responsibilities such as family or work means that adolescence can be a point at which the world appears most transparently and glaringly not as it should be, and one's place in it most difficult to find.

In his cultural study *Teenage,* Jon Savage traces the development of the concept of adolescence as a separate stage of life, subject to particular stresses and with its own particular sensibility, epitomized on one hand by the Romantics and revolutionary youth of the late eighteenth century and on the other by America, the rising power of the new century. By the middle of the twentieth century, the angsty adolescent tropes of European Romanticism had given way, against the post-war spread of American values, to the idea of the Teenager—now a marketing demographic at whom advertising could be targeted rather than a cultural archetype. The Teenager was considered to be

> the ultimate psychic match for the times: living in the now, pleasure-seeking, product-hungry, embodying the new global society where social inclusion was to be granted through purchasing power. The future would be Teenage.
> (Savage 465)

The Romantic sense of adolescence as a time of both transformative power and listless disaffection, which the early Manics tapped into, could at certain historical junctures become a source of threat and instability. As radical doctrines of class equality and sexual and racial liberation established themselves after the Industrial Revolution, young people were frequently in the vanguard of movements for social change. At times and places when participation in mass movements for change were less possible, the "classic mode of the impatient adolescent" was impotent frustration. The writer Richard King has described the South Wales valleys as "a locus in permanent adolescence" (see "Studio Hiraeth"). The impact of post-industrial stasis in their place of origin, and the economic and psychological arrested development it produced, seemed to inspire the band in both a practical and a creative sense. It not only intensified the urge to escape, but much of their image and music drew on previous cultural explosions of militant adolescence: the fusions of youth culture and political protest which gave rise to Paris in '68 or Italy in '69, in which "the contradictions of class and capitalism [...] explode *directly* in the behaviour, styles and consciousness of youth" (Thompson 12).

In this as in so much else, the band was a deliberate throwback, their radical nihilism the revival of a kind of youth consciousness that remained a minority taste in the 90s, which was a decade marked more by youth as cheerful marketing target, comfortable and consuming rather than restless and rebelling. The early Manics' admiration of historical alliances between youth subcultures and radical politics—the 50s Beat Generation, the student uprisings of 1968, punk's roots in deteriorating material conditions and subversion of the consumer culture young people were expected to swallow whole—clearly influenced their conception of the cultural influence their own band could wield. Their idealistic expression of adolescence as generational consciousness, as a point of radical opposition to a conservative, compromised and corrupt—and, simply, square—adult world, was a deliberate strategy from the band's inception:

> Richey: "rock n roll is meant to be this great force for change. It still can be. You can reach a young audience that are untainted by all the bullshit that's gonna come their way later on. The first thing we set out to do was recreate the generation gap and I think we're succeeding. All our fans are really young. From thirteen to sixteen. And most people know what we're about, we are a really/obvious/band.

But even if people just know that we're pissed off that's more than most bands."

(qtd in Smith, "Outrage")

If *Generation Terrorists* and the early Manics expressed a kind of militant Teenage angst, *The Holy Bible* is steeped in adolescence—not the mid-century celebration of the Teenager, but the earlier, restless and despairing Romantic-Gothic kind.

I KNOW I BELIEVE IN NOTHING BUT IT IS MY NOTHING

Listening to "Faster" effortlessly transports me back to my teenage years, which are easy to remember but more difficult to describe. There was an inescapable daily routine—school, home, homework, tea and TV, bed—accompanied by the knowledge that all you were doing was moving incrementally towards a stage of life where your daily routine—commute, work, commute, home, sleep—would be merely different by degrees. For me, the early Manics captured the longing for another era—the tragic glamour of James Dean or Marilyn Monroe, the political thrill of Parisian barricades—and the wish for adventure while fully aware of how difficult it would be to come by in such a drab and diminished time and place. There were occasional moments that punctured this boredom and despondency, and almost all of them—a gig, a new album, discovering a new band—revolved around music. I recall thinking of rock 'n' roll itself as fundamentally an extended adolescence, but an adolescence to aspire to rather than escape: a state in which adult responsibilities, pressures and repercussions could be delayed, if not indefinitely evaded, and in which, since music outlasts its creators, mortality itself might be outrun.

Emerging from childhood and facing adulthood, you think you know what's coming. You are aware of the adult world, but not allowed to engage in it, and your criticism of it is received in condescending terms. To be told that once it comes to you (once you "grow up") you won't mind the grind, the boredom, the acceptance of mundanity, the settling, is not a comfort but a counsel of despair. Irvine Welsh's 1993 novel *Trainspotting* follows a group of heroin users living in urban poverty and squalor in "culturally rich" Edinburgh. It maps forgotten areas in an "all middle-class now" Britain—like the Welsh Valleys, post-industrial blackspots given over to escapism and addiction. One of *Trainspotting*'s best-remembered quotes is a subversion of the 80s conservative slogan CHOOSE LIFE, which, originally drawn from the Book of Deuteronomy, was coined in opposition to drugs and abortion. Welsh's character Renton reinvents the slogan as a scornful anatomy of what adult life has in store for those who follow its rules:

> Choose life. Choose mortgage payments; choose washing machines; choose cars; choose sitting oan a couch watching mind-numbing and spirit-crushing game shows, stuffing fuckin junk food intae yir mooth. Choose rotting away, pishing and shiteing yersel in a home, a total fuckin

embarrassment tae the selfish, fucked-up brats ye've produced. Choose life. (187)

This paean to rejecting convention for addiction—for being a dutiful consumer, but consuming a product not sanctioned by tax and marketing—was in one sense a weaponized reconfiguring of teen angst, a twisting of Romantic myth. In April 1994, Cobain's borrowing for his suicide note of Neil Young's line "it's better to burn out than to fade away" (effectively, to die in the summertime) also called to mind the petty-heroic posturing immortalized in songs like the Clash's "Death or Glory," the idea of dodging the inevitable fading of one's potential and one's talent, rejecting the idea of "striking a bargain with the world" as one of compromise and mediocrity. There has always been a certain seductive pull to this line of argument—just as there was to *Trainspotting*'s grimy anti-glamour. Why do anything when you can forget everything? Against this smack-imbued stagnation and the urge to succumb to it, to me as a teenager "Faster" was, instead, speed and focus and acceleration, the setting into motion of possibility, the lifting of restriction.

Released on June 6th and reaching #16 in the UK charts, "Faster" was the album's lead single, backed with "P.C.P." Both songs were clattering, lacerating strokes of sound and fury, lashes of whips dipped in similar vitriol. As the vanguard of such an extraordinary record, and the first we heard of the band's new direction, "Faster" carried the shock of the new. It had something in common with early outings like "Motown Junk," but while the latter was described as "ragingly half-articulate," "Faster" seemed more like a case of something being fully articulated while the listener was at fault for only being able to understand half of what they were hearing. As befits its namechecking of Mensa, Miller and Mailer, "Faster" is intimidatingly, bruisingly articulate, a battery of weaponized words. Even its co-author commented that it was "probably the first time that we've written a song and not completely understood what we've written." Still, what I wanted most as a teenager was to be entertained. The more dramatic, extreme, loud, shiny and glam the entertainment, the better. A guitar riff as big as the Ritz. Add to this an adolescent appetite for the Romantic appreciation of what Jon Savage termed "accelerated life sealed by an early death," and *The Holy Bible* and everything surrounding it in 1994 seemed fatally attractive, its acceleration as dramatically unsustainable as Yeats' widening gyre.

NO HORIZONS

Self-harm is a means of attack and defence. When you feel the world is likely to do violence towards you, it can feel perversely logical to pre-empt this by doing it to yourself. Self-harm can also feel like the only possible way of expressing what feels inexpressible, calling attention to pain or protestation that cannot be expressed in words. Enacting harmful or destructive behaviour on oneself can feel like the only logical way to carry on, to cope, to tolerate. Coping mechanisms which set in during adolescence—cutting, binge-drinking, disordered eating—can be pursued into adulthood, of course, but they tend to be associated with the process of growing up. Some teenagers do grow up and change their minds and their methods, while some don't. The stark and simple stab of "Faster"'s opening line was explicitly associated by Nicky with Richey's methods of self-harm, something which Richey himself tended to downplay by insisting on the impulse's universal quality:

> When I went back home after I cut my arm, I would bump into people in the street, and they'd say, 'Yeah, I did that as well', and they did it because they were so fucking bored. It's not something that's out of the ordinary, because everybody recognises it, everybody sees it in their own lives.
>
> (qtd in Selzer 49)

Before "Faster," there was 4-REAL. Richey's decision in 1992 to prove to a doubting journalist his own and his band's sincerity, authenticity and commitment by carving the sentiment into his own forearm, retains a hallowed place in the band's mythology and was a formative part of Richey's mystique. Rather than the "easy and cheap" recourse of physical violence towards his antagonist, Richey chose to perform an almost ritualistic act, submitting to his own trial by ordeal. After his disappearance, the incident was brought up as an early illustration of his alleged instability and wildness, his unpredictable rock 'n' roll volatility—when in fact the incident, though not premeditated, was calm, deliberate, and thought-through. Driven to A&E directly afterwards, Richey insisted that others without self-inflicted injuries should be seen before him. For all the incident's shock value, for him it was something routine, spectacle turned almost mundane.

Pain is intolerable at some levels; at others, it can be borne. When I cut myself as a teenager, I did not know the word *sublimation,* or *catharsis.* This was *translation,* or it felt like it: the translation into a readable symbolism of something you cannot articulate—and even if you could, you have no hope that anyone would listen. In the temporary sanctuary of my room, I swiped razorblades, scissors, kitchen knives and the point of my school compass back and forth across my skin, feeling as exhilarated as if I were conducting a symphony. Over hours, days and weeks, I would observe the way in which bright beads of blood would fade to softly pink slices of scar tissue. There was an obvious and precise logic to what I did, it seemed to me, although I couldn't get it out in words. Listening to "Faster" was the only thing that struck the perfect chord. When I heard the whole album, "Yes"'s pivotal line "I hurt myself to get pain out" provided as disarmingly simple an explanation as any analyst or spectator could require.

"We enjoy playing 'Faster'," Bradfield explains, "because we think it epitomises something about Richey's lyrics in that there's not a lot of self-pity there. It's all about discipline, and there's still a certain positive energy in playing that song, whereas a lot of the songs on *The Holy Bible,* of course, just sound like the anthology of a self-fulfilling prophecy."

(qtd in Eccleston)

"Faster" displays not just an absence of self-pity but a perverse kind of pride, swerving at times into arrogance. Lines like "I've been too honest with myself, I should have lied like everybody else" transform the protagonist's self-confessed flaws into virtues. A backhanded salute to the strength of mind and principle required to remain "too honest," presenting oneself as the last outpost of integrity in a world sinking into corruption, the line exemplifies the song's earlier observation of self-disgust as a mirror-image of self-obsession. The chorus, described by Wire as "almost heroically self-indulgent," becomes a further affirmation, resounding with what Sylvia Plath wrote of as *the old brag of my heart. I am, I am, I am.*" In "Faster," weakness, loss and instability are turned into triumph and pleasure by sheer force of will.

The lyrical simplicity of "This Is Yesterday"—and of "Die in the Summertime," a song which is nothing if not starkly straightforward—throws into relief the convoluted sentiments and tortured logic that make up "Faster," which Wire considered "the most confusing song on the album":

> I added some stuff about the regurgitation of 20th Century culture and the way that everything's speeded up to such an extent that nobody knows if they've got any meaning any more [...] I don't even know if that's a bad thing, I don't know if we're not on some kind of path to a superbeing where all emotions are lost and everyone finally gets on perfectly because of that. The world is such a violent place. What we experience from the everyday world, what we read and what we see makes you realise that there's worse and worse things happening all the time. "Perhaps," he concludes thoughtfully, "it might reach such a low point of existence something good may come of it."
>
> (qtd in "Manics")

Some of Wire's ruminations here—the anxiety over cultural and technological progress and their potential to produce a jaded and desensitized mentality, versus the more (perversely) positive potential for things to get so bad that they can get no worse—were being voiced by others in the mid-90s. In its nihilistic impulse, "Faster" sometimes displays the lipstick traces of accelerationism. This odd philosophy took Marx's contention that history advanced by the bad side, which welcomed capitalism's ability to dissolve previous socio-economic relations, and combined it with the Nietzschean desire to "break the world in two." It concluded that capitalism, rather than having its course arrested or rolled back, should be expanded, repurposed or accelerated in order to generate radical social change—either by repurposing modern technology to socially beneficial and emancipatory ends, or by hastening the system's collapse by exacerbating its self-destructive tendencies. In its most absurd extrapolation, accelerationists could argue that any beneficial act which contributed to something other than the wholesale degeneration of society—saying thank you, or standing for old ladies, for instance—was in fact a negative act holding back the ultimate cataclysm that would eventually regenerate an unsalvageable system (Noyes). Curiously close to the fundamentalist Christian concept of The Rapture, accelerationism welcomed apocalypse as the ultimate sign that Things Can Only Get Better.

Since the 90s things have only gotten, not better, but certainly ... faster. Technology gets speedier, attention spans get shorter, news cycles turn over ever more rapidly. Things remain stable, new or satisfactory for vanishingly small amounts of time. In a world so obsessed with speeding up, is it any wonder that refusing to keep pace has some appeal? Conversely, accelerationism's contrarian impulse, a point at which left-wing thought can become indistinguishable from right, may have held the same passing influence on Richey's thinking as the right-libertarian contrarianism that fed into "P.C.P." *The Holy Bible* is poised between the accelerationist impulse—a kind of appetite for destruction—and the equally destructive appeal of arrested development. In "Faster," the album, with Blakean alchemy, achieves the marriage of Nietzsche and Marx.

NUMBER ONE I WOULD REGRET MY ENTIRE LIFE

The spine of "This Is Yesterday" is a bright and brittle guitar figure, gentle and relaxingly regular. The song sinks in like a cooling balm on "Faster"'S fevered brow. Its lyrics written entirely by Wire, the song's atmosphere of bittersweet retrospect would show up later in the more sophisticated militant melancholia of albums like *Rewind the Film,* with the elegiac "A Design for Life" a significant step along the way. It strikes a balance between regret and reassurance. The sudden sadness of "houses as ruins and gardens as weeds" make the song as despondent as it is euphoric, despite the lullaby quality of the chorus and the music's sustained calm. (In fact, "houses as ruins and gardens as weeds" seems more in keeping with the desolate imagery of "Die in the Summertime," just as that song's sunlit glimpse of "whole days throwing sticks into streams" seems to belong with the melancholy memories of "This is Yesterday.")

"This is Yesterday" is strategically and mercifully situated, providing a breathing-space between the onslaughts of "Faster" and "Die in the Summertime." The latter two songs sound suitably like high drama, the personal crisis expressed in their lyrics echoed and underlined by rocketing guitars and soaring, nastily anthemic choruses. But if "Faster" finds manic euphoria in the passing of time, "Die in the Summertime," like "This is Yesterday," mourns it. One of the first songs written for the album, "Die in the Summertime" has a spine-tingling opening —drums and guitars prowling and skittering until the song sounds like jangled nerves feel—which introduces some of the album's most self-consciously ghoulish imagery: the gothic horror of rusty nails scoring flesh, crabwise crawling, shrunken hearts and curled-up animals. Bradfield's uncanny enunciation on the final word of each verse turns "ideal" and "streams" into free-falling wails of almost gleeful catharsis, his delivery both taut and precarious like a rope-bridge over a ravine.

The Holy Bible's central theme of childhood as an idyllic period, contrasted with the horrifyingly inevitable ageing process, is a longstanding preoccupation of both the band's lyricists. On their 1994 tour, Richey annotated a set-list by scribbling in its margin the first stanza of Shelley's "A Lament":

> O World! O Life! O Time!
> On whose last steps I climb,
> Trembling at that where I had stood before;
> When will return the glory of your prime?
> No more—Oh, never more!

The Holy Bible is suffused with the same idea of ageing as not only inevitable, but also as inevitable weakening, corruption and decline from a state of innocence, contentment and potency, whether explicitly expressed as in "Die in the Summertime" or in asides like "She is Suffering"'s "no thoughts to forget when we were children." This is of course a somewhat rosy view of childhood, verging on the Victorian, and Edwards acknowledges it as idealized rather than accurate. His notes for the song state "Condition of old age-youth always remembered fondly ... Adult memories tawdry, of little value," clarifying that this is the protagonist's perspective and not necessarily that of the lyricist. However, several quotes attest to Edwards himself holding a comparable view. Not quite Disraeli's maxim "youth is a blunder, manhood a struggle, old age a regret," but both "This is Yesterday" and "Die in the Summertime" bring to a head the album's distinction between a childhood state of grace and a corrupt apocalyptic adulthood which offers only terror, loss, failure, disappointment and exploitation. Adolescence, the no-man's-land between these eternally warring forces, therefore appears as a liminal space in which, irresistibly propelled towards the adult world, one must choose whether to resign oneself or to resist.

In his counter-cultural memoir *Bomb Culture,* Jeff Nuttall explained William Burroughs' *Naked Lunch* as art which presented "existence as a nightmare obscenity [and] described accurately how we felt the world to be" in the early 1960s (116). The same could be said of *The Holy Bible*'s relationship to the end of the twentieth century. Its adolescent rejection of the adult world is far darker and more pessimistic than the convictions of *soixantehuitards* that, with their elders' generation overthrown, they could build a better world for all. In 1994 the Manics, as this album makes clear, had no more time for the political alternatives which appealed to some 60s intellectuals and activists on the left than they did for those on the right. Instead, the weapons reached for are those of cathartic self-directed violence or of even greater, nihilistic extremes ("all I preach is extinction"; the desperate, annihilating ecstasy of "Faster"). Like the self-harm it describes, *The Holy Bible* is an attempt to express trauma in order to exorcise it. If adolescence is on one level a search for the worst in everything, yourself included—the quest and challenge of asking "what's the worst that can happen?"—then *The Holy Bible* answers this question comprehensively. Its trauma is the trauma, at once generational and universal, of having to grow up.

CHAPTER 4
New Moral Saviours

Ifwhiteamericatoldthetruthforonedayitsworld wouldfallapart – Revol – P.C.P.

"Moral certainty is always a sign of cultural inferiority. The more uncivilized the man, the surer he is that he knows precisely what is right and what is wrong."
– H.L. Mencken

"Take away the right to say 'fuck' and you take away the right to say 'fuck the government'."
– Lenny Bruce

US AGAINST YOU

The Holy Bible was released in a historical interlude marked by the search for new meaning. In his notes for the album, Richey demonstrated a concern with the concept of "New Moral Certainty" which he saw solidifying in 90s culture, politics and society, regardless of its basis in fact or rationality. In the vacuum left by the apparent end of geopolitical battles based on ideology, it was culture, rather than politics or economics, which became the primary battleground. As the decade progressed, a new moral certainty began to shape itself in both Britain and the US which blended religion and politics to justify an aggressive foreign policy of imperialist intervention and a domestic policy which lauded "Victorian values" or "family values" over the post-60s advance of civil rights and struggles for racial and sexual liberation. A decade after *The Holy Bible,* Tony Blair's "new moral certainty and his burning desire for a place in history" would lead him to follow the US into war in Iraq, dragging with him a country which had expressed its resistance in the biggest civil unrest in living memory (Baldwin). In the years leading up to this, pop culture continued its historical role as an arena of conflict, subject to racial and social anxieties as it became a means for the oppressed to express themselves, and for this expression to provoke outrage and condemnation from those in power.

The Manics' relationship with the US had always been ambivalent. Like the Clash, who chased American success despite the hostility evinced in songs from "I'm So Bored with the USA" to "Washington Bullets," the Manics' official disdain may have masked the understandable yearning for the lucrative US market to which a majority of bands, and certainly their labels, have always been vulnerable. It should also be viewed alongside their idolization of US bands like Guns n' Roses and their admiration of the social critiques and political consciousness (as well as the sampling techniques) of Public Enemy. Their early ambition—to become a cross between both bands—was framed in purely American terms, since they had grown up in a time and place where the US was synonymous with both ambition and success. The dark side of the US was something that involved conscious engagement, looking deeper than the shiny surface you were sold and looking beyond the country's marketing of itself. The Manics' opposition to the US had a multitude of facets, from the country's pop-cultural domination to its hawkish foreign policy to its historical—and ongoing—exploitation and oppression of many sections of its own population. In 1992 the reference-heavy b-side "Dead Yankee Drawl" had anatomized all three aspects, and in some ways "Ifwhiteamerica" is a slightly more sophisticated retread of the same terrain, right down to Moore's marching-band beat, Bradfield's breathlessly sneering verses and the song's *West Side Story*-esque chorus.

"Ifwhiteamerica" situates several of the album's general themes within a specifically US context: military atrocities, imperialism, a foreign policy that interferes with the sovereignty of other countries from Cuba to Poland, censorship, nationalism, restriction of civil liberties and entrenched social and racial inequality. The song critiques both US cultural hegemony and the attempts to impose a US-led moral mindset on the wider world. However, both Thatcher's spectral presence and the chorus' excoriation of the union flag besides the stars and stripes make it clear that this malaise is not confined to the US itself.

The song's opening sample is taken from a 1983 broadcast by the Republican Party mouthpiece, GOP TV (everything, including political endorsements, is for sale). This both locates the song in the Thatcher-Reagan era and acknowledges this period's abiding influence on the age of Clinton and Blair. Both men presented themselves as heralds of a new era of social liberalism and post-80s, 60s-style cultural harmony, but both did little below the surface to ameliorate the economic damage done by their predecessors. The 90s saw increasing collusion between previously divergent political parties, as social democratic parties abandoned their commitment to economic change and adopted the 80s monetarist consensus. Richey's notes for "Ifwhiteamerica" sceptically dismissed those who "still believe Democrats are an alternative," offering a relatively early example of the disillusion that set in, in both the US and UK, when the decade's change in governments did not automatically lead to a better world for all.

ANOTHER AUTO-DA-FÉ

"There has been from Henry Miller to Norman Mailer to Charles Manson a logical progression. The Miller-Mailer-Manson 'man' [...] was born, emigrated to America, killed Indians, killed blacks, conned women ... righteous murder stalks the land."

– Gore Vidal, 1971

"Ifwhiteamerica" presents popular culture as a distraction from political atrocities, a papering over of abyss-sized cracks with celebrity gossip, consumer goods and performative confessional tales. Along with patriotic fervour and the tactics of divide-and-rule—especially along racial lines but also through demonization of the poor and unemployed—these superficial concerns are kept at the forefront of public awareness. There, they overshadow the aggressive foreign policy, whether imperialist exploitation of resources or anti-communist "containment," pursued by US forces in Grenada, Haiti, Poland, Nicaragua and beyond. In the chorus' sardonic hat-tip to Tipper Gore, co-founder of the Parents Music Resource Center, pop culture is invoked as another arena of conflict and suppression, where the interaction of class, race and culture plays out.

In the culture wars of the 80s and 90s, with the spectre of communism diminishing as an excuse for cultural censorship, surveillance and regulation, lobbyists and moralists seeking the next available threat to America began to target music. The PMRC committee was formed in 1985 with the aim of increasing parental control over children's access to music considered to promote—or merely to depict—sex, violence, drugs or the occult. Many record stores refused to sell albums containing the black-and-white Parental Advisory sticker, and others limited sales to adults. The PMRC's original concerns were with rock 'n' roll and heavy metal, but, as rap and hip-hop artists began to gain a mainstream audience, their music was targeted too. As rising crime, riots, school shootings and workplace killing sprees across the US expressed an unacknowledged malaise at the heart of the country, its causes were sought not in politics or economics but in the alleged pervasive effects of pop culture.

Such anxieties had a long history. At the turn of the twentieth century, moral panic over popular music increased in the UK as jazz and blues grew in popularity, with young white audiences developing an affinity with music by black and particularly US artists. In 1965, when the Pulitzer Prize jury wished to mark the contribution to music of Duke Ellington, the Pulitzer Board rejected the notion, claiming that jazz existed beyond the pale of "respectable" high art. As the century progressed, British critics, couching their opposition in concern with "obscenity," regarded US pop culture as a corrupting lowbrow influence promoting amorality to working-class youth. The PMRC, although claiming to be politically neutral, found itself making common cause with reactionary fundamentalist groups who saw "immoral" popular culture—and its associated crossing of racial, class, and cultural lines, its links with desegregation, women's rights, and gay liberation—as part of a communist plot to destabilize America. As several US artists pointed out, the PMRC's real uneasiness appeared to lie with the popularity of rap and hip-hop, their empowering of black artists and entrepreneurs and their ability to resonate beyond black US audiences. As a result, the idea of morality became "the instrument of a kind of political racism in whose name part of the population is irretrievably condemned" (Yves Lemeunier qtd in Chastagner 189).

Even left-leaning critics like Richard Hoggart, in his study of working-class culture *The Uses of Literacy,* could condemn the US gangster novels of Mickey Spillane as "daydreams for the frustrated and the sick" (268). Hoggart's description of Spillane's world as one in which "there is no horizon and no sky" (340) employed strikingly Holy Biblical language, and "Ifwhiteamerica" often seems anchored in Spillane's world of pulp and noir, or the semi-fantastical whirlpool of images plumbing the depths of American life in Burroughs' *Naked Lunch*. The song's landscape is both literary and cinematic: Bradfield reels off fragmented flashes of inner-city deprivation and depravity like Travis Bickle in *Taxi Driver*—or, more precisely, like Joe Strummer's pastiche of Bickle on the Clash's "Red Angel Dragnet." Like "Yes," "Ifwhiteamerica" has a hard-boiled, world-weary narration in which sex and violence have been assimilated in a manner too jaded to be salacious: there is no pleasure in this pain, no lust in this coma. This is a more nuanced, street-level view of the febrile and flammable US than Gore's top-down editorial, and it apportions blame for the social crash-and-burn it observes to systemic causes rather than to culture.

TOO MUCH WHITE IN THE STARS AND STRIPES

The effect of US culture in the UK has been condemned by the right as vulgar and damaging, and by some of the left as merely "sex in shiny packets." But, as proven by artists up to and including the Manics, it could prove complementary rather than diluting or disruptive to British oppositional culture and consciousness. The Manics' affinity with US black radicals from Paul Robeson to Public Enemy, their shared critique of white corporate America, was a function of the band's anti-racism, which in turn stemmed instinctively from the internationalist working class perspective they absorbed while growing up. This perspective contradicts class-essentialist assumptions on both right and left—either that the white working class will necessarily be bigoted and reactionary, or that it will require a middle-class vanguard to articulate its desires. Gun ownership in particular tends to be thought of as a right-wing shibboleth, but "Ifwhiteamerica" advocates it from a left (or at least anti-imperialist) position by recognizing the intersection of racial and class discrimination.

Oriented around the arguments of Marx and Malcolm X that capitalism and racism are intertwined, and taking its title from iconoclastic stand-up and free-speech martyr Lenny Bruce, "Ifwhiteamerica" also tips its hat to Paul Gilroy's 1987 work *There Ain't No Black in the Union Jack,* which addressed the interplay of race, class and nation. Although institutional slavery and direct colonial rule has been abandoned, economic exploitation and inequality, frequently justified by racist narratives, remain entrenched. Even in "rich" countries, black workers tend to be among the poorest and most disadvantaged sections of the working class, with correspondingly high rates of addiction, crime and imprisonment. The focus by government and media on these symptoms of poverty and discrimination ignores both the structural disadvantages which give rise to them and the institutional biases that make them worse. 1980s America saw its inner-cities ravaged by unemployment, poverty and government neglect. In early-80s Britain, meanwhile, cities from London to Liverpool were convulsed by rioting, ignited by police violence but fuelled by systematic deprivation and discrimination. Documents released in 2015 uncovered the depths of the then Conservative government's indifference or active callousness towards these populations, and a willingness to attribute some inherent "violence and criminality" to working-class and black communities, rather than regarding their actions as valid social protest (see comments by Thatcher's advisor Oliver Letwin following 1985 riots on the Broadwater Farm estate in Piggott and the then Chancellor Geoffrey Howe following 1981 riots in Toxteth, Liverpool in "Toxteth").

A decade on from this—and two years before *Melody Maker*'s Neil Kulkarni would describe the Manics as sounding like "the last honest white band"—their 1992 US tour found them "in miserable form" after the Los Angeles riots. The city of Compton "was literally still smoking—and they felt that the actions of a little Welsh band were pathetic in comparison" (Bailie, "Traumatic"). The five days of rioting in April and May 1992, stemming from years of police brutality, racial profiling and interracial tension in South Central

LA, had been sparked by the beating of a black motorist, Rodney King, by white police officers and their subsequent acquittal by a mostly-white jury. The endemic police racism and corruption which the riots revealed was not limited to Los Angeles. Over two decades later, the momentum gained by the Black Lives Matter movement against entrenched discrimination in the US police, courts and prison complex reveal how little has been done in the intervening years to do more than paper over the cracks.

This is the context in which "fuck the Brady Bill" becomes an anti-capitalist sentiment. The Brady Handgun Violence Prevention Act, which required all gun owners in the USA to have a license for their firearm, came into force in February 1994, and generated concern that its effect would be to remove the possession of handguns from poorer citizens, especially those of colour, who would find themselves unable to afford the license, leaving access to weaponry in the hands of the rich. Richey noted, as did many US observers, that this was a characteristic example of nothing being done about a social problem largely affecting the urban poor, until more affluent white areas also became affected: "typical – glorify gun culture until The Massacre gradually moves from the inner cities to the suburbs. The consequence arrives." In this line and throughout the song, "Ifwhiteamerica"'s consideration of context and circumstances is notably at odds with the moral absolutism expressed in "Archives of Pain," a song in which actions are divorced from their context and judged in isolation against an abstract moral framework. If one accepts the latter song's extremism is primarily performative, this becomes less of an anomaly.

LAST JET TO LEAVE MOSCOW

"Revol," like "This is Yesterday," feels like a bright spot at the album's storm-centre, a lightning-fast break in the clouds after "Archives of Pain" and before the skies darken again for "4st 7lb." Whereas "This is Yesterday" is mellow and melodic enough to make a listener overlook its melancholy subject matter, "Revol" is harshly, brutally energetic, its chorus hitting like a sledgehammer, imbued with an infectious enthusiasm (not to mention Bradfield's ludicrous, life-affirming "Sha-na-na" in the final chorus). The lyrics, juxtaposing political figures with images of sexual and emotional dysfunction or debauchery, explicitly blend the personal and political. Oscar Wilde, whose radical politics are still under-acknowledged, derived a positive energy from the tensions between "decadent debauch and socialist utopia" (Savage 26). In "Revol" a similar tension occurs, but the result is sexual dysfunction and its political counterparts of corruption and sleaze.

Presenting power with its pants down has been a time-honoured method of mockery and opposition, from Marie Antoinette to Bill Clinton, and the hypocrisy of politicians who engaged in moral grandstanding by which they did not personally abide was a major theme of the 90s. The Major government's Back to Basics campaign, which attempted to rehabilitate the moral standards of pre-60s Britain, was made a national laughing-stock by a succession of sexual and financial scandals involving its ministers, a cluster of which took place in 1994. "Revol" expresses its personal and political scepticism with, at times, a comparable kind of tabloid glee, by depicting as all too human the leaders we have been encouraged to place on godlike pedestals—implying, perhaps, that if one cannot succeed in finding happiness and fulfilment in one's personal life, then one cannot expect to successfully shape the conditions in which others live.

"Revol" was *The Holy Bible*'s second single in August 1994, charting at 22 in the UK where it sat bizarrely among the year's array of imperial-stage Britpop. The single's sleeve featured a quote from the conclusion of Orwell's *Animal Farm,* in which the degree to which the revolutionary oppressed have become the oppressors is revealed:

> Twelve voices were shouting in anger, and they were all alike. No question, now, what had happened to the faces of the pigs. The

creatures outside looked from pig to man, and from man to pig, and from pig to man again: but already it was impossible to say which was which. (89)

Looking from East to West in the 90s, like Alice through the looking-glass, one could feel as confounded as the residents of Animal Farm. The Russian premier Boris Yeltsin spent the 90s spearheading "shock therapy" for the former Soviet Union. This process of economic liberalization, privatization and asset-stripping led to the concentration of wealth and power in the hands of an oligarchic elite, leaving the rest of the country to impoverishment, psychological shock, endemic organized crime and corruption. To the benefit of its leaders and the detriment of its people, the East became a mirror-image of the West's worst excesses. The Manics' critique of Western capitalism and its turbocharged adoption by the East, allied to their lack of faith in the practical application of communist ideology—though not the ideology itself—makes "Revol" an extension of the axiom of post-communist cynicism which states that Soviet leaders "were lying when they told us about communism, but were telling us the truth about capitalism."

The Manics' use of Soviet imagery in a post-Soviet world was not new, but *The Holy Bible,* with its lyrical preoccupations, the band's adoption of military uniforms and the semi-logo of a Soviet war medal, saw it become something more definitive. How much of this was aesthetic opportunism, and how much politically earnest? Like the Manics, I grew up in impeccably Old Labour territory and, way before discussions on how to be a fan of problematic things, remember being starry-eyed about the Soviet Union. Any yearning for the USSR, though, had less to do with the reality of its final days and more to do with its symbolic opposition to a Conservative regime which was then laying siege to the industry, economy and community of my part of the country. I looked East in the way one might look to the stars in the hope of arbitrary rescue by occupants of interplanetary craft, with expectations about as realistic.

What had been a source of fear and fascination in the 1980s was, in the postmodern vacuum of the 90s, safely powerless and therefore kitsch. Fascination with the communist past—dubbed *Ostalgie*—tended to be denied any political dimension, allowed to manifest only in ironic or mocking forms, and very rarely linked with contemporary anti-capitalist critique (Pyzik, *Poor*). *The Holy Bible*'s suffusion in Soviet chic, though, had more to it than ironic recuperation. Nicky Wire, when asked, "What do you think makes sense?", responded: "Certain kinds of socialism, where everyone is given a chance. A true egalitarian society where everyone is offered an education." As basic and uncontroversial as this is—and note the cautious "certain kinds" of socialism, pre-empting the conflation of socialism with Stalinism—it highlights the band's commitment to keeping the idea alive in politics and culture. The later Manics' Labourism appears almost uninterestingly mellow in comparison to *The Holy Bible*'s morbid fascination with the extremes of Soviet communism, but neither approach denies the contemporary relevance of political history, or presents it merely as kitsch.

BIGOTS AND BIG BROTHER

"P.C.P." is, all puns intended, a high note on which to end. From the accelerating opening to the needling guitar solo to Bradfield's final line, in which he chews up the word "amnesiac" and spits it back with six extra syllables, *The Holy Bible*'s last hurrah is feverish and compelling. Hearing the tonal shift from the previous song's creeping horror feels like shaking your head to clear it of fog. Like "Revol," "P.C.P." exhibits a fine sense of its own absurdity, not least through some of the most incongruously chirpy backing vocals since Magazine's "Rhythm of Cruelty." Like "Archives of Pain," it probes the sore point at which left-wing rhetoric and dogma can cross that of the right. Like "Faster," it has an Orwellian undertow; the former's themes of surveillance and restriction of thought, speech and behaviour are enlarged in "P.C.P."'S dazzlingly dystopian depths.

The song's trigger was apparently Richey's reading of an anti-"political correctness" article in *Living Marxism*, the journal of the tedious career-contrarian outfit formerly known as the Revolutionary Communist Party. In 1994, Nicky Wire identified the impulse behind political correctness as an "inherently good idea" which, like socialism, was open to abuse by the unscrupulous:

> I think that's more than anything about the right to freedom of speech, and freedom of the media. Once the state gets control of that in a country, you know everything's fucked. That's the one thing that I think is really frightening about Political Correctness – the eradication of words.
>
> (qtd in "Manics")

The danger identified here—as with Soviet communism—is not the idea itself, but its misuse and corruption by institutional power. "P.C.P." constitutes a relatively early objection to what in the 90s was a project largely confined to US campuses, where it had arisen to combat an atmosphere of rape apologism, harassment and assault. In taking aim at extreme and almost self-parodic manifestations of this, "P.C.P.," like "Archives of Pain," walks a fine line between the contrarian and the conservative.

"P.C.P." brings out the album's—or Richey's, at least—sporadic libertarian leanings. The Manics' early courting of controversy was not entirely a pose: the band were out of step in many ways with 90s cultural conventions, and what they said and its reception reflected that. Their attitude was solidly rooted in the level-headed social morality of the Welsh Valleys, in which political (as opposed to personal) offence was not easily taken. At another level, of course, the band were in thrall to the attention-grabbing allure of Situationist provocation. Their almost compulsive commitment to going against the grain could lead them into recursive contortions of diminishing return—from the sublime and diamond-hard "P.C.P." to its ridiculous soft-centred descendant "The Love of Richard Nixon."

Part of "P.C.P."'S greatness is that its full-throttle fury is entirely indiscriminate, at times sounding like a particularly eloquent and high-concept pub rant. It is the sound of a subject driven to the end of their tether by great and petty insults and injustices, insisting that the outside world consists of a confederacy of dunces. Some of what the song denounces is not immediately recognizable as politically correct, or else the lyrics are so densely incisive—or so tied to the 90s—that their precise meaning is obscured. (Is "pro-life equals anti-choice" offered as an example of P.C. rhetoric, or an attack on it, or simply an anti-conservative interjection? What was the ten-foot sign in Oxford Street? Were the overweight genuinely denied medical help or was that some tabloid fever-dream?) "King cigarette snuffed out by her midgets," a line which seems particularly to baffle listeners, is an absurd but surely relatively straightforward presentation of the increasing power of the anti-smoking lobby: King Cigarette, an industrial tyrant like King Coal or King Cotton before them, has been brought low through the collective efforts of those with far less individual power. This image is an instance of the logical knots one can tie oneself in via contrarianism: an industry—a monarchy, no less—overthrown by a collective of comparatively powerless subjects is usually something the Manics would celebrate, but in "P.C.P." the toppling of King Cigarette's throne becomes another outrageous example of the world turned upside down, classed alongside teachers depriving children of intellectual nourishment and doctors ushering patients towards death.

The song's recurrent medical/pharmaceutical images reflect—besides, presumably, Richey's personal preoccupations at the time—90s debates over the right to treatment according to need, the NHS' founding principle, which has been gradually chipped away by the insistence on blaming individual illness on lifestyle choices, whether smoking or obesity. The relative prevalence of such illnesses in poorer communities, where nicotine and junk food often offer relief from a depressing existence and "healthier choices" are often unaffordable, is rarely factored in. They also reflect the 90s focus on "designer drugs" like Prozac, which enabled the rise of a multimillion-pound "depression industry" complete with novels, films and memoirs. This industry revolved around the attempt to medicate the symptoms of depression, stress and anxiety rather than dealing with their underlying causes, which could be as much socio-economic as psychological. Elsewhere, the very 90s cult of "self-esteem," whose intellectual godfather was Ayn Rand's former acolyte Nathaniel Branden, insisted that positive mental attitudes could counter one's desperate economic circumstances, using psychological bootstraps in place of monetary ones. Across the board in the 90s, symptoms of frustration, unhappiness or anger—from self-harm to rioting—were seen as irrational and as deviancies to be punished or corrected, rather than as legitimate expressions of the conflict generated by the inconsistencies of advanced consumer capitalism. Caught in the centre of this web of contradictions, "P.C.P." flails and rages with magnificent abandon.

BEWARE SHAKESPEARE

James Dean Bradfield: "Britain, as a pop music nation, used to have this very 'empire' kind of attitude. We used to 'invade' the world with our bands, you know? That's obviously changed, because in Europe they're much more interested in bands speaking their own language."

(qtd in JereC7)

At the heart of P.C., and of "P.C.P.," is a belief in the power of language. *The Holy Bible* attempts to give a voice to the unheard and the silenced, and to oppose the mechanisms which would enact this silencing, whether linguistic, cultural, economic or political. Its reference to bi-lingual signs invokes—for me at least—the English and Welsh road signs in the Manics' native country. The "systemised atrocity" behind them may be imperialism, colonialism, the attempted eradication of the Welsh language, the destruction of the mining industry, or all of these at once. A specifically Welsh-nationalist—as opposed to Valleys—consciousness is almost totally absent from the Manics' early work, though something like it would inform the later albums *This Is My Truth, Tell Me Yours* and *Rewind the Film.* But the idea of one's own language, and of being denied it, figures highly in the band's self-image and is strongly tied to their sense of class and regional identity. Nicky Wire, commenting on the "Roses in the Hospital" line "This century achieved so much to make a voice no voice at all," described it as one of the best Richey had written, noting that the sentiment "seemed to apply to the whole working class [in] a direct line from [miners' leader Arthur] Scargill to us."

"Language" here is not a literal one but a collective mode of expression, and "P.C.P.," like many Manics songs, recognizes how the end of the twentieth century silenced the working-class voices that had been gradually gaining in volume since its beginning. In the line "bow to the bland" it targets, from a position of relative non-privilege, the cultural and political loss occasioned when language is flattened to an inoffensive and homogenous background noise. This process has been, and is, used by cultural gatekeepers to erase the creative expression of the marginalized, justifying this suppression by stressing the ability of language—whether written, rapped or sung—to incite, corrupt and offend. Recognizing the power of speech does not automatically imply a wish to censor it—indeed, the use of words as weapons is a longstanding cultural tradition among those with little other social or political power.

In 1994, three decades after the Pulitzer board had refused the call to honour the "vitality and originality" of Duke Ellington's work, the year's prestigious Booker Prize was controversially awarded to James Kelman, a writer from inner-city Glasgow whose sharply intelligent chronicles of the overlooked underclass had polarized opinion. His novels were condemned and derided for their disrespectable language; critics, like those of *The Holy Bible,* complained that "every other word is 'fuck.'" At the black-tie award dinner, before raising a clenched fist in salute, Kelman spoke about the writer's duty to stand up to oppression:

> My culture and my language have the right to exist, and no one has the authority to dismiss that [...] A fine line can exist between elitism and racism. On matters concerning language and culture, the distance can sometimes cease to exist altogether.

As he finished, Kelman's speech was denounced as "a bloody disgrace" by one of the award's corporate sponsors. Although in many ways an exception that proved the rule, Kelman's shock win also provided a reminder that, alongside what would become Cool Britannia, 1994 saw the blooming of a popular culture whose mood was "much angrier, darker and more radical than we have come to remember" (Niven). Kelman's work, like *The Holy Bible,* both contains this unsettling cultural undercurrent and displays an atmosphere which more sympathetic readers identified as one of "gnarling paranoia, imprisoned minimalism, the boredom of survival" (Wood).

Today, the world of culture wars is as through-the-looking-glass as it was in 1994. An absence of alternatives to capitalist hegemony means the continuation of economic and social problems, while government and media refuse to acknowledge their roots and, through generating superficial moral panics, redirect attention from economic and political causes to social and cultural symptoms. In "P.C.P", attention to the interplay of class, ethnicity and language steers the song away from kinship with the kind of anti-liberal backlash which transfers resentment at a lack of economic power to the cultural arena. "P.C.P." condemns the language-policing attempted by the PMRC—a confluence of middle-class liberal and conservative attempts to control the popular production and consumption of culture which, as Richey noted, "aimed at the working class [and condemned] the very people it aims to save"—but also condemns the religious right's Leviticus-based homophobia and opposition to 60s-led advances in civil and reproductive rights. The friends of Tipper Gore introduced in "Ifwhiteamerica" re-emerge in "P.C.P." as a more clear and present danger.

CHAPTER 5

Archives of Pain

Of Walking Abortion – Archives of Pain – Mausoleum – The Intense Humming of Evil

> "I did not wish to be accused of dark, twisted inventions, or of misrepresenting the human potential for deplorable behaviour. The group-activated hangings, the tearing apart of human beings [...] the forbidding of literacy, the denial of property rights: all had precedents, and many were to be found not in other cultures and religions, but within western society, and within the 'Christian' tradition, itself."
>
> – Margaret Atwood

> "The interconnexion between sadism, masochism, success-worship, power-worship, nationalism and totalitarianism is a huge subject whose edges have

barely been scratched, and even to mention it is considered somewhat indelicate."

– George Orwell, *Decline of the English Murder*

THE RESPECT THEY DESERVE

After the personal self-laceration of "Yes" and the political wrecking-ball swing of "Ifwhiteamerica," "Of Walking Abortion" blends and distils both. It begins to expand the album's themes beyond explicit political critique and personal crisis towards the deeper philosophical questions asked of human nature in "Archives of Pain," "Mausoleum" and "The Intense Humming of Evil." After the rapid-fire pace of the first two tracks, the creeping first few lines of "Of Walking Abortion" also provide a momentary breathing-space, despite offering little else in the way of relief.

The song's opening samples the US writer Hubert Selby Jr, whose 1964 puritanical panoply *Last Exit to Brooklyn* is similar in atmosphere and concerns to some parts of *The Holy Bible*. Book and album walk a similar conflicted line between morally absolutist horror and morbid fascination with the squalor and venality among their cast of "junkies, winos, whores." Selby's imagery finds its closest echo in "Yes" and "Ifwhiteamerica," both songs seemingly set in the same overcrowded cityscape, their busy, bristling lines both pitying and contemptuous. After these, "Of Walking Abortion" is starker and sparser, its world far less densely populated. What was claustrophobically intense in "Yes" is here spaced-out and strung-out, viciously precise rather than breathless and chaotic. The song's towering contempt, its arm's-length alienation from humanity, is such that the mass of corruption which "Yes" and "Ifwhiteamerica" anatomized in lurid close-up has now, observed from a suitably disdainful distance, dwindled to the size and moral value of maggots. The terrain feels almost alien—we might be standing outside the universe, in horrified but implacable judgement.

"Of Walking Abortion" is merciless. Its musical bludgeoning and lyrical bleakness (Richey's notes for the song open with "There is little hope...") make it feel apocalyptic in parts. Against the spitting of Moore's off-kilter percussion and staticky scrawls of guitar, Bradfield's delivery is white-hot and scourging, the abrupt self-criticism of "loser, liar, faker, phoney" striking like a slap to the face after the drawling and stilted first verse. The cumulative condemnatory fury of the song's final lines is immense: Bradfield's growled "little people in little houses" and suddenly slicing guitar as sinister as a shark's fin cutting through water. "The massacred innocent blood stains us all" is a line which, like many on the album, could sound wildly overblown or parodic in the wrong hands, but Bradfield's delicate and raw delivery manages to set it down unscathed before the final, clanging back-and-forth of "WHO'S RESPONSIBLE? – YOU FUCKING ARE," Bradfield berating himself like a late-night drunk in the street.

And what are we responsible for? The song's targets range from mass murder, torture and incarceration by Hitler, Horthy, Tiso and Mussolini, to

Western consumers buying branded baseball shoes made by underpaid workers in developing countries (and, through the recuperation of radical icons or imagery—Malcolm X in this case—adopting moral or political causes as fashion accessories). The song neither admits nor allows neutral ground. The taut, ruthless economy of "pure or lost/spectator or crucified" underlines its view of life as a zero-sum game. In 1994, the era of Clinton and Blair's cozily compromising Third Way, the album's rigid logic is defiant, both continuing the divisions of the Cold War and anticipating the with-us-or-against-us mentality which spread, in the US at least, following 9/11—perhaps still this century's defining New Moral Certainty. The song recognizes 90s liberal triumphalism as disingenuous, a historical glitch.

Those on the losing side of the twentieth century's political battles, facing the sudden absence of previous certainties with nothing to replace them, could just as easily convert this sense of loss into nihilism and self-destruction—and, in places, an attraction or resignation to resurgent totalitarianism. "Of Walking Abortion"'s second verse observes this danger in the political backlash which formed part of de-communization in Eastern Europe and led to the rehabilitation of former fascist leaders, including Hungary's Miklós Horthy and Slovakia's Jozef Tiso. But the song, like the album as a whole, goes beyond this to suggest that fascist figureheads merely write large the things of which every individual may be capable and in whose crimes every individual may be implicated.

The song's title comes from Valerie Solanas' 1967 polemic *The SCUM Manifesto,* seen by some as a wholly sincere call for the eradication of men and by others as a more subtle critique of patriarchal control, comically and grotesquely exaggerated for effect. After shooting and wounding iconic pop artist Andy Warhol at his New York studio—thereby attaining minor iconic status herself—Solanas spent years in and out of institutions before her death in 1988. Like Selby's moral tracts, her story can be used to illustrate the dark side of the 60s, junctures at which the era's lifting of restrictions spiralled into social and psychological anarchy. Arguably, the song either weakens or subverts Solanas' critique by expanding its target from men to humanity as a whole. Unlike some of the band's hit-and-miss earlier efforts, this is not primarily a song of male self-loathing or feminist solidarity, but a comprehensive condemnation of human nature. The song's canvas is vast and its vision too single-minded to be concerned with nuance: everyone is guilty and blood stains us all. The rest of the album explores the uses to which this absolutist perspective, for good or ill, may be put.

THE GRIEF OF THE MOTHER IS THE PROSECUTOR

Between the murky "She is Suffering" and the relatively perky "Revol," "Archives of Pain" swirls, boils and seethes like a red-hot whirlpool. Anchored by a muscular bassline, it bobs between extremes, between the revving, slamming urgency of the chorus and the languorous, incongruously dreamy-sounding bridges (the line "a drained white body that hangs from a gallows" itself seems to lazily twist like the hanged corpse it describes). The song grounds the album's abstract concerns in a concrete context, its chorus naming a litany of state and civilian offenders both historical and contemporary, both iconic and relatively obscure. By marshalling these names together, as "Revol" does more playfully, "Archives of Pain" challenges the distinction between personal and political wrongdoing. As the album as a whole is conscious, the state can kill on a far greater scale than the individual, and often with impunity—with the claim to right, morality and justice on its side.

"Archives of Pain," seemingly advocating retributive justice in its most terminal form, raised eyebrows at the time and continues to do so. The band themselves were anxious about its reception. Britain in the 90s, particularly after the murder of two-year-old James Bulger by two other children in February 1993, saw an increasingly stormy debate on crime, with the right focusing on punishment as deterrent and justice being seen to be done, the left on understanding, rehabilitation and viewing crime in its socio-economic context. The Manics' intervention came down jarringly on what seemed an unexpected side. Although on this album the song's moral grandstanding and merciless absolutism is hardly out of place, its embrace of the state's potential power and duty to punish its citizens seemed unprecedented, and lyrics condemning Hindley's crochet lectures felt uncomfortably close to the manufactured outrage of the *Daily Mail*. Regardless of where one stood on the song's argument, the argument itself seemed uncharacteristic of the band.

"Is revenge justified?" asks Richey in his notes for "Archives of Pain." "Nothing in common with Manson or Dahmer cult and its current fashionability. There is no glory in innocent death." Bradfield's explanation of the song, drawing on Camus rather than Foucault, was that in the absence of visible manmade justice, a dissatisfied citizenry will turn from the state and back to god to see retribution exacted (see *No Manifesto*). "Archives of Pain" complicates the idea which is developed throughout the rest of the album, of collective responsibility for humanity's atrocities and corruption. If we have already established that everyone is guilty—and we will, ultimately, all be buried in the same box—then why the emphasis, so luridly expressed here, on punishing individuals? Why insist on enacting "justice" against one, if we all—through passivity, through spectating, through turning away—are equally deserving? Foucault's deep ambivalence to the state and state power makes the title's hat-tip to him seem like another of the song's logical fault-lines.

As both Edwards and Bradfield suggest, the desire for vengeance is not quite the desire for justice, and the heart of "Archives of Pain" is not merely the unexamined bloodlust that the *Daily Mail* et al thrive on. On the chorus' hit-list is the High Court judge James Pickles, notorious for dispensing the kind of hardline, zero-tolerance punishment that "Archives of Pain" is held to support—yet here he is, indicted alongside Dahmer, Le Pen and Milosevic. In the 80s and 90s, Pickles was notable for his contemptuous remarks towards survivors of rape. He accused one woman of "asking for it," another of "clever manipulation," and another of dressing in a manner "calculated to invite attention." A female hitchhiker, who had been raped by the man who gave her a lift, was deemed guilty of "contributory negligence" and her rapist merely fined accordingly. ("A lot of people," Nicky Wire mused in a 1994 interview, "don't like to see rapists getting off with a £25 fine.") The song's singling-out of Pickles, whose idiocy might also have inspired the climactic shout of "STERILISE RAPISTS," is a more helpful statement of feminist solidarity than anything in "She is Suffering." This aspect also complicates the song's critique, recognizing the flaws and biases of judicial institutions even while it advocates their strengthening.

Also notable is the song's opening sample, taken from a report on the trial of Peter Sutcliffe, who between 1975 and 1981 murdered thirteen women and left seven others for dead. In the recording, the mother of one of the women killed by Sutcliffe speaks to a camera outside the courtroom in Leeds. Most of Sutcliffe's victims were sex workers, as are a large proportion of the victims of serial killers, along with homeless and transient populations—those who are already economic and social casualties. Police investigations into the Sutcliffe case were hindered by the notion that such women were less of a priority and that injury and death were practically a hazard of their job. The socioeconomically weak and marginalized die young and, overwhelmingly, unheard. "Archives of Pain," by prioritizing the voices of sex workers and condemning both their predators and subsequent victim-blaming, illustrates *The Holy Bible*'s commitment to amplifying the voices of victims rather than "martyrs." This principle aligns the song against the artistic tradition which romanticizes murderers as martyrs, outlaws and libertines, while ignoring their (often more deprived, invariably less powerful and romanticized) victims.

Nicky Wire has stressed that "Archives of Pain" "isn't a rightwing statement, it's just against this fascination with people who kill." In the tradition to which the song objects, murderers have been viewed as iconic outsiders who have shaken off the constraints of "civilization," as the extreme, obscene expression of a general social malaise, and as lesser criminals in a society which applauds and rewards the larger criminality of capitalism and imperialism. This was in fact the attitude taken by the Manics in their 1993 b-side "Patrick Bateman," a song which lauds the *uber*-80s anti-hero of Bret Easton Ellis' *American Psycho* as a manifestation of the horror endemic to Reaganite capitalism, and which sees individual psychopathy as the logical conclusion of such a dysfunctional system. Bateman's victims, like Sutcliffe's, are already the casualties of brutal economics and urban alienation, but "Archives of Pain" sheds any exculpatory romanticism when dealing with real life rather than literature.

From the Marquis de Sade to Patrick Bateman, the male serial killer in particular has been a figure of fascination and almost preternatural power in popular culture, with the taking of life frequently mythologized as a path to some kind of immortality. Ian Brady, an admirer of both de Sade and Nazi Germany, claimed his killings granted him an "expanding sense of omnipotence." Brady's associate David Smith, the "tearaway" brother-in-law of Myra Hindley, wrote in his adolescent diary some lines which found their way not into "Archives of Pain" but "Of Walking Abortion":

> Rape is not a crime, it is a state of mind.
> Murder is a hobby and a supreme pleasure
> God is a superstition, a cancer that eats into the brain
> People are like maggots, small, blind and worthless.
>
> (see Wilson and Seaman)

The solipsistic sentiment expressed in the verse's last two lines pervades much of the album, and its loftily contemptuous perspective lends "Of Walking Abortion" much of its impact. But, in "Archives of Pain," the sub-Sadean attitude behind the first two lines is violently rejected with the same distaste for "edginess" which antagonized Wire on hearing the Therapy? lyric "I know how Jeffrey Dahmer feels."[1] A similar uneasiness at outrage-courting art was evident in 1997, when the Young British Artists *Sensation* exhibition included Marcus Harvey's reproduction of Hindley's iconic police photograph, composed from the multiple layering of an infant's handprints. The exhibition was greeted by pickets and protests, and Harvey's work was vandalized twice by other

---

[1] Wire's evaluation of the line was "I don't fucking want to know how Jeffrey Dahmer feels, and I think it's quite appalling to put yourself in that position." Therapy?'S response was, to my knowledge, not elicited, but relations between the bands seem to have remained friendly, with Andy Cairns joining them onstage for at least one gig on The Holy Bible twentieth anniversary tour.

artists. The *Sun* newspaper, oddly echoing the gallows-vs-crochet imagery of "Archives of Pain," wrote that "Myra Hindley is to be hung in the Royal Academy. Sadly it is only a painting of her."

"Archives of Pain" disdains the idea of murderers as Genet-like antiheroes, and of murder as glamourous rebellion in a meaningless universe. This insistence on a moral framework may be striking—*square,* perhaps, and at odds with the often nihilistic tendencies of adolescent romanticism—but it is consistent with the album's recognition of humanity's unsettling tendency towards Nietzschean self-aggrandisement by some and power-worship by others, the sadomasochistic "worm in human nature" described by Wire. If the album condemns institutional political sadism and its apotheosis in the Holocaust, then it must also condemn the same principle where it identifies it on an individual level—even if, in songs like "Of Walking Abortion" or the Übermensch impulses of "Faster", there is the suggestion that what is being condemned has been explored from inside as well as out.

REGAIN YOUR SELF-CONTROL

The Holocaust is a shadowy presence throughout *The Holy Bible,* briefly glimpsed on "Of Walking Abortion" and thrown into starkest relief by "Mausoleum" and "The Intense Humming of Evil." The subject had been one of Richey's areas of interest as a student, and the Manics had joined in the anti-fascist activism that formed part of 90s alternative culture. Alongside the band's commitment to firefighting its ongoing manifestations, *The Holy Bible* was a deeper-rooted attempt at processing the phenomenon of fascism. The album's "brother-sister songs" are contrasting treatments of the same subject: "Mausoleum" is all speed and fury, a blazing rage against the same dying of the light that "The Intense Humming of Evil," with its atmosphere of banked fire, slowly and clinically anatomizes. *The Holy Bible* deals with the Holocaust as apocalypse, its particular horror blended into both the horror of the world in general and the horror experienced in coming to terms with this.

On *The Holy Bible,* the band take a far more serious approach to Holocaust representation than they did with the sub-Pistols provocation of "celebrate Buchenwald as Her Majesty's heir" on early b-side "We Her Majesty's Prisoners"—or indeed their debut album's "you love us like a holocaust." The Second World War, and specifically the Holocaust, as cautionary tale, as a gothic horror story that defines the limits of what can be called civilization, is how the narrative has passed into twentieth-century history. *The Holy Bible* both draws on this lesson and complicates it. Matthew Boswell has identified the album as an example of "Holocaust impiety"—a counterpoint to works of "holocaust piety," exemplified by *Schindler's List,* whose redemptive and optimistic retellings can only be achieved by "resisting the basic facts of [...] good failing to triumph over evil." In retrospective representations of the Second World War, public preference for positive messages has led creators to focus on stories of "escape, survival and heroism [rather than] slavery, disease, suffering, moral compromise and mass death." By contrast, works of Holocaust impiety "deliberately engineer a sense of crisis [...] by attacking the cognitive and cultural mechanisms that keep our understanding of the Holocaust at a safe distance from our understanding of ourselves" (1–6).

Octave Mirbeau's novel *The Torture Garden* was written partly to allegorize the hypocrisy of European civilization. It was published at the height of the Dreyfus Affair, a judicial scandal rooted in anti-Semitism and still often referenced as a universal example of injustice. The book is ironically prefaced: "To the priests, the soldiers, the judges, to those people who educate, instruct and govern men, I dedicate these pages of Murder and Blood." (Mirbeau's character Clara, who reaches orgasm over the torturing of prisoners, might have felt at home with "Revol"'s political perverts, not to mention certain fans of "Archives of Pain.") This quote from the book, appearing on the album cover and gabbled by Bradfield on an unreleased version of "Revol," sums up much of the album's atmosphere:

> You're obliged to pretend respect for people and institutions you think absurd. You live attached in a cowardly fashion to moral and social conventions you despise, condemn, and know lack all foundation. It is that permanent contradiction between your ideas and desires and all the dead formalities and vain pretenses of your civilization which makes you sad, troubled and unbalanced. In that intolerable conflict you lose all joy of life and all feeling of personality, because at every moment they suppress and restrain and check the free play of your powers. That's the poisoned and mortal wound of the civilized world.

The Holy Bible's indictment of history, however, admits no distinction between the civilized and uncivilized world. Civilization can contain the worst of human impulses and achievement: murder, war, enslavement, exploitation, mass imprisonment, torture and execution have all, at one point or another, been carried out under the banner of advancing civilization, and are still. *The Holy Bible* argues that even the worst excesses of humanity must still be recognized and acknowledged as human. In her report on the trial of Adolf Eichmann, Hannah Arendt coined the term "banality of evil" to emphasize that everyday human mindsets, rather than malevolent individual psychologies, can enable an environment where atrocities are possible, and that this environment is not confined to the context of World War II. The human propensity to take pleasure and even sexual gratification in killing, interrogation and torture has been testified to in accounts from Central America, the former Yugoslavia, Africa, Vietnam, Iraq and Afghanistan (see Winlow and Atkinson). Far from presenting "civilization" as a restrictive barrier to utopia, *The Holy Bible* documents what can result from the unchecked "free play of your powers."

After the dreamlike delicacy with which "4st 7lb" fades out, "Mausoleum" is a crude and furious reawakening.

Guitars insistently jab throughout the song, a constant wounded throbbing, as though to reinforce the lyrical revulsion. As the J.G. Ballard sample dropped in halfway through makes clear, "Mausoleum" is primarily a song of outraged indictment. Addressing himself more to perpetrators than victims, but also taking aim at a culture of moralistic voyeurism, Bradfield revs through the breakneck chorus with contempt, tearing into the lines as though he cannot empty his mouth quickly enough of this particular subject matter. He ends it with another of the album's extraordinary vocal moments, a repetition of "winter" that becomes a wordless cry pitched halfway between anguish and disgust.

"The Intense Humming of Evil" is pure atmosphere, a deliberately uneasy listen in which silence is as effective as sound. (It cuts in abruptly after the final, choked-off "I want to die–" of "Die in the Summertime." So much of this album has been concerned with suicidal ideation, the idea of having nothing to live for, and the means of fashioning one's own exit from the world through starvation or self-destruction, that a song which focuses so suddenly and unflinchingly on the deaths of those who did not choose, welcome or enact it on themselves might give us pause.) The album's emotional palette, which on other songs might have blended rage, anxiety, mania and despair, here concentrates on painting only horror and abhorrence with relentless, suffocating strokes. Death again becomes a relief from suffering, but in this chillingly altered context. The sonic landscape is disturbingly industrial—metallic, cinematic horror redolent of doors clanging shut and the grinding of conveyor belts. A brilliant and harrowing invoking of the factory-line processing of humanity, it is the sound of human beings dehumanized, of individuals becoming numbers, products, matter to be mechanically rendered.

"Mausoleum," its imagery drawn from the band's visit to Hiroshima's Peace Museum as well as from Dachau, questions the narrative which places one instance of mass death on the side of good and another on that of evil. In *Bomb Culture*, Jeff Nuttall connects the "modish fed-upness" of 60s counter-culture to living, post-Hiroshima, with the constant possibility of death. For the Western world to have embraced the use of the atomic bomb was, he considered, to have espoused an evil as great as the Nazi genocide, which induced a crisis of identity: "[if] we were also wrong, who was ever right? If no one was right, what was right [and] what could guide us through the terrifying freedom such a concept offered?" (21). Rather than embracing the "terrifying freedom" Nuttall sees in the expanded possibilities produced by World War II—a world of no horizons—*The Holy Bible* regards them with a mixture of mourning and fatalistic dread. The album's perspective is still a Cold War one. The threat of nuclear war had burdened previous generations with the imagined horror of nuclear holocaust, an apocalyptic winter which would eradicate without discriminating by ideology or ethnicity. In 1994, that threat may have been lifted, but in its place was a burden less nameable and barely acknowledged: the burden of disbelief in "the end of history."

DESIGNER AMNESIAC

Nicky: "The lines: 'Churchill no different/Wished the workers bled to a machine' are about how Britain always thinks that it has a superior attitude. But as soon as the war was over, the attitude was: 'Let's go back to normal and exploit as many people as we can again. Keep the proles happy, tie them to their machines and then send them out to war again to be killed when we need to'."

(qtd in "Manics")

"The struggle of man against power is the struggle of memory against forgetting."

– Milan Kundera

In 2002, the Jewish Museum of New York's *Mirroring Evil* exhibition included an artwork with the very early-Manics title of *Prada Deathcamp,* consisting of a model of Auschwitz made from a designer hatbox. Its artist, Tom Sachs, who claimed the work sought to challenge the coercive logic of consumer capitalism, was accused of producing "holocaust agitprop" which "failed to grasp the gravity" of the events it referenced (Solomon). Sachs' choice of Prada may be baffling when a more direct connection is available via Hugo Boss, a company which in 2011 admitted its founder's enthusiasm for Nazism and its wartime use of forced labour. Fascism involves, classically, the merger of state and corporate interests, and, in an age of mass processing and industrial exploitation, mutual admiration existed between Hitler and Henry Ford (see "Hugo" and Dobbs). Rather than constituting a return to pre-modern barbarism, Nazism had a peculiar industrial character which was inextricably linked to twentieth-century progress and modernization, the advancement of design, engineering and construction, and the subordination of individuals to the demands of mass production. In 1932, the UK's Trade Union Congress produced a report on the productivity-maximizing Bedaux system, the brainchild of French-US industrialist and management consultant Charles Bedaux. Bedaux was to die in prison in 1944, after several years collaborating with the Vichy regime and the Nazi government itself. Criticizing the implementation of Bedaux's scheme in British factories, the TUC reported:

> ...the worker under such a system is made to feel that he is a cog in a machine for increasing output. The tendency is to obliterate individuality and craftsmanship and make the worker merely a machine.
> (Savage 298–99)

If it takes a certain *chutzpah* to end a remembrance of the Holocaust with the bait-and-switch "Churchill no different," it also displays a valid understanding of twentieth-century history, in which Churchill's views on imperialism and white supremacy were seldom far away from those of many fascists. In the hands of other bands, the lyrical sideswipe might have been a failed attempt at iconoclasm, as faux-edgy as "I know how Jeffrey Dahmer feels," but as a summation of the century-long war in which the class from which the Manics arose found themselves unwilling conscripts, it makes grimly perfect sense. After Churchill's dispatching of troops against striking miners in the Rhondda in 1910, the subsequent skirmishes of industrial history and their bloody 1980s finale fed into a certain perception that the country's ruling class regarded provincial Britain as a restless colonial population, to be governed like an occupied territory. The late-Manics song "30-Year War" encapsulates this, but all their work bears traces of the same perspective. In the 90s, these resentful regional folk-memories stood in direct contrast to Britpop's lionizing of national triumph—two world wars and one world cup—as a reminder that Britain remained a country divided. *The Holy Bible* is rooted in the 80s and their aftermath, which were foreshadowed in the economic crisis and struggle of the 20s and 30s. The album telescopes the twentieth century, with its brutal beginning and end for the working class and the Second World War as its cataclysmic centre.

James: "I didn't think the first draft of Intense Humming of Evil was judgmental enough. It's a song about the Holocaust and you can't be ambivalent about a subject like that. Not even we are stupid enough to be contentious about that."

(qtd in Maconie, "Smile" 35)

While most totalitarian regimes have been marked by an enforced forgetting, an erasure of the past, consumer capitalism has often seen memory and history as an enemy too. The Manics' politics have always been tied to a concern with their own history and that of others, and both "Mausoleum" and "The Intense Humming of Evil" demonstrate anxiety over historical memory of the Holocaust and how this relates to our understanding of ourselves. Richey observed that attempts to qualify or erase the Holocaust were an example of "even truth being questioned," which he considered more dangerous than the election in 1993 of Derek Beackon, the neofascist British National Party's first local councillor (Bailie, "Traumatic"). The BNP's rise in early-90s Britain, an example of the turn among the far-right from street violence to electoral politics, served as a reminder that fascism had not begun or ended with the Second World War, but merely reshaped itself.

Anti-fascist and anti-communist conflict in the 1930s had formed the backdrop to the Spanish Civil War, which drew volunteer fighters from all over the world, not least the left-leaning Welsh coalfields. After the defeat of Fascist Italy and Nazi Germany, military dictatorships and corporatist authoritarian regimes remained in power in Spain, Portugal and Greece until the mid-70s, a decade in which Britain itself faced the possibility of a right-wing coup against its Labour government from panicky anti-communist elements (see for instance Beckett). The persistence of popular anti-fascist cultural alliances and street politics across most of postwar Europe to check and contain the resurgence of neofascism demonstrates that the liberal utopia of peace and stability only ever ran as deep as the surface. None of this diminishes the Holocaust's unique dimensions, but rather lends them context as the apex of twentieth-century fascism and the nadir of the historical cycle of violence and victimization which *The Holy Bible* documents. "Of Walking Abortion" recognizes that the totalitarian impulse has guided far more of the twentieth century than the democratic principle has. Far from being dead and buried certainties, in the year of the album's release these issues were still live.

Both "Intense" and "Mausoleum" are marked by gnawing self-doubt and internal dispute over the meaning and significance of what they describe, what they present themselves as having documented and witnessed, as well as their capacity to do it adequate justice. This uncertainty reflects the 90s as a time of recalibrating, of abandoning the stability of twentieth-century narratives. In a postmodern age, every tear may be false. Truth could indeed be questioned, and was. In a series of essays, published in 1991 as *The Gulf War Did Not Take Place,* Jean Baudrillard argued that Western military action against Iraq was an atrocity masquerading as a war, in which it was impossible to tell the "real" experience of the conflict from the stylized and supervised media broadcasts through which it was presented to Western viewers. During the civil war and genocide in the Balkans, the accuracy of reported events was endlessly disputed.

In 1994, Stjepan G. Meštrović, in *The Balkanisation of the West,* predicted that rather than the liberal ideal in which democracy and capitalism spread to the former communist world, we were witnessing the incipient dissolution of the rest of the world, including the US and western Europe, into the kind of ethnic, religious and other pre-modern conflicts which were fragmenting the former Yugoslavia and which could easily be co-opted by fascist principles. Meštrović attributed this to postmodernism's undermining of Enlightenment rationalism and the philosophical basis which democracy derived from it. With no secure moral foundations and no guiding narratives, as "Archives of Pain" argues, power—and, consequently, concepts like justice and truth—can revert to those strong enough to appropriate them.

The Holy Bible is conscious of the need to memorialize the particular impact of Nazism, but also recognizes the dangers of reifying it as the only form of fascism that matters and therefore as a dead and buried ideology, leaving us unable to recognize it in resurgent forms. In addition to revisionist accounts of the twentieth century which obscure or downplay the dimensions of the Holocaust, the twenty-first century has seen both the rise of neofascist movements and the rehabilitation of twentieth-century fascism. "Of Walking Abortion" describes the public veneration of the corpse of Hungary's far-right ruler Miklós Horthy; in 2013 a bronze likeness of Horthy was unveiled at a church in Budapest (see Schiff). Across eastern and western Europe, parties extolling solutions adjacent to fascism have all seen notable electoral success, built on both postcommunism and, after the 2008 financial crisis, on the effects of rising wealth gaps, precarity, impoverishment and the imposition of austerity.

Disadvantaged outgroups—refugees, claimants of welfare, the long-term unemployed—as well as women and minorities have become lightning-conductors for a build-up of unfocused resentment, in the absence of any concerted attempt at (and perhaps, any faith in) more progressive solutions from the left. As "Mausoleum" warns in what may be its most resonant line, prejudice burns brighter when it's all we have to burn.

CHAPTER 6
Images of Perfection

Yes – She is Suffering – 4st 7lb

"In the 19th century, it seemed as if everyone was slowly dying of consumption. Consumption came to be viewed not in medical terms (medicine had little to offer anyway), but in popular terms, first as romantic redemption, then as reflection of societal ills. The consumptive prostitute, for example, could be a moral deviant redeemed by suffering and death. [...] The pallor and wasting, the burning sunken eyes, the perspiration-anointed skin—all hallmarks of the disease—came to represent haunted feminine beauty, romantic passion, and fevered sexuality, notions reinforced by the excess of consumption deaths in young women."
– David M. Morens, "At the Deathbed of Consumptive Art"

> *"Don't be misled: The imperative to 'Enjoy!' is omnipresent, but pleasure and happiness are almost entirely absent. We can have as many vibrators as we like, and drink as much booze as we can physically tolerate, but anything else outside the echo chamber of money-possessions-pleasure is strictly verboten."*
>
> – Nina Power, *One Dimensional Woman*

END OF THE CENTURY NAUSEA

> *Richey: "The only perfect circle on the human body is the eye. When a baby is born it's so perfect, but when it opens its eyes it's just blinded by corruption and everything else is a downward spiral."*
>
> (qtd in Bailie, "Traumatic")

Itself a downward spiral, a ring of Dante's inferno, *The Holy Bible* is also full of smaller circles: an animal's defensive coil on "Die in the Summertime," the navel-gazing that concludes "4st 7lb" and, on "Yes," the cyclical routines of sex work and wage labour fused into purgatory's circle. "Yes" sets the tone for *The Holy Bible* well: a song, like the album, full of sunless afternoons and plagued streets, disease, fever, nausea, swarming insects and ambulances at the bottoms of cliffs. Bradfield's vocal is notably restrained throughout, almost cautious, fraying at the edges as the choruses conclude, suggesting a narrator beaten-down and hemmed in by pressure and powerlessness, but it also expresses a quiet stamina and focused flexibility when delivering the intricate lyrics—a feat not always matched during live renditions. The song's breathless and raw reportage contains some of the album's most evocative lines, mixing panic attack, personality crisis, prurience and pity.

Saying thank you and offering your seat to the elderly float incongruously in "Yes"'s stew of mental collapse and bodily degeneration, but they fit logically into the song's themes of keeping up appearances through rituals and coping mechanisms so deeply embedded in everyday life that they become automatic. Adherence to social conventions of politeness and courtesy are one way for an individual to retain some measure of control over a disintegrating interior landscape, and for a society to avoid falling into Hobbesian chaos. The greater the internal churning, the more important it becomes to maintain an external facade in which rules are obeyed, orders followed and individuals presented as upstanding members of society. Like "Faster," "Yes" takes defiant, exhilarated pride in just about holding itself together, in keeping the cracks just about adequately papered over. With the unsettling inclusion of self-harm among these accepted conventions and coping mechanisms, the album starts as it means to go on.

"Yes" employs its sex work metaphor as a tool of social criticism, blending it with a veiled critique of the music industry—MSP as "the band that like to say yes"—as well as broader social and economic power relations. Something that makes the song's chosen metaphor particularly eyebrow-raising is the furore over Richey's acceptance of a handjob from a sex worker on the band's troubled April 1994 tour of Thailand. Adding to their manifold points of crisis in that year, the tour was described by accompanying *NME* journalist Barbara Ellen as "a morality coma" (19). Less shocking than it was exasperatingly predictable, the behaviour Ellen records in the city's red-light district and strip clubs cleaved to a certain tedious archetype that was depressingly endemic in the newly laddish 90s and which jarred with the band's ostensibly progressive politics. Was it naïve to expect any different? Ellen's interview makes clear the context of imperialist, racist and sexist power relations in which the Thai sex industry is mired, and the complicity of Western tourists in this. Richey attempted, when challenged, to counter these concerns by invoking an equivalency in exploitation between East and West:

> All developing economies abuse their young. When Britain was a developing economy we sent our children up chimneys and down coal mines and out into the street to

steal. This is just abuse on a wider scale. When we ask the Thai people about these girls they say that most of them want to be here. [...] It's hard for us to imagine what it's like to live in a zinc hut in 125-degree heat with no sanitation and basically no future. Who can blame these people for getting out any way they can? (17)

This justification ignores the fact that some parties have the agency and power to enjoyably or profitably participate in such "abuse"—whether capitalism or sex work—while others can only take part as the exploited party. This is the dynamic which "Yes" mercilessly outlines rather than obfuscates. The song's broader point is the fine line between exploiter and exploited, and how the same individual may be both in different circumstances. "Of Walking Abortion" excoriates Western consumers who feel themselves oppressed while benefiting from the exploitation of sweatshop labour. In "Ifwhiteamerica," domestic racial oppression runs parallel to a foreign policy of imperialist exploitation. The album's blurring of totalitarianism and sadomasochism also blurs the line between atrocity and pornography—in both cases, power produces desire and the results are shocking and transgressive. In the libidinal economies mapped by "Yes," celebrity, sex work and wage labour merge in a perfect storm of mutual exploitation. Power in *The Holy Bible* is inescapable and infects all relationships—there will always be someone or something to submit to, and someone or something to exploit.

LOVE IS FOR THE COLD MADE WARM

Richey's fatalistic attitude towards his use of prostitutes was of a piece with the posture the band had adopted since their early days, in which sex and love were considered distractions at best and destructive at worst. A number of Manics lyrics express pessimism or disdain towards relationships and seldom make any distinction between good relationships and bad, assuming that both love and hate will end in abandonment. The negativity Richey could demonstrate in the same interview towards committed relationships ("I've seen so many people get left or hurt. It looks terrifying") and towards groupies who expected some level of affection ("There's no passion involved for me so it would be immoral to pretend there was") displays a contradictory attitude in which sex and love are at once valueless—and therefore hold no power—and powerfully terrifying, a source at once of boredom and of fear.

This psychosexual tension runs throughout the album. While "This is Yesterday" and "Die in the Summertime" uphold an ideal of childhood purity against the adult world's corruption, "Faster" begins with a sample of John Hurt balefully intoning Winston Smith's line from *1984:* "I hate purity, I hate goodness, I don't want virtue to exist anywhere, I want everyone corrupt." Smith's contempt here is towards the Party, loyalty to which requires a corrupted idea of purity as political conformity. The rejection of purity, the acceptance and promotion of corruption, can therefore become a means of social and political rebellion, whether against Big Brother or the PMRC. But the use of sex as political weapon need not imply any personal tenderness or connection; indeed, in *1984* it is Julia's recklessly rebellious commitment to sex for its own sake that brings about the downfall of herself and Smith. Elsewhere on the album, "4st 7lb" ecstatically records the disappearance of the protagonist's secondary sexual characteristics and their "sex" itself, the deliberately reduced body "naked and lovely" in contrast to the tears and tension induced in "Faster" by the uncensored naked form.

In this shrinking from sex we are now, of course, floundering in the stagnant waters of "She is Suffering," the album's third single release, which reached #25 in October 1994. The song is dripping in disdain for "nature's lukewarm pleasure"—a line I'm happy to believe targets sex itself rather than women, but a song doesn't have to be misogynist to be boring. Richey may well have explained that "she" in the lyrics is not female *per se,* and that the song is concerned with the

Buddhism-inspired need to free oneself of desire in the pursuit of peace. Beauty as terrible and as terror may well allude to Yeats and Dostoevsky. None of this improves the plodding, murky drudge of "She is Suffering," which comes close to sounding like filler, or at least a *non sequitur,* with little connection to the rest of the album. Its polished precision seems to give it more in common with *Gold Against the Soul*—it particularly recalls "Life Becoming a Landslide"—or the later bombast of *Everything Must Go.* (Incidentally, it's interesting to note that charges of misogyny are hardly ever laid against "P.C.P.," even though that song pointedly characterizes the shrill, shrewish and censoring voice of political correctness as "she" and "her." This might simply be down to "P.C.P." being a far more enjoyable song.)

24-7 ALL YEAR LONG

The artist-as-prostitute is a laboured simile, but "Yes" makes sex work a metaphor for labour of other kinds, painting all aspects of modern existence as a kind of prostitution. In the universe of "Yes," the idea of Everything for Sale has taken on the feel of a religion, or a dystopian law by which the song's narrator, although exhausted by obedience, must abide. The line "to show displeasure's shame" had multiple resonances in a decade that relentlessly focused on euphoria and hedonism, on getting loaded and having a good time, and in which one's personal happiness was also a high-stakes game of conspicuous display. "Having it all" became an instruction to be unescapably obeyed, not a potential choice that one could take or leave. Work (production) and play (consumption) fused into a compulsory, mutually-reinforcing round of obligations and performance.

Two years before *The Holy Bible,* the band had hired businesswoman and former underage porn star Traci Lords as a guest vocalist on "Little Baby Nothing." "We wanted her or Kylie," remembers Richey, "because at the time they were both women that were perceived as puppets. No one could imagine that they might have their own vision on how they wanted to be sold." Hearing the song at the age of thirteen or so, I had no idea of Lords' history, and received her only as a compelling vocal counterpart to Bradfield. On the single's publicity photos, I saw her as a proponent of the same fake-fur wrapped, glossy-lipped glam aesthetic I admired in Courtney Love or, closer to home, Kenickie, or indeed the *Generation Terrorist* era Manics themselves. With Richey and Nicky to either side of her in similar leopard-print and eyeliner, she looked entirely at home. Her look for the single was a feminine reclaiming of sleaze and camp, an unfashionable identity in the 90s which differed from that of Riot Grrl, from "ladettism" and from the heroin-chic look of Kate Moss. By the time of *The Holy Bible,* though, the images associated with the band seemed far more vulnerable, frail and subjugated than this—it was hard to imagine any of the girls or boys in the lyrics of "Yes" being able to transcend their exploitation, to be able to sell themselves instead of being sold.

Richey's introductory note for "Yes"—"The majority of your time is spent doing something you hate to get something you don't need"—could have been taken from several recent analyses of twenty-first century capitalism. Wage labour can feel not merely dislikeable and alienating but actively pointless and damaging to self-development and community, which are eroded by the focus on producing and consuming for the profit of a few. By conflating sex work and wage labour, and suggesting no meaningful distinction can be drawn between the two, the song reflects some feminist arguments that sex work should be regarded as little different from other kinds of labour, in a similar way to how the unpaid "emotional labour" undertaken overwhelmingly by women under capitalism should also be counted as work.

In an increasingly squeezed and unstable job market, the act of compiling a CV or attending an interview has become an exercise in "selling oneself" both personally and professionally as a desirable worker—an exhausting process in which qualifications must be offered alongside an accommodating, dedicated personality; a willingness to please. This is an act that much of liberal "one percent feminism" does not challenge or criticize but actively encourages, seeing the gaining of high office or getting rich as feminist ends in themselves (see Power and Foster). The idea that empowerment or liberation for a female artist like Kylie or Traci Lords would constitute having "their own vision of how they wanted to be sold" demonstrates the degree to which this perspective had become embedded in 90s ideas of female empowerment. Even if women were offered the opportunity to "take charge" of our sex and sexuality, it was in the expectation that we would oversee its being sold to the highest bidder, that we would find empowerment and enjoyment in the ability to extract a high price for ourselves. The idea of not selling, of taking ourselves off the market, was never presented as an option.

In a decade marked by debates on whether the presentation of female sexuality was empowerment or exploitation, the possibility of being sexual on our own terms was repeatedly denied. Women could say yes to being "protected" by a paternalistic authority from the corrupting and exploiting influence of "raunch culture," or we could say yes to engaging in and conforming to its ideals. What we couldn't seem to do was opt out of both: when competition is everything, and someone else will always say "yes" if we don't, we are denied the choice, the right and the relief of saying "no."

CHOICE IS SKELETAL IN EVERYBODY'S LIFE

Anwen Crawford: "My favourite song on The Holy Bible *is, I think, '4st 7lb.' What a turn around from the lyrically patronising, musically plodding misfire of 'She Is Suffering'! The lyric still astonishes me. The music still astonishes me: the way it slows into that terrible, final reverie [...] I think it is an entirely truthful song – artistically truthful and ethically truthful. It tells the truth about how that disease feels from the inside."*

In a world where someone will always say yes, saying no—denial, abstinence, resistance and withdrawal—takes on greater significance. "4st 7lb," the seventh track of thirteen, is in many ways the heart of the album. Its lyrical invocations of stalled growth and arrested development mark a digging in of adolescent heels, a refusal to be dragged into the next stage of life, to "bud and never flower." Whereas most of the album sounds as brutal and distasteful as its subject matter, and unequivocally pities or condemns what it describes, "4st 7lb" is devastating in the lush, daydreamy torpor it creates, seeming to luxuriate in its own malaise. Its frank explicitness defies definition, blending reportage, fantasy, voyeurism and exhibitionism. The idea of choice is woven throughout the lyrics, insisting on the narrator's agency even as it brings her closer to death. "4st 7lb" is a significant song for many fans, whether or not they can identify with what the lyrics depict.

The historical ebb and flow of anorexia is difficult to trace, particularly given the lack of recognition of the disease before the later twentieth century. A flood of stories on the dysfunctional relationship between young women and food appeared from the mid-90s onwards, with tentative medical findings giving way to lurid sensationalist accounts and intrusive speculation over celebrities, giving the impression that self-starvation was endemic among young women in 90s Britain. Analyses often blamed this on the proliferation of unattainably perfect media images of women, to which "ordinary girls" struggled to live up. The emotions and motivations that inform "4st 7lb," however, do not merely stem from a refusal of adulthood or passive imitation of media images. Those who have experienced anorexia characterize it similarly in more complex and often politicized ways, as recognition and refusal not of adult sexuality itself, but of the mantle of social obligations and objectification that comes along with it.

In 1993, Jeffrey Eugenides published *The Virgin Suicides,* a novel which, although set in the 1970s, managed to capture a very 90s impression of doomed female youth in stifling suburbia. A sample from its film adaptation would appear, alongside some of Richey's unused lyrics from this era, on the Manics' 2009 album *Journal for Plague Lovers*. The novel's title characters, five sisters suffocating in domestic isolation, range in archetype from "cherubic misfit" to "carnal angel." As the story unfolds, their horrifying, cinematic self-destruction cannot be understood by outsiders, who, like listeners of "4st 7lb" and like some observers of Richey's decline, can feel by turns like archivist, obsessive, confessor and creep. Like *The Virgin Suicides,* "4st 7lb" invokes the potent mystical-horrific power of the unhappy teenage girl, in which strength, control and empowerment can paradoxically be expressed through a militant show of weakness, denial and refusal, up to and including death. It also suggests virginity—defined not necessarily in sexual terms, but in terms of remaining untouched and apart from the outside world—as a state of strength, to be aspired to and permanently maintained rather than lost.

Richey's notes for "Faster" include the phrase "strength through weakness," but in "4st 7lb," too, physical weakness—and the mental self-discipline its attainment requires—is perversely celebrated as a sign of power, superiority and impending triumph. Vanishing breasts and hands like trembling stalks become beautiful medals of honour. The protagonist's ecstatic masochism, and the song's unflinching cataloguing of progress in destruction, also bear traces of an earlier medieval tradition of female self-starvation. At a time when fasting was held to denote female holiness or humility and underscore purity, as well as constituting a means for women to exert some measure of control, the phenomenon of *anorexia mirabilis* saw women spend long periods in pursuit of spiritual enlightenment by taking in no food but the Eucharist. In "4st 7lb," the narrator remains precariously anchored to her dissatisfying earthly form, in no way reconciled to the idea of recovery. Like "Faster," the song takes pride in falling apart, presenting self-destruction as the only logical reaction to an unbearable world—and as superior to submission and acceptance of it. From this perspective, as with "Faster," by losing one can "win." Locked in the song's deadly logic, by taking in nothing of the outside world and therefore remaining uncorrupted by it, one can become a martyr, a sacrifice, a saint.

HANDCUFFS NOW PEARL BRACELETS

Nicky: "Anorexics do see themselves as having complete control, wanting to withdraw into themselves so that the 'state' – banks, shops, everything is obliterated and they feel some self-control, which has always attracted Richey."

(qtd in Double 12)

The 90s were bizarrely balanced between the pushing of female empowerment through entrepreneurship and ambition and the pull of constant arguments within politics and academia that, despite legal and material gains, girls were drowning in unprecedented levels of anxiety and despair, expressing this in the rise of eating disorders, cosmetic surgery, self-harm and depression. As anyone who's been a teenager will tell you, the anxiety experienced in growing up is nothing new; a 1950s study found "widespread dejection and a desperate striving for perfection" among British youth, with "very few girls content with how they looked" (Dyhouse 212–16). The 90s, though, saw an explosion of awareness and interest in teenage female angst, into which were woven the threads of disordered eating, binge-drinking and self-harm. The patron saint of female neurosis was of course Princess Diana, her loneliness and unhappiness in a loveless marriage manifesting in self-harm and bulimia, a struggle for control over her body as she felt control over her life increasingly taken away. The themes of isolation, breakdown and despair expressed in books like *The Bell Jar* found an echo in the self-conscious confessionals of Tori Amos or Alanis Morissette, and in the revelation of dependency on medication and therapy described in Elizabeth Wurtzel's *Prozac Nation* and Susanna Kaysen's *Girl, Interrupted*. Media handwringing over supposedly screwed-up and starving girls was in some ways the flipside to concern over loud, binge-drinking ladettes—either female bodies were taking up too much space in 90s Britain, or they weren't taking up enough.

A 2005 study suggested rates of anorexia had in fact remained stable in the 90s, while bulimia—characterized by cycles of binging and purging—had risen dramatically (Currin et al.). But even if there was no actual epidemic, the reproduction everywhere in media and culture of smack-skeletal, pale and hollow-eyed young women certainly contributed to the impression that there was. It's difficult to say (it was certainly difficult to say when I was fourteen) whether the sudden visibility of female self-harm, disordered eating, and half-articulated generalized despair made us feel as though cracking up was somehow a new normal, that having no wounds to show meant you fell short of the fucked-up female ideal—or whether seeing these things acknowledged, in however sensationalized a way, made us feel less alone in our own unarticulated discomfort. At any rate, Richey's expression of dissatisfaction, and his chosen methods of self-harm, made him a rare male exponent of what was held to be a typically female malaise.

In his part of Wales, Richey once observed: "the women are as bored as the men, but the men will go out to the pub and beat the shit out of everyone else; the women will stay at home and concentrate on surviving" (qtd in "Preaching"). Male rebellion against domesticity and conformity has often involved identifying these things with women: the nagging wife or girlfriend, the stifling mother, the trap of fatherhood. Female rebellion, as a consequence, has had to follow a less straightforward and ready-made path, and is often seen as passive and internalized rather than active and external. "4st 7lb" expresses rebellion and rage in a feminine register, weaponizing the things that have historically been used to control and restrict women: adherence to physical ideals of youth and thinness, taking up little space, coping and carrying on until it kills you.

At a point where the internalized violence of self-harm and disordered eating was seen as a female preserve, Richey's use of it to express personal crisis unsettled these boundaries, as did his decision to "speak" through a female protagonist. Female listeners who identified with Richey—particularly traditionally unlistened-to teenage girls—could partake of this tragic-heroic identity in a way that might otherwise be denied to them, or could simply see their feelings reflected in a way that would not be automatically disbelieved, dismissed or derided. Throughout the album, however, there remains a tension between depicting feminized suffering as a point of solidarity between artist and audience, and appropriating or fetishizing it.

Looking at Jenny Saville's cover art for *The Holy Bible*, entitled *Strategy (South Face/Front Face/North Face)*, the listener cannot help but associate and contrast the woman depicted in "4st 7lb" with the images of starved, injured and exploited female bodies more generally contained within the album. The painting's title becomes significant in this respect: disordered eating can be a strategy of resistance, a refusal of the consumption otherwise encouraged at every turn. It is a strategy which can give the appearance of conforming to physical and social expectations of thinness, obedience and self-discipline, while taking them to extremes in order to use them as a tool of resistance. From this perspective, the central impulse of anorexia is not weakness but subversion: the anorexic channels their energies into producing a dysfunctional parody of the feminine ideal. It is, to adopt an industrial analogy, the same kind of passive resistance as working-to-rule: we refuse to do what we should by doing only and exactly what we are told to.

CHAPTER 7

Won't Die of Devotion

"Era-defining icons like [Clara] Bow and Valentino might have escaped blasted backgrounds for a glittering realm, but at considerable personal cost [...] Yet their luminous presence helped to introduce new archetypes: in their particular case, a blurring of gender roles that evoked the androgyny associated throughout many societies with young deities and talismanic performers."
– Jon Savage, *Teenage*

"Girls can be unhappy without needing rock stars to tell them to be, y' know?"
– Anonymous female fan in a letter to *Melody Maker*, 1996

CHILDHOOD PICTURES REDEEM

When I think back to buying *The Holy Bible* in 1994, the picture looks so quaint it should be sepia-toned. Much of the album's context is now part of a lost world, the current consumption of pop culture vastly different: Woolworths was scrubbed from the high street in 2009, *Top of the Pops* had its last weekly broadcast in 2006 and online communities have replaced the networks through which I used to communicate. With a day-job, gig-going can no longer be a day-long ritual. Now that the Manics are so well-established, it's hard to express how uncertain their continued presence felt in 1994. When later fans relate the band's history, they've seen it play out like a drama, a legend, a story to which they know the ending in advance. Manics mythology is now something set in stone to be read and recounted, no longer living history in the process of taking shape around you.

Manic Street Preachers were, for me and for others, an inextricable part of the process of growing up and becoming reconciled to the world we were growing up into. I am continually surprised, humbled and inspired by the level of devotion the band attract and the amount of analysis and scholarship their work has generated, sometimes in print but more often online. In the process of putting this book together, I heard from individuals of all ages and from all over the world whose interests, tastes, and in some cases lives, have been shaped by the band's influence. Appreciation of *The Holy Bible* is much bigger and better in retrospect than it was at the time. But for many mainstream critics, while the album is generally held to be Manic Street Preachers' masterwork, this praise is predicated on a view of the band as a slightly embarrassing curio, interest in which is somewhat unseemly and inexplicable after adolescence. The album is supposed to—barely—justify the band. To those outside the fold of fandom, the Manics remain a band largely brushed under the carpet, due both to their culturally anomalous nature in 90s Britain and to critical distaste at the significantly teenage and significantly female nature of their "classic" fanbase.

Richey Edwards became a particular point of identification for female fans through his androgynous self-presentation, the confessional nature of his later material, and his use of traditionally female-associated methods of self-harm, which amounted to a feminized spin on the historically male trope of heroic (as opposed to tragic) self-destruction. These tendencies reach their apotheosis on *The Holy Bible.* This identification accompanied the idolization or sexualization traditionally present in the dynamic between rock star and fan, which it would be foolish to pretend was never there. The depth of feeling that can attach to a star, the explosive level of emotional investment, is of course age-old, and rooted both in sublimated sexual attraction and the hedonism and escapism that music can provide.

FRAGMENTS OF UNIFORM

Wire: "I have a lot of traditional male traits, most obviously my love of sport. But as a kid, I was very close to my mother so I think I acquired a real fascination and kinship with the female side. I would always rather stay in and piss around with make-up in front of the mirror than go down the pub. I still try Rachel's dresses on and stuff like that even though they're miles too small for me. All that is part of who I am."
(qtd in Maconie, "Everything"102–103)

The origin of the band's rockstar personas can be glimpsed in the escapist glamour they had begun to use while growing up, rooted not only in contemporary hair-metal but also in the homegrown glam tradition which produced fellow Valleys boy Adrian Street. Born in 1940 in the industrial town of Brynmawr, Street became a professional wrestler who made overt sexual ambiguity and outrageous attire into professional trademarks. His most iconic appearance is in a photograph taken on his return to the mines in which his father worked. Posing in claustrophobic darkness, in full tinfoil-and-feathercut regalia, his homecoming stance is as defiant and heroic and proud and absurd as Nicky Wire onstage in his feather boa and Kylie t-shirt. His appearance does nothing to compromise his masculinity. Similarly, the happily married and staunchly heterosexual Wire, dressing in glam-rock uniform, frocks and headscarves, lining his eyes and fetishizing housework, was able to complicate his identity without calling it into question.

James Dean Bradfield is a sharp and underrated analyst of contemporary masculinity and his own relationship to it, an aspect often overlooked in his superficial contrast with Richey and Nicky's performative androgyny. For all his occasional adherence to the laddish booze-and-birds stereotype, Bradfield makes it clear that an admirable bravery—or recklessness—is attached to his bandmates' defiance of other masculine conventions. (In 2016 on their *Everything Must Go* anniversary tour, Bradfield affectionately compared his bassist to Kathryn Hepburn and Dorothy Parker.) When remembering his bandmates' adolescent dressing for attention, he glosses it more as a heroic outsider stance than a threat to his own security, and emphasizes the strength it took:

> to walk through a town like that, looking like a West Coast androgynous mess with slogans painted all over you, in a hardcore working-class town like Blackwood, where people are stumbling out of the rugby club steaming [...] Yeah it took a lot of guts, especially if you're not used to getting into fights. It might sound dramatic and it might sound as if I'm trying to give it my own cinematic makeover, but it was! Watching Nick and Richey walk through town with that hair and the eyeliner was kind of startling! Richey had a fearlessness and so did Nick. Nick would just walk through town with his Kylie Minogue t-shirt and his skinny white jeans, with his hair all tousled up, and his eyeliner and necklace and

> they thought nothing of it when they were told "If you walk past like that again you big poof, I'm going to give you a fucking slap." They didn't care about those things.
>
> (qtd in Cummins 173)

As the band gained initial press attention, their glam personae, outwardly ambiguous sexuality and All Rock 'n' Roll is Homosexual sloganeering stood in provocative contrast to the dull dressing and leaden machismo of groups like the Farm and the Happy Mondays, who, as Wire noted: "are so drab. They look like my father." In 1992, music writer Richard Smith bracketed the Manics with Suede, Fabulous, Army of Lovers (and, uh, Right Said Fred) in a "new wave of ambisexual acts" whose shock value was a consequence of things having been "disturbingly quiet on this front" since the early 1980s (*Seduced* 11).

By the time of *The Holy Bible,* this new wave had decisively broken, the concept and performance of sexual ambiguity having gained traction in mainstream pop culture as the decade progressed. In 1994, *Select* magazine devoted an issue to "The New Lesbian Cool," following the soap opera *Brookside*'s decision to broadcast a kiss between two of its female characters. From the progressive perspective of today, it may be hard to imagine this as a great leap forward, but in a country emerging from the cultural battles of the 80s and their reactionary effect on culture and society—with Section 28 still in place, with government and media still attributing the spread of HIV to "deviant" lifestyles, with the age of consent for homosexual sex still higher than that for heterosexuals—1994 felt like a breakthrough. Although often presented as having been in the vanguard of this, the Manics' gender politics were more a continuation of the glam tradition than an attempt to position themselves as part of anything either "new" or "cool." Like many of the band's progressive tendencies, it seemed an accidental but welcome result of their scattergun commitment to defiance of existing social convention, rather than a deliberate strategy.

Craig Austin: "I've not sufficiently reflected how overtly sexual the early shows, imagery, and provocation were. Hugely homoerotic in part (though transparently played out by affected heterosexuals). None of that mattered though. It took the foundations of the New York Dolls and the LA glam rock scene and made it more aggressive, more confrontational, more unsettling. It was as far away from the 90s indie scene and its conservative, pedestrian rules as it was possible to be."

Berry Jordan: "The deliberate blurring and exchange of gender norms/signifiers (militaria vs feather boas?!) made it a text to study. [...] They are a political band but there was a sexual undertone to much of what they did and the relationship between Richey and Nicky – I'm not sure where I get that from but that was defiantly there. In a time, as a teenager, when you too are working out your own sexuality and identify, this blurring, this looseness is appealing."

Anwen Crawford: "Our friendship certainly had an eroticism to it [...] And so that homoerotic element to the Manics, particularly that spark between Richey and Nicky, their mutual delight with each other, which seemed so very, very feminine (didn't they call each other "sisters"?), that made sense, too. I think it helped us. We saw ourselves in them."

The complex response of female fans to the Manics highlights the complex nature of female appreciation of male androgyny and homoeroticism. Subscribing visibly to the Manicsfan subculture could be a way of demonstrating the wish to transcend one's surroundings, and one's imposed identity, in the way the band had successfully done. Fans could adopt the band's signifiers—fake fur, white jeans, black eyeliner, sloganized clothing, military regalia—or they could construct a uniform of their own which was equally distinctive and identifiable.

As anyone who's ever over-listened to "You Love Us" will know, antagonism can be life-affirming, and sometimes deliberately adopting a confrontationally extraordinary look can be a perverse form of self-defence. By the same token, though, doing so is at least a gamble, at most a risk, depending on its context, and those who adopt it cannot really bargain for its varying receptions. The lack of everyday space in which to aesthetically experiment was partly why the gigs I did manage to attend as a teenager, and for which I spent whole days ritually preparing, attained such value as safe subcultural spaces where one could dress up and act out. Dressing up for gigs—drawing, like Courtney and Kenickie and like Richey and Nicky, on aggressively feminine signifiers and a brash, ambitious and unapologetic kind of glamour—called to mind the trappings of working-class nights out: the meticulously, ritually constructed approximation of excitement, luxury and sophistication as an age-old reaction to being surrounded by drabness and mundanity. In doing so, it also evoked the escapist and empowering potential of that process. In Celtic mythology, "glamour" can mean a coercively appealing illusion and a protective charm. The band's devotion to dressing up had elements of both.

IDOLS AND ABYSSES

While many fans might have been drawn in wholly by identification with or attraction to Richey, for others this was an incidental or secondary part of the band's appeal. For some fans, it was actively off-putting, and *The Holy Bible*'s primary association with Richey's physical and mental collapse is to its detriment. Fans of Richey in particular and the Manics in general were not limited by gender or sexuality, nor was attraction and appreciation necessarily based on sex. There is a difference—overlooked or elided in studies of female fans with depressing regularity—between wanting to be one's musical idol and wanting to fuck them. For many fans, male and female, the appeal of the Manics was not (or not just) sexual, it was aspirational, to the point of imitating them in style, dress and mannerisms. Fans adopted the band's aesthetic and signifiers as methods of identification, escapist aspiration and occasionally empowerment.

If the success of *The Holy Bible* had a downside, for both the band and a significant part of their fanbase, it was its encouragement of a solipsistic inward-turning tendency which prioritized self-absorption above critical engagement with the outside world.

> Nicky: "Originally the band was never about self-hate anyway, it was about injustice in society, and with The Holy Bible it became so inward looking, too inward looking for my liking, to be honest. It was never the intention to carry on in that vein, but now we're destined to be frozen in time as this myth. And the only way we could ever break out of that now is to completely shed all our old fans, which I don't want to do. Well ... let's say, a section of our old fans ... those Cult Of Richey people."
>
> (qtd in Parkes, "Escape" 30)

Originating with the band themselves, the Cult of Richey label became a negative stereotype among fans and observers, attracting criticism which ranged from valid critique to condescension and abuse. At the more constructive end of the scale, *Melody Maker*'s Taylor Parkes denounced it as a "sick, inverted celebration" which, besides running counter to much of the life-affirming resistance that the band stood for, was also unhelpful in overcoming the very disadvantages it was based around. In a line which transformed my own perspective on the matter, Parkes wrote: "you don't deal with depression by making it the focal point of your personality, you have to rage against it, perpetually." On the other hand, the same paper's running-joke feature "Diary of a Manics Fan" drew on clichés—in fact, just the one cliché, repeated week after week—of the spoilt, pretentious schoolgirl with no "real" problems, no wounds to show, who wrongly thinks herself above her hormone-addled peers. Through such media caricatures, the archetypal Cult of Richey member came to embody the most despised aspects of any theoretical fan: dim, obsessive, creepy, hypocritical, hysterical and—needless to say—female.

There is a tension between the band's understandable discomfort—which many of their fans shared—with the increasingly ghoulish veneration of Richey that developed throughout 1994, and the equally uncomfortable dismissal or mockery of young female fans which it made possible. The Cult of Richey stereotype, rightly or wrongly, played into the traditional dismissal of female rock fans as air-headed, self-absorbed, shallow and oversexed spoilt little girls—when, you know, some of us were and some of us weren't—whose attachment to bands is therefore less credible and legitimate than that of male fans. It also reinforced the idea that there is a right way and a wrong way for a woman to be a music fan, and that right and wrong are decided by a majority-male criterati.

Today, this stereotype is less representative than ever, and tends to function more as a strawman—or straw-fangirl—against which other fans justify their own excesses or are able to laugh at themselves. The majority of past and present listeners recognize that *The Holy Bible,* in common with the band's entire career, is as much rage and resistance as wallowing and despair, as much waving as drowning. The last word should go to them.

Kasper Wibe Solheim: "'Self-harming teenage girls' was the go-to phrase back in the day, no? What I'm interested in is what it says about their detractors that it's so easy to dismiss a fanbase – and, by extension, a band – by painting their fanbase as teenage girls and young women who cut themselves. [...] I find the fairly transparent misogyny inherent in the lazy stereotyping of Manics fans incredibly grating at times, and I think a much more interesting question is 'why did these four dudes, and in particular this one dude, seem to resonate so deeply with a bunch of unhappy young women?' And a lot of the answers are probably very obvious, and some of them are maybe less so, and basically what I'm saying is that while Manics fans are certainly a lot more diverse than 'self-harming-teenage-girls,' I'm not really interested in pretending those girls weren't there, because they were, and their stories are as important as anyone else's."

Rebecca McCormick: "We were all just stupid girls in the eyes of 'real' music fans – we were only in it for the pretty boys in eyeliner, the feather boas, etc. Female fans of music get put down ALL THE TIME and as a young female Manics fan that was definitely my experience. I think the Manics gave me the confidence to say Fuck 'em."

Works Cited

Arnopp, Jason. "Depression = Drink = Mutilation!" *Kerrang!* (December 4, 1993): 38–43. Print.

Atwood, Margaret. "Haunted by the Handmaid's Tale." *Guardian.* Guardian News and Media Limited, 20 Jan. 2012. Web.

Bailie, Stuart. "Interview with Richey Manic." thisisyesterday.com, Tom Hatfield. 1994. Web.

_____ "Manic's Depressive." *New Musical Express* (October 1, 1994): 32–34, 61. Print.

_____ "Traumatic for the People." *New Musical Express* (December 23, 1995). Print.

Baldwin, Tom. "Religion in Every Orifice." *New Humanist.* Rationalist Association, 31 May 2007. Web.

Baudrillard, Jean. *The Gulf War Did Not Take Place.* Trans. Paul Patton. 1991. Bloomington: Indiana UP, 1995. Print.

Beckett, Andy. *When the Lights Went Out: Britain in the Seventies.* London: Faber, 2009. Print.

Boswell, Matthew. *Holocaust Impiety in Literature, Popular Music and Film.* Basingstoke: Palgrave, 2012. Print.

Chastagner, Claude. "The Parents' Music Resource Center: From Information to Censorship." *Popular Music* 18.2 (1999): 179–92. Print.

Cummins, Kevin. *Assassinated Beauty: Photographs of Manic Street Preachers.* London: Faber, 2014. Print.

Currin, Laura, Ulrike Schmidt, Janet Treasure, and Hershel Jick. "Time Trends in Eating Disorder Incidence." *British Journal of Psychiatry* 186 (2005): 132–35. Web.

Dobbs, Michael. "Ford and GM Scrutinized for Alleged Nazi

Collaboration." *The Washington Post.* The Washington Post, 30 Nov. 1998. Web.

Doody, Margaret Anne. "Deserts, Ruins and Troubled Waters: Female Dreams in Fiction and the Development of the Gothic Novel." *Gothic: Eighteenth-century Gothic: Radcliffe, Reader, Writer, Romancer.* Ed. Fred Botting and Dale Townshend. London: Routledge, 2004. 83–122. Print.

Double, Steve. "Don't Give Up the Deity Job." *New Musical Express* (August 27, 1994): 12–13. Print.

Dyhouse, Carol. *Girl Trouble: Panic and Progress in the History of Young Women.* London: Zed, 2013. Print.

Eccleston, Danny. "Unrepentant Manic Street Preachers: Their Appeal is Becoming Less Selective." *Q Magazine* (June 1997). Print.

Ellen, Barbara. "Siamese Animal Men." *New Musical Express* (May 28, 1994): 16–19. Print.

Forrest, Emma. "Cut and Run." *The Independent.* Independent News & Media, 20 Jan. 1993. Web.

———. "Preaching to the Converted." *Sunday Times* (January 23, 1994). Print.

Foster, Dawn. *Lean Out.* London: Repeater, 2016. Print.

Gilroy, Paul. *Ain't No Black in the Union Jack: The Cultural Politics of Race and Nation.* London: Hutchinson, 1987. Print.

Hoggart, Richard. *The Uses of Literacy: Aspects of Working Class Life.* London: Transaction, 1958. Print.

"Hugo Boss Apology for Nazi Past as Book is Published." *BBC News.* BBC, 21 Sep. 2011. Web.

JereC7. "James Dean Bradfield Interview." thisisyesterday.com, Tom Hatfield. Web.

Jones, Rhian E. *Clampdown: Pop-Cultural Wars on Class and Gender*. Winchester: Zer0, 2013. Print.

King, Richard. "My Little Empire: Interview with Rhian E. Jones." *Studio Hiraeth*. 24 Jan. 2013. Web.

Kulkarni, Neil. Rev. Manic Street Preachers at the Astoria, London. *Melody Maker* (December 24, 1994). Print.

Maconie, Stuart. "Everything Must Grow Up." *Q Magazine* (October 1998): 98–101. Print.

———. "Smile, It Might Never Happen." *Q Magazine* (October 1994): 34–35. Print.

Manic Street Preachers. *The Holy Bible: 10th Anniversary Edition*. Columbia Records, 2004. CD.

"Manics' New Testament." *Melody Maker* (August 27, 1994). Print.

Meštrović, Stjepan Gabriel. *The Balkanisation of the West: The Confluence of Postmodernism and Postcommunism.* London: Routledge, 1994. Print.

Milne, Seumas. "Back to Basics." *Guardian.* Guardian News and Media Limited, 10 Feb. 1994. Web.

Mirbeau, Octave. *The Torture Garden.* 1899. Sawtry: Dedalus, 2010. Print.

Moers, Ellen. *Literary Women.* London: Doubleday, 1978. Print.

Morens, David M. "At the Deathbed of Consumptive Art." *Emerging Infectious Diseases* 8.11 (2002): 1353–358. Print.

Niven, Alex. "Forget Cool Britannia-We Should Reclaim the Subversive Spirit of 1994." *Guardian.* Guardian News and Media Limited, 13 Apr. 2014. Web.

No Manifesto: A Film About Manic Street Preachers. Dir. Elizabeth Marcus. Wibbly Wobbly, 2014. DVD.

Noyes, Benjamin. *Malign Velocities: Accelerationism and Capitalism.* Winchester: Zer0, 2014. Print.

Nuttall, Jeff. *Bomb Culture.* London: Paladin, 1968. Print.

Orwell, George. *Animal Farm.* 1945. London: Penguin, 2000. Print.

Parkes, Taylor. "Escape from Our History." *Melody Maker* (June 11996):28–30. Print.

_____. "Manic Depression." *Melody Maker* (August 20, 1994): 12–14. Print.

Piggott, Mark. "Oliver Letwin at Centre of Race Row over Comments Made about Black People in Memo." *International Business Times.* IBT Media, 29 Dec. 2015. Web.

Power, Nina. *One Dimensional Woman.* Winchester: Zer0, 2009. Print.

"Preaching Revolution for Real." *The Times* (December 5, 1992). Print.

Price, Simon. Rev. of *The Holy Bible*, by Manic Street Preachers. *Melody Maker* (August 27, 1994). Print.

Pyzik, Agata. "Orgreave and Other Battles-Interview with Jeremy Deller." *Nuits sans Nuit et Quelques Jours sans Jour.* 9 Apr. 2013. Web.

———. *Poor But Sexy: Culture Clashes in Europe East and West.* Winchester: Zer0, 2014. Print.

"Richey's Last TV interview." thisisyesterday.com, Tom Hatfield. 1994. Web.

Savage, Jon. *Teenage: The Creation of Youth: 1875–1945.* London: Chatto & Windus, 2008. Print.

Sawyer, Miranda. "James Dean Bradfield of the Manic Street Preachers on a Year of Hospital Horror." *Select* (January 1995). Print.

Schiff, András. "Hungarians Must Face their Nazi Past, Not Venerate It." *Guardian.* Guardian News and Media Limited, 11 Dec. 2011. Web.

Selzer, John. "A Working Class Hero Is Nothing To Be." *Lime Lizard* (August 1993): 46–49. Print.

Smith, Richard. "Outrage and Boredom just go Hand in Hand." *Gay Times* 1991. Print.

_____. *Seduced and Abandoned: Essays on Gay Men and Popular Music.* London: Cassell, 1995. Print.

Solomon, Deborah. "Questions for Tom Sachs; Designer Deathcamp." *New York Times.* 10 Mar. 2002. Web.

"The 331/3 Author Q&A: Anwen Crawford." *331/3 Sound.* 6 Feb. 2013. Web.

Thompson, Paul. "Youth Politics & Youth Culture." *Revolutionary Socialism* 2 (1978): 11–15. Print.

"Toxteth Riots: Howe Proposed 'Managed Decline' for City." *BBC News.* 10 Dec. 2011. Web.

Turner, Alwyn. *A Classless Society: Britain in the 1990s.* London: Aurum, 2013. Print.

"Waxing Body Company with Richey and Nicky Manic." thisisyesterday.com, Tom Hatfield. Nd. Web.

Weight, Richard. *Patriots: National Identity in Britain 1940–2000.* London: Macmillan, 2002. Print.

Welsh, Irvine. *Trainspotting.* London: Secker & Warburg, 1993. Print.

Wilson, Colin, and David Seaman. *The Serial Killers: A Study in the Psychology of Violence.* London: Virgin, 2011. Print.

Winlow, Simon, and Rowland Atkinson, eds. *New Directions in Crime and Deviancy.* London: Routledge, 2013. Print.

Wood, James. "Away Thinking About Things." *The New Yorker.* 25 Aug. 2014. Web.

Acknowledgments

Fans' quoted contributions are from interviews conducted by the author in 2015, with thanks.

Richey Edwards' "pass notes" for the songs of *The Holy Bible* are taken from the 1994 tour programme, accessed February 2016 at <http://4.bp.blogspot.com/-rE0zkCj0T2w/VgyGqLdvbCI/AAAAAAAArQ/oZ9OFPlJEds/s1600/THB%2BProgramme%2Bscan%2B6.jpg>.

I am also grateful for the interviews, reviews, and articles archived at foreverdelayed.org.uk, thisisyesterday.com, and richeyedwards.net, and to manicsdiscog.wordpress.com.

PART II

Fragments Against Ruin: The Books of Manic Street Preachers' The Holy Bible

DANIEL LUKES

*"Everybody is a book of blood;
Wherever we're opened, we're red."*

– Clive Barker

CHAPTER 1

Comfort Comes

My first encounter with Manic Street Preachers I hated them—before even hearing a note of their music. I saw a photo of them—the press shot used for *The Holy Bible*— it must have been in the *NME* or *Melody Maker,* in summer of 1994, while I was in the UK for the holidays. I blacked out their faces with marker. They were pretty boys with cheekbones: they looked arrogant. I hated a lot of British bands with pretty boys in them in those days: Blur, Placebo, Suede. I had liked Take That briefly, earlier on, but something had changed. Thin, good-looking guys: how could they speak for me? I was fat, felt ugly, hated myself, not just my looks but my social inability, my abject failure with girls, my difference: I felt I was different from everybody else.

When I was a teenager I discovered my voice through Nirvana: I came into being through the pain of Nirvana's songs. I was full of self-hatred at the time: not just an almost constant feeling of misery, but this sense of being a miserable old soul that came through so well in the music of Nirvana. I knew that Kurt Cobain understood what I was going through, I was not alone. When I heard he was dead and had killed himself it was like a punch in the gut. I blacked out pages in my diary in mourning, and after a while, went in search of more music like Nirvana. I was on the hunt for it, and that's what I did in the summer of 1994. Cobain's death had created a void I needed to fill with more music. I was discovering rock, pop and rap, but that stuff, the music of pain, held a special place for me: Stone Temple Pilots, Tool, Alice in Chains, Nine Inch Nails, Melvins. The darker the better: it needed to be music that was dark and was about suffering, made by miserable men singing about their misery and sadness and confusion and pain. It was one of the few things that provided some respite.

So it was autumn or end of summer of 1994 when, back in Italy where I was growing up, I saw the "Faster" video on *Videomusic,* and fell mesmerized by it almost immediately. Wow. That song, that video, understood those feelings within me. I watched the video and I was reading the words, the key words of the text, the fragments of lyrics printed up on there. So strange to hear such words in a pop song: "acne" for example. Soft skin now acne. Yes, I had acne: as many teenagers do. I was conscious about it, I had spots on my nose; kids in my class mocked me, called me a witch. But this song, this band, knew about acne, and were singing about it, in the context of a body lived as a horrific thing. A burden of everyday misery, felt deeply, overwhelmingly at the level of the body. They may have been beautiful pretty boys, but they knew about the horror of life, and so their beauty was not so much forgiven, but irrelevant. Their beauty had been ugly to me, offensive, but they knew about *it,* so of course they were friends now.

Who were these guys? It didn't matter. All that mattered was that they knew about *it.* "Faster" interpreted and gave voice to—gave words to and put into words—these searing emotions that I had been carrying around with me. It spoke to me in that special way where I was being interpellated, called upon, directly addressed by a kindred spirit who *knew*. The loneliness, the pain, the misery, the yearning, the agony. When you are an angsty miserable teenager living in a world of pain, these are the moments you live for, the ones that make a difference.

So I fell in love with "Faster" and *The Holy Bible* with a devouring passion. It became my nightly bible, to listen to and pore over in bed before going to sleep. I had found what I had been looking for. And it was something more than the lazy apathetic languor of Beck's "Loser": this was urgent, this was awake, this was fury and anger and clear-sightedness, and determination—to do serious damage, against the self and everything; to enjoy that damage, and the brutality and destruction of truth. The lyrics, and their delivery, merciless in their bludgeoning of the self and everything else, which are the same thing when you're in that teenage monad world.

There is nothing but my pain. To me "Faster" made perfect sense. I was waiting for it and it spoke to me when I needed someone speaking to me in that way.

Mensa, Miller, Mailer, Plath, Pinter. I had no idea who they were talking about. I mean I had *heard of* some of them, but what were they doing here? I needed to find out. Actually, some years before, I had been to a garden party where Harold Pinter had read out a poem about his cock. I remember my mother disliking Plath for some reason, which surely made her work all the more appealing to me. *The Bell Jar* managed to worm its way into my life, and what a shocking, revelatory experience it was for me. How cruel and brutally exquisite it was to suffocate in silence alongside Sylvia Plath in the reading of that book. I remember riding into school in February, the day after finishing it, still reeling from the iron-gloved blow it had dealt, in awe that there was someone out there who understood. And then, killed herself, in February. Years later, I'd stay at the house of a friend of my dad's, in Chalk

Farm, in the winter, right near where she died, and frequently cross the bridge where Ted Hughes once encountered a man with a baby fox under his coat. I heard what sounded like cats killing each other outside in the gloom there one night.

Around the same time that I discovered *The Holy Bible* I was also getting into literature, moving beyond the children's books on my bookshelf—like Leon Garfield's *Devil-in-the-Fog,* which I read in June 1994 —toward edgier stuff, like Ira Levin: I pulled an all-nighter reading *Rosemary's Baby.* Rock music helped to open up adult literature for me, the literature of disgust and sex and transgression: I recall a review of AmRep band Cows' *Orphan's Tragedy* album that compared the band's sick and twisted sense of humour to that of Hubert Selby Jr. I remember reading about the "cruelty" of Ian McEwan, and picking up *Black Dogs* and *The Innocent,* and being hooked. Baudelaire, Bukowski, Burroughs all followed. I was attracted to literature opening up forbidden scenarios, and with *The Holy*

Bible I was starting to realize that the sick truths contained in my rock music songs were also there for the taking in literature too. *The Holy Bible* was my awakening, in many ways, my education. It set the ball rolling: it was a gateway drug.

Literature can be big and scary and boring and towering and intimidating, but in the context of a shouty rock song like "Faster" the Plaths and the Pinters are brought down to size, and I'm so grateful someone did that for me, made literature cool to me in that way. I would have got there anyway perhaps, but *The Holy Bible* certainly helped, setting a precedent by which literary recommendations from rock stars would then carry much weight for me: Tool's Maynard James Keenan recommending Iain Banks' *The Wasp Factory* back in 1998, Nine Inch Nails' Trent Reznor recommending Cormac McCarthy's *The Road* in 2006. What *The Holy Bible* did is collapse the artificial distinction between literature and rock, high and low culture, serious business and mindless rubbish. *The Holy Bible* showed me I could love both, and that literature could be as cool as rock. That rock could puncture a hole in the literary fabric and catapult me into that world, and that I needed literature as much as I needed rock.

In the section that follows I'm going to try, and surely fail, to do two things. The first is to explain what *The Holy Bible* meant for me, and why it was so important. This is doomed to failure: twenty odd years have gone by, and it's not easy to remember exactly what I was feeling as a miserable, angsty teenager, and what *The Holy Bible* did for me, no matter how many times I listen to "Faster" or re-read my old diaries. Secondly, I will attempt to read and discuss the books that are referenced by and were an influence on *The Holy Bible,* reading them through the album and in turn the album through them. Some I haven't picked up in twenty years, others I've re-read over the years, some are new to me. How did these books and writers influence *The Holy Bible?* How does *The Holy Bible* treat its literary sources, how does it select them and how does it read them selectively? How does it recommend and disseminate, cite and construct itself as a patchwork assembly of literary references? How does it use literature as a way of staving off horrors personal and historical? Why does it choose certain literary texts to make certain points? Why does it hang its observations on literary precedents at all?

At some point during the process I realized with dismay that I had set myself an impossible task. For each book I read, countless others opened up. Eight months in and I'm still swamped by books I haven't read: twenty *years* in and I still haven't read Norman Mailer's *The Naked and The Dead*—some books invite you in, others turn you away. The books pile up around me: I can't wait to sweep them back to their shelves and libraries, put them out of sight again. It's not just a matter of quantity: it's also the content. Books related to *The Holy Bible* are a gloomy bunch, and reading this type of material over a matter of months takes its toll. Reading about Richey's disappearance, about rock musicians and writers and suicide; reading about

Sylvia Plath and Primo Levi's last days; reading about the Holocaust for weeks on end. It was February, I was cold and miserable, and I had to put it all aside for a while, for my own sake.

What follows then is a chronicle of what I read. It's neither impartial nor exhaustive. I've gotten distracted, gone off on tangents, seduced into thinking not just about books, but also about films and other records to compare with *The Holy Bible.* As I read and read with *The Holy Bible* and Richey's story in my mind as central organizer of all these texts, I felt two movements occur. The first is a depressive deepening of some the album's themes, a pulling inwards and downwards, a morbid extension of the album's malignant spirit back onto the texts that had inspired it: they were innocent before; now, read back through *The Holy Bible,* they seem corrupted, their inner corruption drawn out. The second has been an outward movement, a sense of fragmentation and multiplicity, an opening up to so many other texts, so many avenues to disappear down: I watched Pinter films repeatedly, obsessively; I put myself through Mike Leigh's *Naked*. I listened to Joy Division and New Order and Throbbing Gristle with new ears. I fell back down into a hole that was my 90s self, and found the experience awkward and discomforting—I wanted to get out and be free to read other things again. I felt I could keep going and never stop, but the path was tightening, my readings constrained and limited by *The Holy Bible*'s narrow remit.

As I disentangled songs and lyrics, a sense of fragmentation set in, a feeling that *The Holy Bible* gathers these fragments against its ruin, pulls together disparate (and desperate) texts; it struggles to make sense or a totality of these fragments of texts, it knows it can't, not really, it's all too overwhelming, the horror, the pain, the misery, the despair. That's part of its appeal, surely: this unresolved struggle, this gathering everything together, the Important Books of the Twentieth Century, but the centre cannot hold. The album's formal structure, its framework, organizes everything admirably, but cannot quite contain itself, cannot stuff into its tight suitcase all the screams of the twentieth century. *The Holy Bible* struggles, and convulses, and squirms and explodes, and it cannot, it just cannot keep the lid on its flood of voices, its overflow of pain-driven energy, no matter how much it tries to affix that flood with fragments like shards. The holy unity of the book and all books has been shattered, and what's left are sharp pieces you can see yourself reflected in or cut yourself on. *The Holy Bible* cuts up literature to cut up the world and you. It steadies itself on these shards of literature, balanced between being overwhelmed by the weight of their indictments and falling into its accelerating overflow of words. On some level it might be a cautionary tale of the overly literary life, the life lived too bookishly and by the books. The life taken too literally, too by the letter.

The Holy Bible shines through its fragments. "The whole is the untrue," writes Theodor Adorno, "The fragment is that part of the totality of the work that opposes totality" (45). Modern art displays a "compulsion toward disintegration […] in the surplus of organization and regimen." In this spirit of fragmentation, my section that follows is a collection of fragments, linked by the act of reading with *The Holy Bible,* itself a collection of literary fragments shored against its and our ruin, a little library for dark times.

CHAPTER 2

Reading Too Much into The Holy Bible

Manic Street Preachers weren't the first, and won't be the last rock band for whom literature and books are of fundamental importance. They came at a point in which popular music had fallen out of love with literature again. "Richey's time as a prolific artist," writes Stuart Bailie in his 2002 *Mojo* cover story, "was book-ended by Shaun Ryder singing, 'I don't read, I just guess' and Liam Gallagher admitting that he'd only ever read one book, *The Lion, The Witch, And The Wardrobe.* In contrast, Richey and Nicky used their library tickets with intent" (78). Manic Street Preachers were from the start a fiercely bookish band, peppering their lyrics and album artwork with snippets from the big guns: Friedrich Nietzsche, Primo Levi, Albert Camus, George Orwell. *The Holy Bible* is their most literary work: an album named after the most influential book of the last two thousand years of Western history. It is arguably the case that never before and never since has a rock album so brilliantly put into practice T.S. Eliot's famous line at the end of *The Waste Land* (1922): "These fragments I have shored against my ruins." Not just a concept album, but also a book of books, *The Holy Bible* functions as a work which demands to be read as well as listened to. "It's not enough just to listen; you also have to read," says Mick Middles, in his 1999 book *Manic Street Preachers* (129).

The early 90s had their fair share of rock albums envisioned as altars to pain, and I consumed them avidly: Nirvana's *In Utero* (1993), Tool's *Undertow* (1993), Nine Inch Nails' *The Downward Spiral* (1994), Therapy?'S *Troublegum* (1994), Korn's self-titled (1994). The crucial difference between *The Holy Bible* and its (mostly American) counterparts is that many of those albums' musical odes to pain, depression and misery were often expressed through a wide-reaching and generalized sense of numbness and confusion at the world—Kurt Cobain has a political conscience, but frequently seems to genuinely not know what the fuck is going on. The Manics took a different route, dissecting the misery of modern life with the discipline and rigour of an academic dissertation. *The Holy Bible* politicizes pain, making it blossom into forms of self-awareness through a meticulous work of contextualization, carefully stitching together its genealogies not merely from the interior world of the self, but from the words of other witnesses: the insight, misery and catharsis of other writers, artists and thinkers.

Literary rock and pop are nothing new. Led Zeppelin put Tolkien to music, Kate Bush adapted *Wuthering Heights*, and Joy Division turned J.G. Ballard's voice into gloomy, stilted anthems. *The Holy Bible* takes its own literariness to a different order. The Manics had employed literary cut outs since their inception as witty sloganeering glam-punks (I wasn't there to see it in real time), but on *The Holy Bible* they structured an album around twentieth-century literature in a newly comprehensive way. According to Nicky Wire, Richey was reading "five books a week" at the time of its creation: in its artwork, its samples and its lyrics, the album gives us snippets, suggestions, acting as seminar in album form.

Jeremy Deller's *The Uses of Literacy*, first an exhibition (1997) then a book (1999), gathers Manic Street Preachers fan art and contributions, and illustrates the extent to which fans of the band constitute a community of people who share a cultural framework, which is defined in part by a particular set of texts. The item "Books that have been acknowledged by the Manic Street Preachers as being influential, subsequently collected and read by Donna Marshall" (which includes Sylvia Plath's *The Bell Jar,* Philip Larkin's *Collected Poems,* William Wharton's *Birdy,* Henry Miller's *Black Spring,* and Primo Levi's *If This Is a Man*), comprises a particular canon of twentieth-century literature across fiction, philosophy, drama and agitprop. That Deller's project references Richard Hoggart's 1957 book of the same name—a founding work on cultural studies, working class youth and mass culture—underscores the proliferating nature of the intertextual uses that the Manics' works lend themselves to, offering themselves as a bibliography or library of suggested readings.

Brought to life through an interview sample on the song "Mausoleum," J.G. Ballard had with *The Atrocity Exhibition* explored literature as manifesto: unequal parts shock tactics, para-academic objectivity and black humour. Following Ballard's lead, *The Holy Bible* presents itself as unconventional bibliography for the twentieth century, summarizing and passing judgment on it in the form of a document which groups together key twentieth-century texts linked not by logic or the rigid categories of genre, but according to a sensibility or worldview defined by sensitivity to historical and personal atrocity and disaster. The album is an atrocity exhibition, a collage of jarring and disjointed fragments that collude to produce a picture of ultimate pain and despair. The signs it posts throughout perform an act of political collage, and assemble an armour of charms against evil. Visually, between its covers, images of religious icons, tombstone angels, totalitarian aesthetics and childhood innocence accompany and illustrate the lyrics like postmodern versions of medieval manuscript illuminations. *The Holy Bible* belongs to the genre of the anti-or para-bible. A desacralized book of songs; book of books. Though it doesn't mention it by name, one book it resembles is Dante Alighieri's *Divine Comedy* (1308–21), also the story of a young man who has lost his way in life. Into its own judgmental *Inferno* it casts dictators and serial killers alike, in an indictment of our worship of strength, violence and domination.

Its contribution as a work of literary criticism lies in its textual juxtapositions, sculpting between decadent literature and social critique the idea of truth as a kind of cruelty. Bookended by a quote from Octave Mirbeau's *The Torture Garden* ("You live attached in a cowardly fashion to moral and social conventions you despise, condemn, and know lack all foundation...") the album channels Foucault's explorations of how the modern world leads us to experience our enslavements as pleasures. *The Holy Bible's* cruelty is desacratory, desacralizing, a tearing down of the sacred cows of democracy, capitalism and individualism performed through a militant dysphoria: a calculated rejection of contemporary modernity from a place of a political, aesthetic and personal total dejection, forging an ideological purity that cannot but collapse in on its rotten self. Gazing sadly on the burning scrap-heap of twentieth-century history, *The Holy Bible* forges a bond through an aesthetic performance of pain between band and fan, embodied in the humanized trinity of the cover art: Jenny Saville's obese woman contemplating herself, and looking out at the world.

Musically, *The Holy Bible* saw the Manics step up and finally become a great band. Sharply canning the polished glam rock gloss of *Gold Against the Soul,* their third album brought the quartet home. Sonically as well as conceptually, the Manics looked to classic British punk and post-punk: The Clash, Wire, Magazine, Gang of Four, the metallic din of Killing Joke, the gaunt and stripped-down alienations of Joy Division, PiL's dubby explorations, the industrial smear of Throbbing Gristle, who had also flirted with paramilitary aesthetics in their war on civilization. The product of a regime of hardship and discipline, its sonic framework was tight and coiled, grimy and thrillingly raw.

The alignment of its form and content, the apparent seamlessness of its influences, musical and literary, into a vision coherent through its own fragmentation, are what enables it to be such a compelling teacher of literature. Its impassioned, often euphoric performance is an act of interpretation which brings twentieth-century literature to life in new ways, for new ears and eyes. It sent my teenage self off on all kinds of investigations, effectively allowing me to discover for myself the voices I came to need. I have come to see the textual community of like-minded souls that *The Holy Bible* sets up as a necessary antidote to the dangers of depressive solitude and isolationism.

The section that follows is an attempt to re-visit some of those investigations, purposefully reading too much into *The Holy Bible*. It is also something of a thought experiment: an attempt at reading the album as if it were a book. If *The Holy Bible* were a book, what kind of book would it be? Perhaps a novel, an experimental novel, in which a tortured young man loses his way, inhabits a variety of characters and voices, tries to find his way again through books, scraps of texts, that tell him of great horrors taken place. He orders them sadly, and looks upon this ruin. A warm, nauseous breeze begins to blow the fragments away; a storm is coming but he can hold on, just a bit longer, just enough time to sketch out a plan, to make of them a meaningful and beautiful message. A set of instructions, a mad idea perhaps, but worth a try. A device, a tool for historical, political, aesthetic and self-knowledge. Even, dare I say it, a moral compass in a mad world.

CHAPTER 3

Against Literature: Therapy?'s "Potato Junkie"

Therapy?'S early music, in particular their 1993 album *Troublegum*, articulates feelings of loneliness, self-loathing, and anger comparable to those of *The Holy Bible*. There are songs about stalking, serial killers, struggles with depression and mental health. Yet the place of literature in Therapy? is sometimes one in which literature is rejected. In "Potato Junkie," on 1992'S *Pleasure Death*, Andy Cairns sings: "I'm bitter, I'm twisted/James Joyce is fucking my sister." The point of the song is that James Joyce doesn't mean shit to him; literature is a tourist attraction, or something dead. "I can see you, I can read you, I won't be you," he sings, shoving Joyce in with 1690 (The Battle of the Boyne and the Orange Order), and the colour green, a composite caricature of Ireland that Cairns rejects: "I'm trying hard just to survive/To keep myself alive." Literature as antique, as heritage material, is inimical to the business of living, the daily struggle with being alive. It's an anti-intellectual, anti-literary approach that sees canonical literature, especially high-brow modernism celebrated as regional historical heritage popular culture, to be rejected as an authority and desecrated with a shocking sex reference. Joyce becomes the opposite of something liberating, something alive, something which can be used to liberate yourself.

The transformation of literature into heritage tourism can be irritating—I have the same feeling when I see the statues of Fernando Pessoa in Lisbon. In his writing Pessoa complains of being a nobody all the time; there is something painful in the fact that after his death he is an everybody sitting on the bench in public, has been made into a product to be publically enjoyed. There is an irony in that Therapy? bring Joyce to life in a rock song by rejecting him obscenely, and so the song performs the double function of rejecting literature as heritage, and re-making it as rock song: a rousing disavowal and rejection of literature that turns into a twisted affirmation of the literary. Therapy? will reprise this trick (in 1995's "Jude the Obscene"), and in their later career appear to make peace with the high-brow and the literary: the title of 2009 album *Crooked Timber* references Kant's notorious view on humanity, and that of 2012 album *A Brief Crack of Light* is a Nabokov quote.

The Manics, from the beginning, know better. They know that literature represents a freedom from whatever situation you find yourself in, it offers a way out of your predicament. From their very inception, they openly embrace literature, regardless of how unfashionable and dangerous it is, or inimical to that stereotypical view of working-class identity as anti-intellectual, the type that doesn't think about life and only wants to get drunk described and challenged in "A Design for Life." For the Manics, and for *The Holy Bible*, literature is life. It is a means to construct community, on the small scale—"We were like magpies, collecting information. We had intellectual meetings. Discussing books," recounts James Dean Bradfield of the band's early days (qtd in Middles 44)—and on the larger one, inserting yourself through literature into the framework of cultural and political conversation: "That was a fantastic achievement, finding that higher ground" (45).

CHAPTER 4

A Heap of Broken Images: T.S. Eliot's The Waste Land

"The repudiation of conventionally 'poetic' imagery, the organizing of symbolic images, incidents, fragments of conversation or of memory without any explanatory links that would lower the pressure of meaning, the arresting of attention by imagistic shock or emotional anticlimax, the purging of self-pity by irony as well as the complete suppression of the poet's own personality and his appearance only through the *persona* of his invented character," writes David Daiches (1132). He's not talking about Richey Edwards, though on some level it feels like he could be. He's talking about T.S. Eliot.

The title of my section is a re-arrangement of part of a verse from the end of Eliot's *The Waste Land,* that modernist work that re-invented poetry for the twentieth century. The poem shows how a broken, fragmented, vortexing world needs a suitably broken and crushed-up poetry through which to express itself. At the end of the poem, when the speaker has morphed into the old, castrated Fisher King, he refers to "these fragments I have shored against my ruins." This verse is often understood as reference to the various fragments that make up the poem: it expresses the notion that there may nothing in the world but broken fragments, torn off from their wholes, untethered and blowing and flowing about a wrecked landscape, that "heap of broken images" that appears toward the beginning of the poem. These fragments of poetry and text and culture and literature and religion from all over the place, having made their way here, to where I am sitting by the river which flows by me full of trash and corpses, I have shored up, here kept, buried in the sand and earth around me, to help me get by in this shuddering world, remind me of who I am. My land is in ruins, and that's fine:

these fragments will help make sense of it all.

The poem is thus a machinery for memory, an archive of seemingly useless bits that remind us of what happened. Notes, scribbled furiously on scraps of paper that flutter away in the wind. Ballard floats above, deconstructing explosions into mechanical parts. Solanas ready to castrate the male body, as it slithers away in abject disappearance. Texts and authors flow through *The Holy Bible,* animating its innards with twisted literary visions, mapping the empty space between the silence of literature and the joyous noise of music: rock, noise, industrial, metal, pop. Literature comes alive spoken by—sorry, spat out by—the interpreter, the adaptor, the curator, the archivist. And the old friends from the library pop down with snippets and their samples. The ghostly archive of literature's dead or soon-to-be-dead. The old gods with their voices and worries and woes.

The young writer joins them. *The Waste Land* has a lot in common with *The Holy Bible:* the fragments of conversation, overhead as the narrator moves through the unreal city; whispers glide along the surface of the river, rolling in like a fog. Eliot's speakers are working-class women, aged by childbirth and poverty, cups of tea in dirty caffs; they are the ennuied middle classes with their orientalist interior design. Eliot the eavesdropper, sucking in and churning out their words in broken form, garbled poetry to delight the mind. *The Waste Land* is polyphonic: it chastises the protagonist for his self-obsession, his unhealthy focus on himself and his own supposed problems. Prufrock, the poet's youthful alter ego, has had his say, and now it is time to empathize with other voices. Eliot's wastelander surveys it all and takes it all in, sees a world, the vision of a world filled with holes and each hole is a screen into which you can peer ... or maybe it is a shard of glass, in which you can see your own reflection—and cut yourself if you're not careful.

Daiches is but one of many critics who objects to Eliot's wilful obscurity: this poem stitched together by fragments who knows where from.

Obscure, *The Waste Land* certainly is. It is a text that flaunts its inscrutability, seeming to proffer the laconic message that these clues will lead you nowhere useful. They're just there to amuse, they mean nothing, coalesce nowhere insightful. Daiches enters into a discussion about whether we need an external critical framework through which to appreciate *The Waste Land* more fully, and concludes that in some cases it does help. The poem grasps out, pulling in its own critical apparatus, and its citational quality, mimicking academic citationality, makes it thus a work of creative academic criticism.

The obscurity of the poem has irked many readers over the decades. This, I believe, is where *The Waste Land* and *The Holy Bible* differ and diverge in their impulse, methodology and goal: they are both journeys through hell by the lost young man, who returns and recounts his infernal visions; but the attitude is different. In Eliot's case the narrator is bitter, frustrated that he has not found knowledge and serenity (he will later, with the religious poems that follow). All he's found are false and dead ends, myths, all myths. He has no answers for you, reader, except that there are no answers. He has no books that he recommends you read, because reading books is a waste of time: they do not have the answers for you. Only a pack of cards, perhaps, can tell you whether you will live happy or die at the bottom of the ocean. The poem considers yet rejects the idea of having a framework into which it can joyously insert itself, a network of allies, a community of like-minded souls that recognize each other with outstretched arms across the void. It scorns and sneers at company. It says, no, misery does *not* love company. It is an anti-social poem, an irritable misanthrope tending toward the hermit life. It impersonates people with a sort of compulsive chatter, a roving audiovisual recording device that transforms trash into art and high legend into babble. It enters into the brains of men and women, and knows that sexual difference is a big source of pain and conflict among humans. It becomes Tiresias, neither man nor woman but both, with knowing eyes that have seen all. Its tongue wraps itself around the consonants and rhythms of the people, other speakers: it "do the police in different voices." But it keeps to itself, it will not explain to you what's going on, what it chatters about. It has lost connection with itself, it does not know what it does and why. It has lost the gift of intellect and is now speaking in tongues.

The Waste Land demands and imposes its own mythical framework; has itself become a legend; "makes necessary dependence on a synthetic myth," notes Daiches (1134). *The Holy Bible* is different: it shares its sources, and it does not guard them as preciously meaningless, but hurls them at the reader-listener, warmly presses them on you. Read this: you're going to *love* it. It is an open platform invested in sharing knowledge as a vital act. We're going to *need* these books for our survival. Look, let's stock the ark with these, let's build bookshelves inside the cabin. The hurling wasteland will be out there soon, but we should keep these texts to keep us warm. Nevermind that they'll be painful reading: we'll find pleasure in that pain, because that's what literature does, isn't it? Transforming pain into pleasure through carefully positioned words.

It's not like *The Holy Bible* doesn't also sometimes reach unintelligibility, but when it does it, it's maybe because it's tripping over itself with too much to say, too little time and space; it gets over-excited, and splices in all these ideas and words and perspectives, but not because it's trying to turn you away with obscure in-jokes that you will never understand, and not because it's flinging obscure and arcane and bejewelled quotations at you in foreign languages, or cowing you with literary references in a performance of elitist superiority, as an act of violence upon the reader. *The Holy Bible*'s foreign words—*lebensraum, kulturkampf, raus raus, fila fila*—are words you need to look up. It shuns and turns such elitism inside out, transforming citationality performed as an act of hermetic and arcane literary misanthropy into an egalitarian and pedagogical framework, informed by the divulgatory quality of hip-hop sampling culture, which gives old songs, riffs, hooks, basslines new leases of life, and anticipates the Internet's encyclopaedic tendencies, salvaging key fragments, alchemically re-working them into aestheticized links to further knowledge. "I never knew who Horthy was," says Nicky Wire in the liner notes to the twentieth anniversary edition of *The Holy Bible*. "To chuck that into a lyric, this obscure Hungarian reference, seems so mad in the era of *Parklife* and *Definitely Maybe*. In a pre-digital world, the amount of research powers that Richey was attaining just staggers me."

CHAPTER 5

Holocaust Pop: The Holy Bible's Nazi Materials

In his wonderful piece "There Are No Horizons: *The Holy Bible* At 20," Taylor Parkes mentions "issues which, generally speaking, no band should even contemplate writing about, issues no pop song could ever contain." How do you square the Holocaust with a pop song? How do you speak of the holocaust in a pop song? Matthew Boswell's *Holocaust Impiety in Literature, Popular Music and Film* (2012) looks at how it's been done, examining the lineage of The Ramones, the Sex Pistols, Joy Division and Manic Street Preachers. Boswell goes as far as to say that "the impact of the Holocaust on punk was total," and "central to the formation of the abrasive, disenchanted punk world-view" (130).

The Holy Bible is deeply imbued with Nazi and Holocaust subject matter: not merely the two songs traditionally understood as explicitly dealing with the Holocaust, "Mausoleum" and "The Intense Humming of Evil." The topic frames and permeates the album in a totalizing way, becoming on some level an ultimate evil to which all other themes converge. Personal depression is thus also rooted in an awareness of the Holocaust, an event which appears to negate any possible hope or optimism in humanity.

With the concept of "Holocaust impiety," Boswell builds on Gillian Rose's critique of "Holocaust piety" which he summarizes as "overly sentimental or sanctimonious approaches to the genocide" (130) that are solemn, self-righteous and lead to a notions of Holocaust ineffability and unrepresentability. Holocaust impiety represents a rupture with Holocaust piety on the part of artists and writers, in particular in the field of popular, even low culture, such as *stalag* Nazploitation B-movies: an irreverent use of the Holocaust, that breaks with and challenges the pietist tradition in order to make fantastic, jarring, speculative or otherwise creative uses of it. Having become a sacred cow itself, the Holocaust is fertile ground for imaginative deconstruction: its fixed and monolithic message of ultimate and inexplicable horror an opportunity for re-imagination. Boswell mentions the Chapman Brothers in passing. They are a clear example of Holocaust impiety. Their *Hell* (1999–) installations model a grotesque fairground Holocaust landscape, in which Ronald McDonald and Stephen Hawking jostle for space amid Nazis, skeleton zombie Nazis, and victims in Games Workshop-like scenarios of torture and death. The Holocaust has not ended, does not end, in this vision of endless hell: the Holocaust is displaced from its historical context, its podium as historical and politicized artefact, and through the teenage-angst eyes of the miniature gamer, who would lord over fantasy future wars and *Warhammer 40,000* Space Marines, is exploded into a wicked commentary on our world today. Holocaust Nazism as not a distant or historical aberration, but rather as the underlying premise to how we do things today.

Boswell's seven pages on *The Holy Bible,* in particular his close reading of "The Intense Humming of Evil," offer some of the most insightful and productive readings of the album. Boswell's analysis of the song makes the case for its belonging to the genre or mode of Holocaust impiety by noting how it rages not merely at the perpetrators, but also at the victims themselves. Whilst the intro sample "vocalises the anger of the victims and their claim to retribution" (127), the actual verses turn their anger on the victims themselves, attacking the idea that their suffering somehow ennobled them, and scathing at their deaths as pointless. Boswell contends that the song offers a conflicted view that wrestles with and performatively calls attention to its own "insidious Nazification" (128), especially where it seems to adopt the point of view of the Nazi in the lyric "you always mistook fists for flowers." Levelling blame and anger at the victims, as the song does, feeds from the long-standing and dubious tradition of casting Holocaust Jews as passive, almost willing participants, lambs to the slaughter. The song, according to Boswell's reading, offers a laconic, nihilistic take on Holocaust butchery, by which the speaker rejects any form of lesson to be drawn from their deaths: "6 million screaming souls · maybe misery – maybe nothing at all · lives that wouldn't have changed a thing · never counted – never mattered – never be · arbeit macht frei."

"The Intense Humming of Evil" and "Mausoleum" may be read as a response to Primo Levi's 1985 poem "Song of Those Who Died in Vain," which is reprinted on the back cover of *Gold Against the Soul*. The content of Levi's poem is a challenge to its title's negative assertion: those who died in vain are ghosts huddled around the living, pressing upon them the challenge that their deaths be not in vain. They died in vain, but there is still a chance to change that, to make their deaths mean something, and use them to change the world. The ghosts order the living to sit down and "bargain," to figure out a way to configure global human society free from the massacre of innocent people. If you do not achieve this, "if the havoc and shame continue," warn the ghosts, "we will drown you in our putrefaction." We will have died in vain if you cannot solve the problem of the slaughter of innocent lives. The poem is a challenge to the politics of today and its "never again." But in 1994, in the middle of the Sarajevo siege (1992–96), with the images of Bosnian prisoners, victims of Serbian "ethnic cleansing," on television and in the newspapers, recalling with their ribcages and barbed wire photos of Holocaust concentration camps, how could those "never again" exhortations not ring entirely hollow? While we were busy believing in "never again," here it was happening again in front of our eyes. That humans fail to learn the lesson—are resolutely set against doing so—cannot but obliterate any meaning those deaths may have ever hoped for. Thus, in answer to the "Song of Those Who Died in Vain," we have failed, and are drowning in your putrefaction, and your curse is nihilism made flesh. *The Holy Bible* is the sound of that drowning.

CHAPTER 6

Sylvia Plath: Holocaust and Self

One of the major critiques addressed to Sylvia Plath is that her poetry utilizes Holocaust suffering inappropriately. These critiques argue that her poetry on some level does not have the right to explore Holocaust materials in the ways that it does: that it is a form of immoral cultural appropriation. Furthermore, they contend that she is appropriating a pain that is not hers in order to illustrate her own inner states; that she is somehow misusing the Holocaust in order to discuss her own depression. Critics have countered this in various ways, arguing that this is an overly biographical take on her poetry, and that Plath's first-person speeches are dramatic monologues for different characters in Europe. The critique that Plath is somehow misusing Holocaust imagery for her own ends, and that these ends are somehow unacceptable, opens up various avenues for unpacking her poetry, and larger questions about ownership of Holocaust representation: to whom does the right to aesthetic or literary representations of the Holocaust *belong?* What does it mean to talk of appropriate and inappropriate uses of Holocaust materials in art?

There is anger against Plath's often deliberately flippant use of the Holocaust in her poetry from various quarters: Jewish critics who see her as unable to capture in her poetry the brutality of an experience she did not live through; Harold Bloom and Seamus Heaney's contentions that they are aesthetically unsuccessful and harness the Holocaust to self-justifying ends. The idea that Plath misuses the Holocaust for her own personal gain does several things: for one, it relies on the notion that as a gentile, she is not granted access to a specifically Jewish suffering. How could a relatively privileged girl from Wellesley know the pain of the Holocaust victim? How could her suffering possibly be on the same level or comparable to those of Holocaust victims? In the light of her suicide, it is certainly questionable to suggest that her suffering was somehow insufficient. It also hinges on a narrowly autobiographical idea of the literary, and its imaginative and ethical capacities for, as Hannah Arendt puts it, "being and thinking in my own identity where I am not" (241).

The critique presupposes a distinction between Plath's gentile suffering and the Holocaust victim's Jewish suffering which her poetry arguably seeks to collapse. Poems such as "Daddy," "Lady Lazarus," and "Mary's Song" identify with Jewishness and with Jewish Holocaust victimhood. "Daddy," in particular, does this in a patently flippant way: "I think I might be a bit of a Jew," the speaker announces at one point. It is as though she has plucked the idea off the top of her head, and then gradually falls in love with it throughout the poem, pushing this bad taste thought further and further, defying the reader to call her out on it (which critics then did). The flippancy of this identification is fully aware of the taboo of doing such a thing, and the pleasure of disobedience is built into the childish nature of the rhyme; Plath's speaker is being naughty, and enjoying it, and pushing limits. Herein lies the impious quality of the poem, which carries within its shock charges deeper meaning: the affiliation is playful and is expressed playfully, but beneath the playfulness there is more serious intent. According to dominant Jewish self-identification processes, one cannot be "a bit of a Jew," one is or one is not. Being "a bit of a Jew" in Nazi occupied Europe could get you deported to a concentration camp, depending on which side of the line of arcane Nazi racial classifications you fell. Declaring that you might be "a bit of a Jew" in this context makes a willing mockery of a multiplicity of positions: of Jewishness self-defined as racial difference, of Nazi anti-Semitism's ideological biological spuriousness, of Jewish suffering as unique practice of ethnic self-identification, of cultural, ideological and political ownership of Holocaust representation.

What issues does the question of asking what it might mean for gentiles to identify with Holocaust victimhood open up? Here we also may begin to think with Richey and *The Holy Bible:* what does it mean for the visitor to a concentration camp, the tourist, to make pronouncements on it? Holocaust tourism is predicated upon a certain type of emotional experience that the visitor will undergo. How might this private catharsis be translated into a response? Claire Brennan's overview of critical responses to Plath's poetry discusses the shift away from thinking about the appropriateness of Plath's use of the Holocaust, and James E. Young's suggestion that rather than "asking whether a writer coming after the Holocaust should be traumatized by a memory she may have inherited only literarily, we might ask to what extent the writer was traumatized by her literary historical memory of the Holocaust" (Brennan 72). The Holocaust has become, by Plath's time, public, shared memory. The poet organizes her inner private world by way of this shared historical imagery:

> If "The public horrors of Nazi concentration camps and the personal horrors of fragmented identities become interchangeable,"

as Arthur Oberg suggests, it is not because they are actually analogous; it is just that the movement between public and personal horrors is at once historical and private. As long as these images of the Holocaust are public, they inevitably enter the private imagination at some level, where they are invariably invoked to order personal experiences.

(Brennan 75)

This gets closer to what I have in mind, but I need to push it even further. Plath constructs her poetic characters, or the poetic self she channels through them, as being in the lineage of the Holocaust, products of it, made by it. There is no self in Plath's poetry that reaches for and makes appropriate or inappropriate use of the facts of the Holocaust that are external to it: but rather, the poetic self is informed by and formed through its knowledge of and reaction to the Holocaust.

This brings us to understandings of depression that de-politicize it as primarily a private, inner, personal matter: a failing of the individual to adequately respond to the social world. Some critiques of Plath hinge on this assumption of depression as a personal matter. The young woman from Wellesley (and in different ways, the pretty boy rock star from Wales who has *made it),* is thus seen as depressed because of some defect within them: depression as a private sphere, an intimate disease of failing, which is somehow contained within the individual. Plath's novel *The Bell Jar* disputes this view. The book begins with a preoccupation about the Rosenbergs, Julius and Ethel, convicted of spying for the USSR, being executed, and from its first line it is thus haunted by the political aura of 1950s McCarthyism and the global violence and geopolitical tension of the Cold War. Autobiographical protagonist Esther Greenwood's interaction with a fellow intern, Hilda, who expresses joy that the Rosenbergs are about to be executed, is a pivotal moment—followed by the personal, sexual trauma of the attempted rape by a misogynistic acquaintance, Marco—that comes before her breakdown. The personal, intimate dimension is always shot through, occasioned by the political, the ideological: violent sexually abusive patriarchy is inextricable from American political brutality. "Daddy" weaves these connections even tighter, exposing fatherhood's fascistic desires.

Plath's work argues that depression and suicide are not an internal causeless failure to live up to the demands of the world, but in part a justified response to the violence of human society and history. In her poetry, depression is not some purely personal problem (as if such a thing could exist) that has hijacked the Holocaust as a way of expressing and aestheticizing itself, but the depression in the first place is partly caused by the fact of the Holocaust existing; it is not so much a case that the depressed or depressive artist is somehow appropriating the Holocaust to express herself, but more so that the depression to begin with is partly caused by the existence of the Holocaust. In this way, the Holocaust belongs to all of us inasmuch as our identities are forged by an awareness of it, and a coming to terms with its existence; a processing of it, and a reaction to it.

Plath's work impiously desacralizes the Holocaust by being flippant about it, by turning it into a fancy dress game, a gleefully morbid cabaret show. Her work challenges the notion that, as a gentile, she has no right to put herself in the place of the Holocaust victim. By being "a bit of a Jew" with a Nazi dad, Plath's work breaks down dichotomies of Nazi and Jew, in favour of a humanistic and universalizing approach that sees the Jew and the Nazi within the human. *The Holy Bible* rejects Plath's comedic flippancy, but certainly carries over her personalizing, appropriating framework into its Holocaust material and the way in which the depressive consciousness at the heart of the album is understood through reference to the Holocaust. Plath primarily identifies with victims, *The Holy Bible* shifts from victim to the interior vision of an external judge and accuser, whose rage and despair boils over into feeling its way into nihilistic positions that may be read as coming to coincide with the Nazi perpetrator. The girl speaker in "Daddy" relishes the thought of being chuffed off to the concentration camp in a train, in a sado-masochistic death fantasy, re-animating the Holocaust as ongoing event, the engine of the train an anticipation of the camp's ovens. For Plath, the Holocaust is not so much over but ongoing, feverishly living on at the level of inner and interpersonal struggle, winning, in the end, as she submits to its death logic: the choice of suicide by gas oven also cannot help but go noticed.

By the time the speaker of "Mausoleum" and "The Intense Humming of Evil" comes to the same place, it has gone cold and lifeless. In this absence of life, a visitor outside of history, he finds the cold pressure of historical fact, but above all his own all-consuming conscience and guilt.

The Holocaust is a highly touchy subject matter, and the Manics wavered on how to best present this topic, reworking the lyrics of "The Intense Humming of Evil" to make them more judgmental. In interviews they discuss the song as a warning against Holocaust denial historical revisionism, so that it becomes a necessary act of historical memorialization, speaking the truth to the lies of Holocaust denial: "I didn't think the first draft of 'Intense Humming of Evil' was judgmental enough," James Dean Bradfield told *Q* in late 1994. "It's a song about the Holocaust and you can't be ambivalent about a subject like that. Not even we are stupid enough to be contentious about that" (qtd in Maconie). Yet as ever, the interview summary of the song only contains a fraction of its multiplicity of voices and perspectives that cancel each other out in a nihilistic blur. *The Holy Bible* battles its own desire to contain and present that truth, the speaker faltering under the weight of his own judgment, almost succumbing to the very violence it seeks to indict.

The cultural and literary afterlives of the Holocaust are and continue to be an extremely contested area. Writing in 1996, Gillian Rose discusses two Holocaust novels and notes:

The books tell the same story: that impotence and suffering arising from unmourned loss do not lead to a passion for objectivity and justice. They lead to resentment, hatred, inability to trust, and then, the doubled burden of fear of those negative emotions. This double burden is either turned inwards or outwards, but both directions involve denial. It is the abused who become the abusers, whether politically as well as psychically may depend on contingencies of social and political history. (51)

This reads very Richey-esque, a pessimistic take on the notion that victims are capable of learning from their trauma: that it is naïve, if not dangerous, to hope that victims will alchemically transform the suffering they have undergone into a more moral world, one elevated and illuminated by the Enlightenment values of reason and truth. The truth may be too much to bear and collapses into anger and resentment and revenge—a process chronicled by Jean Améry in his Auschwitz survivor memoir *At the Mind's*

Limits (1966). Rose could also here be talking about Israel, and how it has come to be seen as embodying these bitter ironies in repeating as abuser elements of that which its progenitors suffered as victim. In the last two decades, global sentiment on Israel as a colonial, occupying force have continued to grow and polarize. Judgment on Israel doesn't appear *per se* in *The Holy Bible,* though "Of Walking Abortion" can certainly be read as provocatively pairing and blurring two worlds: the safe inhabited world of "shalom shalom" with its love for the children and its limitless horizons, an ideological sublime of the nation state; and the world of violence and death and destruction and fascist dictators and butcher's hooks that it rests upon and disavows.

CHAPTER 7

The Industrial Holy Bible

As I read about *The Holy Bible,* one aspect of it that I find does not receive due coverage is the industrial nature of the album. It's not an industrial album, but it does have an industrial sheen to it, and employs many of the stylistic and thematic tropes common to both types of industrial: the 70s/80s first wave, and the 80s/90s industrial rock scene. These include: a sonic interest in low grade noise, atonality and distortion, disruptive, mechanized sounds, copious use of samples with which to introduce or end songs, drum machines and programmed rhythmic patterns, themes of angst, dread, existential horror, totalitarianism, politics as violence, the surveillance state. Old-school industrial drew directly from the literary and conceptual cut-ups and splicings of William Burroughs and J.G. Ballard, and the idea of Richey as the band's "Minister of Propaganda," though coming from Public Enemy's "Minister of Information" Professor Griff, also makes me think of the Slovenian band Laibach, and their notion of a band as totalitarian state in microcosm.

Old-school industrial similarly juggles a conceptual and literary component different to and alienated from the strictly musical side, forming a deliberately ill-fitting whole: the concept provides a key with which to interpret the music, which can only achieve meaning through the often shocking concepts. What guides the listener through the industrial music of Throbbing Gristle is a conceptual aesthetic predicated upon shock, horror and alienation, shaping the music to meanings that might it might not inherently contain. Lastly, industrial music is obsessively concerned with totalitarianism, and Nazism in particular.

In his informative book *Assimilate: A Critical History of Industrial Music* (2013), S. Alexander Reed discusses the roles played by Nazi imagery and references in industrial music. Reed presents several arguments as to what

Nazi imagery is doing in industrial music, understanding the genre as an often ambiguous one, which coasts along ambivalent uses of authoritarian, even fascistic tropes to "reject the signal clarity that aurally identifies authority" (190). The genre often plays with Nazi and fascist imagery, using cutups, samples and collages, and reproducing images and sounds in a new context which may serve to expose secrets and hidden truths within our socio-political apparatus, providing access to the information that our society is more fascistic than we give it credit for. This is the case of Laibach, who are, as Alexei Monroe puts it, an "interrogation machine" that speaks back to power.

What Laibach do is present themselves as a parody of a totalitarian state, forcing the listener to accept that popular music itself is a totalitarian aesthetic that disavows its own totalitarianism and complicity with capitalist power. The message is thus an educational one, opening the mind of the listener to the fascism that persists in our world. The worry is that the educational part of industrial music, the irony, will go over fans' heads, who will instead indulge and enjoy precisely that fascistic part, reading it unironically as an ode to power. This is part of the point, but it is a risk. The powerful wall of sound erected by Laibach and Ministry has the function of creating a fascistic music, which is macho and tough, taking from heavy metal and from pop—or rejecting pop as Ministry did, and giving the crowd an endurance test. Where Laibach stick in a socialist realist mode, dressing up like the platonic ideal of a Nazi, replete with Heideggerian walks through the forest in the "Life Is Life" video (possibly their pivotal achievement), Ministry go off into the realm of post-apocalyptic science fiction, resurrecting Mad Max for scenarios and worldbuilding.

Industrial metal typically ramps up and constructs hyper-masculinity, with parodic intentions or not. Nine Inch Nails' *The Downward Spiral* can be compared with *The Holy Bible* on many levels: thematic, sonic, conceptual. Andy Johnson's "Five Dark Parallels Between NIN's *The Downward Spiral* and the

Manics' *The Holy Bible*" presents both 1994 albums as belonging to the genre of the young man descending to his own inner hell. Here I'd like to briefly compare the albums' modulation of gender. S. Alexander Reed discusses Nine Inch Nails' performative femininity. The Reznorian character certainly flirts with femininity in new and interesting ways since glam: the fish-netted goth girl persona that it inhabits emphasizes sexiness and vulnerability, harnessing femininity as a way of indulging masochistic and submissive positions. *The Downward Spiral* forges a gorgeous obscenity by feminizing and queering industrial metal's macho tropes, mocking phallic gun culture ("Big Man with a Gun"), and offering breathers of ambient calm amidst the metallic raging riffs. *The Downward Spiral* frequently capitulates to anger and self-destructs, but also pulls itself back from the brink of terminal masculinity ("Mr. Self-Destruct") with redeeming or even womb-like moments ("Piggy" and "A Warm Place"). *The Holy Bible* also modulates and defies industrial and metal, whilst borrowing from both. From its first sample-introduced track, "Yes," *The Holy Bible* twists metal into something softer, as James' vocals and guitar lines present a melodic, plaintive, delicate counterpart to the album's rhythmic barrage and noisy fuzz. *The Holy Bible* bends and prostrates itself, toppling phallic monoliths of sound with fragile, stuttering, stumbling passages. *The Downward Spiral* feeds on alternating contrasts: loud/soft, organic/artificial, rage/release, heavy song/slow song. *The Holy Bible*'s alternations are often internal: the second half of "4st 7lb" with its sing-song unwinding; the dulcet pre-chorus of "Archives of Pain"; the almost bleated opening of "Mausoleum"—soft alternates integrated into the album's wiry shell.

Perhaps following the lead of Throbbing Gristle, whose deliberately sketched songwriting—almost like a child's drawing of pop music—lo-fi muffled sound and vocal performance of slight dementedness conspire to an aesthetic of weakness, so *The Holy Bible,* albeit in a more avowedly rock context, constructs a performance of weakness. It appropriates and advances an agenda of industrial strength metal, "Faster" being its most obvious representative of a phallic wall of sound, to then deconstruct and queer that macho paradigm with concepts and images and songs of becoming-woman and sonic strategies that draw from romantic pop. *The Downward Spiral* presents a struggle between the self-destructive male and a femininity that seems to engulf the singer, to which he succumbs. *The Holy Bible* performs a version of industrial metal displacing the male victim character at its heart with a variety of female voices speaking for the protagonist from a place of pain.

Finally, I would like to compare *The Holy Bible* with neo-folk band Death in June, who in name also "die in the summertime" and construct an aesthetic informed by literary decadents—the band have a song called "The Torture Garden" and express admiration for Yukio Mishima—and have a morbid obsession with Nazism and the Holocaust, which their music takes to very different and contested places.

Death in June also construct a performance of sonic weakness, predicated upon a queering of Nazi tropes and symbols and a perpetrator-identifying sense of Nazi self-pity, and revolving around the central, camo-clad and masked mournful figure of Douglas P., a kind of troubadour forever lost in a melancholic Holocaust world from which he cannot exit. A bit like a lo-fi Nazi Leonard Cohen. With a kind of anxious discomfort, the listener often comes to the realization that the speaker of these morbid acoustic ballads is singing from the perspective of Nazi as victim. "We had our chance/And lost our voice," sings Douglas P. on "Come Before Christ and Murder Love," arguably the lament of a defeated Nazi who now has to live on in a world he despises. When Douglas P. amends and updates "C'est un Rêve"'s gloomy incantation "Òu est Klaus Barbie?" onstage to ask "Òu est Bin Laden?" (the answer is: *"Il est dans le coeur"*—he is in the heart, and *"Liberté/C'est un rêve"*—liberty is a dream), the effect is to plunge the spectator into a horror show in which

Hitler lives on in our hearts and there is nothing we can do about it.

By contrast, *The Holy Bible* treats its Nazi materials with shame and self-disgust, with none of Death in June's ironic distance or posture of bookish amorality. It neither indulges in nor submits to Hitler in the soul, but angrily or wearily indicts it, refusing to accept the fascism of the modern world as a sad but inevitable truth or fact of life. Instead, *The Holy Bible* recognizes it, railing against it to the point of self-implosion. It reaches out into Holocaust consciousness and recoils in pain, shuddering with revulsion and sadness and anger. It sees the paradigm of the concentration camp extended to the rest of civilized modernity (Giorgio Agamben's thesis in *Homo Sacer*) and gasps in horror, struggling against its own complicity in that project, choosing self-annihilation over further insidious self-Nazification. *The Holy Bible* faces the Holocaust as historical fact, imaginatively inhabits its victims, executioners, bystanders, judges, and unable to make moral sense of it, succumbs to the ideal of total annihilation it represents. Where Douglas P. wallows in the Holocaust as spurious kitsch, and makes a career of bad taste Holocaust pop cabaret, *The Holy Bible* submits to the impossibility of averting its gaze from the Holocaust, without ever seeming to find a way out.

CHAPTER 8
Foucault: Archives of Pain

In an oft-quoted remark, Bradfield describes *The Holy Bible* as having been put together with "an almost academic discipline" (qtd in Price, *Everything* 143). Post-punk and industrial have a history of using the concept of discipline in a Foucaultian sense. Throbbing Gristle's "Discipline" (1981) mercilessly parodies, in its distorted, repetitive dirge of barked commands, that rightwing tactic of calling for discipline and order as what's necessary. Post-punk's aesthetic minimalism is a disciplining of punk's anarchic and chaotic impulses, with totalitarian aesthetics and styles mimicked for parodic and satiric effect. Post-punk and industrial constitute and pursue a Foucaultian aesthetic of minimalist rigor, depressed affect and realist content concerned with human suffering and social organization.

Ironically, Foucault does not use the word discipline in his original French title for his 1975 book *Surveiller et punir: Naissance de la prison* (*Discipline and Punish: The Birth of the Prison*). "*Surveiller*" is closer to surveille, monitor, observe: the act of being constantly watched in the panopticon, the surveillance society we are coming to know well. Constant surveillance replaces those spectacles of corporal punishment, torture and execution prevalent before the nineteenth century. This is the thesis of *Discipline and Punish:* the birth of the prison society. *The Holy Bible*'s "Archives of Pain" inserts itself into this discussion by wondering how much of a good thing this is.

Of course, I had to pick up David Macey's 1993 tome *The Lives of Michel Foucault.* The chapter "The Archives of Pain" describes the *Discipline and Punish* years, the preparation and publication of the book. One episode in the chapter recounted by Macey is of interest, especially for its picture of the fascism of everyday life indicted by "Of Walking Abortion." In late 1975, a group of seven French protesters including Foucault, journalist Claude Mauriac, filmmaker Constantin Costa-Gavras and the actor Yves Montand, travelled to Spain to protest the execution by Franco's regime of a group of Basque separatist movement ETA and antifascist FRAP (*Frente Revolucionario Antifascista y Patriotica*) militants (two of whom are pregnant) by garrote. Macey describes the preparation of the trip and the document denouncing the execution that they would read at a press conference there ("Ten men and women have just been condemned to death. They have been condemned by special courts and did not have the right to justice..."), signed, among others, by André Malraux, Louis Aragon, and Jean-Paul Sartre. Once arrived, the French protesters go to the Torre de Madrid hotel bar and are surrounded by the secret police, who demand their flyers and detain them, and then take them back to the plane and send them back to France. We get a vivid feeling, from Macey's narration, of fascism in real life action, with the figure of the actor superimposed on it. The scene in the bar is one of great tension, with a silence descending in the face of the secret police. "Everyone was ordered to remain silent and stay seated." The journalists are arrested and taken away in handcuffs. The French delegation are "held separately and told that they would immediately be put on a flight for Paris" (346):

> Mauriac had the impression of being in a Costa-Gavras film. So did Foucault: [...] "There was something fantastic about the look of these policemen and they found the presence of Montand extremely embarrassing: the man who incarnates the image of the 'resistance fighter' in so many films had suddenly found himself face to face with policemen who recognised him. That gave the scene an extraordinary political intensity [...] It was then that we felt the presence of fascism. The way people watch without seeing anything, as though they had witnessed the scene hundreds of times before. And at the same time the sadness, and probably the

stupefaction, at seeing a very real scene that they had lived through hundreds of times, with the imaginary hero they have seen on the screen as an actor in it. They were seeing a film about their own political realities. And that silence [...] the silence of the crowd, watching and saying nothing." (346–7)

The weakness of human conformity in the face of the spectacular exercise of fascist state violence underlies "Of Walking Abortion"'s indictment of our collective responsibility for allowing the fascism of everyday life to thrive. The lyric "Hitler reprised in the worm of your soul" comes up a lot in literature on the Manics, understandably. Mick Middles is horrified by it: "Who would write such a line?" he asks. I always used to mishear it as "whim" of your soul. Strangely, that doesn't alter too much the meaning that anyone can be a Nazi, that a potential Hitler is within us as humans, and that we cultivate the soil in which that worm grows, that the Nazism of daily life is all around us if we are not too cowardly to look, that this worminess is perhaps some kind of animal quality within us, a disappointing tendency to acquiesce to violence if it suits us and if we can afford it.

John Lennon is purported to have said: "We all have Hitler in us, but we also have love and peace. So why not give peace a chance for once?" On jittery cabaret number "Hitler in My Heart" from 1998, Antony Hegarty of Antony and the Johnsons sings: "As I search for a piece of kindness/and I find Hitler in my heart." Both Antony and *The Holy Bible* may be read as pessimistic responses to Lennon's optimistic question. No, John, we can't.

In his big book *33 Revolutions Per Minute: A History of Protest Songs from Billie Holiday to Green Day* (2011), Dorian Lynskey discusses "Of Walking Abortion" in the context of the protest song, reading it as "the protest song [that] eats itself": the common bond between the protest song and its audience, to bond together against external evils, is shattered here, argues Lynskey, as the protest turns inwards. Of the song he notes:

> The underlying principle of almost every protest song is that people are essentially good and only need to be liberated from a few malign individuals. But "Of Walking Abortion" contends that people are weak and selfish and create these monsters themselves [...] The key image is "Hitler reprised in the worm of your soul," the human weakness that allows fascism to thrive. (484)

The song's message is a universal *j' accuse* which indicts humanity as collectively responsible, rather than othering the Nazi as some demonic presence, some perverted deviation from the norm. Moral contagion is everywhere. As Lynskey puts it, "Moral disgust which would wriggle like a tapeworm [...] hatched in the soil of Belsen and Dachau" (483). Says Wire:

> A band dressed like Guns N' Roses going to Dachau and Belsen. Obviously we'd read about it but to actually go there and experience the silence and the deathliness and the abject horror, it affected us all. I think that was the final piece in

the jigsaw for Richey. There's an overriding philosophy behind the whole album: evil is an essential part of the human condition and the only way to get over it is recognizing all hypocrisies, all evils – recognizing it's in us all – which I guess is not a liberal view. (483)

Lynskey identifies a key aspect of *The Holy Bible:* the extent to which it is contaminated and consumed by the materials it handles. It cannot look into the abyss of human atrocity without being pulled into that abyss, without amplifying and reifying and becoming the horrors which it excoriates:

> It is a song about the evils of fanaticism – the names of Mussolini and Hitler are rat-a-tatted out – but it *sounds* fanatical. It is like the final report of someone who has been commissioned to investigate the causes of an atrocity and who, instead of producing a series of wise, humanitarian recommendations, concludes that the moral contagion is everywhere and the blame is bottomless. The singer delivers the final verdict in

a shrill, distorted howl: "Who's responsible? You fucking are!" (477)

Evil is not some us vs them, but proliferates among us all, especially in the desire for justice and punishment. *Discipline and Punish* chronicles the shift in punishment from the spectacle of torture to the prison state. The book opens with the brutal, visceral images of the regicide Robert-François Damiens, the last person condemned to death by drawing and quartering following his attempted assassination of King Louis XV in 1757. The description of Damiens' last hours is harrowing: as his body is mutilated and tortured, he pauses to look at his own body, as the primary spectator in this spectacle of ritualized pain as punishment. The scene acquires an almost comical flavour. As you read its gruesome details you can't quite believe that humans did and still do this to each other in the name of justice.

Discipline and Punish describes a shift from the brutal spectacle of torture as justice, a system in which punishment is understood to fit the crime, the two connected via a violence that is divinely justified. Throughout the nineteenth century we move to a concept of punishment as an economy of suspended rights; the jail is understood to be so much more civilized, and we begin to look backwards to torture as belonging to an era of barbarity. Torture as a public spectacle, public execution, horror atrocity, power asserted through the spectacle of violence, making an example through terror, are replaced by a change of attitude, a move away from blood, from justice as a vengeance taken out on the flesh, to confinement and surveillance, the gentle way of punishment, the disciplining and individual and collective coercion of bodies, isolation of the convict, prison regime. Writ large, society acquires a carceral texture, as the world moves from a feudal system to a bourgeois and capitalistic and democratic one in which justice is measured out in teaspoons rather than being a divinely-sanctioned retribution on the flesh of the sinner.

The Holy Bible's "Archives of Pain" weighs these two concepts of justice against one another, lurching toward a reprisal of the prior method. It asks why murderers and killers and genocides and dictators should receive the soft treatment, and whether it is fair that those who have taken life away may be entitled to keep theirs. It asks if we should bring back the death penalty, and public torture and execution. The lyric "A drained white body hanging from the gallows · is more righteous than Hindley's crotchet lectures" shuttles between the two positions, positing that the former is morally superior to the latter, and that the latter is not really punishing: any fool can regret yesterday, and it is not really fair to reward killers with a soft place to live for the rest of their lives, but instead, pain should be rained down on them in retribution to their acts, an eye for an eye. "Tear the torso with horses and chains" refers to Damiens, whose body was torn apart according to the practice of being drawn and quartered: the horses were not able to tear his limb from his torso, so the executioners did it instead with knives. The song begins ominous and brooding with *that bassline,* setting its premise, lulling you briefly with a mellow pre-chorus that contrasts starkly with lyrics asserting that violent criminals, murderers and rapists, are not getting their just penance; then it explodes with rage on the chorus, suddenly taking an upward accelerating lurch, onto the target of political leaders, politicians responsible for mass death in war, who kill thousands and sanction mass death in the name of civilization, who it babblingly lists and argues are and should be counted in the company of serial killers, and are not getting their just deserts, not getting the "respect" (said with an utterly sarcastic sneer) they deserve.

Written to mock the worship of serial killers—serial killer culture which vicariously enjoys the acts of serial killers as entertainment, in a mechanism that isolates evil as the domain of a select few, that others serial killers as special individuals deserving fame and fortune and molly-coddling in the carceral soft prison—the song can be read as arguing that this demonizing of the serial killer is part of the process that allows politicians to keep their respectability in civil society. Politicians and serial killers are at two opposite ends of the spectrum, but "Archives of Pain" brings them close together and forces them to share the same circle in hell.

"Archives of Pain" is possibly the song that the Manics have expressed most subsequent unease with. The song transcends its status as right-wing rant in the "abortion language of *The Sun*" (Mankowski, "How to Make") by overreaching to the point of total destruction. It goes way over the top in calling for total extinction—the speaker is consumed with a genocidal zeal that peters out in sarcasm, that "respect" for serial killer politics. The right-wing disciplinarian goes too far, ending up with the death of all human life, his words carved on humanity's tombstone as ultimate judgment of the will to violence that consumed all. In its mimicry and terminal acceleration of right-wing disciplinarian discourse it also recalls the writing of transgressive author Peter Sotos, whose writing screams against a tabloid media that indulges and glorifies serial killers, paedophiles and other forms of moral depravity under the guise of moralistic condemnation. Tabloid readers enjoy and participate in crimes vicariously through a ritual of condemnation, argues Sotos, outsourcing to punished pariahs desires and acts they could never undertake, disavowing their complicity by othering the violence into a "them" rather than an "us." In "Archives of Pain" the combination of recognizing communal complicity (we are all guilty) for murder and genocide and bringing back an eye-for-an-eye punishment (and so must all be punished) necessarily dictates total genocide.

The song is an argument for communal suicide. Yet it begins with a logical premise ("If hospitals cure · then prisons must bring their pain") that I have often found unconvincing, troubling. Just because hospitals cure, it does not follow that prisons must bring their pain. Foucault is a historian who describes and analyses socio-political practice and ideological change over time. His advocacy, where it is present, is subtle and implied rather than boldly stated. "Archives of Pain" builds on and departs from Foucault in ways that Foucault's methodology would never do: a return to the torture garden would necessarily hinge on a return away from bourgeois capitalism and back to the aristocratic feudal world that spawned it. "During the writing of the album, Richey confessed to an appreciation of the aesthetics, if not the ethics, of fascism, and told me of his admiration of Dr Hassan al-Turabi, who had implemented a hardline Islamic code of Shariya law in Sudan (amputation for theft, etc.)," writes Simon Price (*Everything* 142). "Archives of Pain" on some level desires this, even if it means the end of everything. And maybe, in the time of ISIS and online viral beheadings and camera phone videos of young black men shot to death by US police, we have explicitly begun to live in that world again.

CHAPTER 9

Spectacles of Suffering: The Third Man

The image in "Of Walking Abortion" of "little people in little houses – like maggots small blind and worthless" possibly in part comes from *The Bell Jar.* Protagonist Esther watches a friend exit the water at the beach: "His body was bisected for a moment, like a white worm. Then it crawled completely out of the green and onto the khaki and lost itself among dozens and dozens of other worms that were wriggling or just lolling about between the sea and the sky" (160). But another possible source occurred to me: the "dots [...] down there" pointed out by amoralist Harry Lime in *The Third Man* from atop a big wheel, looking at the citizens of post-WWII Vienna below. Lime, accused of stealing and diluting penicillin on the black market, explains his philosophy to his friend and future executioner Holly Martins:

> Victims? Don't be melodramatic. Look down there. Tell me. Would you really feel any pity if one of those dots stopped moving forever? If I offered you twenty thousand pounds for every dot that stopped, would you really, old man, tell me to keep my money, or would you calculate how many dots you could afford to spare? Free of income tax, old man. Free of income tax – the only way you can save money nowadays.

Harry's monologue justifies murder via the principle of scale and the limits of human knowability: we can't know all those people, we can't care for them individually, so how can whether they live or die make any difference to our conscience? "I pushed a button and elected him to office and/He pushed a button and dropped a bomb" sings NIN's Trent Reznor on "Capital G." "I need to watch things die/From a good safe distance [...] Much better you than I" sings Tool's Maynard James Keenan on "Vicarious." All three songs indict the silent acquiescence of the Western citizen: we live in comfort while our governments rain down bombs from above at tiny dots of people in countries far away from us, people we will never know or meet, whose grief we will never know. Is Harry Lime an amoral lone wolf, or the guilty conscience of any of us?

In the end, the film resolves this ethical dilemma by having Martins convinced by British officer Major Calloway to help deliver his friend to justice. This resolution occurs by way of a visit to the hospital, where he will witness in person the sick and dying children that Lime's watered-down penicillin has maimed. This direct contact, this visual witnessing in first person of the effects of Lime's actions transforms those "dots" into living, suffering creatures, human innocents. Martins needs to be shocked by this knowledge into ethical action, and what he sees—which is mostly hidden from the viewer, who sees only shapes and bandages in hospital beds—rouses him from the comfort of amoral apathy and the charisma and appeal of Lime's economic cynicism.

The Holy Bible comes up against the notion, theorized by Baudrillard and others, that we live in an era in which we have become desensitized to the suffering of distant others transmitted by media, that we have surfeit of it and cannot *feel* for victims of tragedies removed from our immediate surroundings. Social media has arguably changed that view. We are much closer connected now, in real time, to the emotional response of others to disaster and collective grieving. *The Holy Bible* re-enacts and intensifies *The Third Man*'s ethical awakening through shock tactics, affirming and overcoming Lime's seductive amoralism, seeming to argue that the role of the work of art is to shock you into ethical action by means of exposing you to the horror that you are complicit in. It takes this to extremes, the shock turning inwards, repeatedly, as it makes human suffering come alive now and forever, amplifying it toward a totality that threatens to occupy the whole of the human soul and consume it completely.

CHAPTER 10

Unrequited Love in The Torture Garden

Octave Mirbeau's 1899 novel *Le Jardin des supplices* (*The Torture Garden),* begins with an evening discussion on the topic of murder, with one character, a philosopher, arguing that the desire for murder is inherent in the human, and that society reflects that by normalizing, even sanctifying that murderous impulse: "Murder raised to the level of duty and popularised to the point of heroism accompanies him at every stage of his existence [...] He is made to *respect* only heroes, disgusting thugs burdened with crimes and red with human blood" (26). I emphasize "respect" to illustrate how this argument underwrites "Archives of Pain"—the outsourcing of mass murder to our political leaders, cleansing ourselves of responsibility.

There is much common ground between *The Torture Garden* and

Foucault's *Discipline and Punish*, especially the central thesis that Western society has moved away from a model of punitive corporal justice centred upon atrocities on the human body, toward the soft punishment of the carceral state. Where Foucault uses a historical analysis, Mirbeau constructs a gendered and Orientalist fantasy, in which an English woman, Clara, and a Chinese Torture Garden embody and enact a performance of the alleged genuine cruelty at the heart of the human, which Western society has come to disavow.

The second part of the novel constructs a kind of Dantean inferno through which *femme fatale* and Virgil stand-in Clara leads the hapless and fretting nameless first-person protagonist on a stroll through a sequence of graphic torture tableaux, in which victims are tortured, suffer and die. This journey purports to enact the violent spectacle of the true meaning of life and nature, which decadent Western society has retreated from acknowledging, attempting and failing to cover it up with Enlightenment's faith in reason and belief that humanity is somehow salvageable and reformable from nature red in tooth and claw.

The passage quoted on the back cover of *The Holy Bible* is part of one of Clara's lectures, and occurs when the two lovers are parting ways, for the time being, at the end of a ship journey from Marseilles to Ceylon. The two had met on board, with the protagonist becoming besotted with Clara and her philosophies of cruelty. Their relationship is a sado-masochistic one in which he acts as Clara's frustrated submissive: he can't keep up with her insatiable appetite for cruelty, he leaves her and then returns, meekly sidelined, confused and emotionally defeated. Clara's pleasure comes first, and takes place between herself and the torture scenes she enjoys; the male protagonist tags along, dog-like, and falters, emotionally overwhelmed.

Reading Richey interviews and biographies, there is a strong narrative of his inability to form meaningful romantic relationships with women. When he sees his bandmates shacking up, and tells Gillian Porter he'll be married within the year, she tells him he doesn't even have a girlfriend yet. His final interviews cryptically refer to a woman who he is in love with, and one of his final acts is to leave her a box in his room at the Embassy Hotel. The band have respected the privacy of this person, and not much is publically known about her. In any case, one of Richey's central tragedies is romantic failure. Yet romantic failure is not one of Manic Street Preachers' central lyrical themes, unlike so many bands in the 1990s, who built their entire lyrical framework around romantic misery and its attendant self-loathings, with an accusatory male ranting against a demonic and unjust female villain who has done him wrong by rejecting or deceiving him (from Nine Inch Nails' *Pretty Hate Machine* to Limp Bizkit and Glassjaw, nu-metal and emo solidify this narrative of the poor, woebegone, self-pitying male me, and the evil, heartless, cruel female bitch you).

The Holy Bible does not do this at all. It contains many female figures and voices, itself performing an aesthetic becoming-woman, from the cover art to the female characters of "Yes," "She Is Suffering" and "4st 7lb," haunted by the Sutcliffe victim's relative and the words and lives of Plath and Solanas. Figures of femininity in *The Holy Bible* are most often emblems of suffering, embodiments of brokenness and pain: the prostitute, the anorexic, the obese woman. *The Holy Bible* depicts an image of abject, fractured femininity, heightening its critique of patriarchal violence by having its male subject self-abjectify by becoming-woman. Though there is certainly space here for these female characters, in loss and failure and defeat and bodily breakdown, to uphold a perverse sense of victory and self-control, what of Clara's assuredness and clarity and philosophical conviction? What of femininity as strength, power, assertion, agency, self-control?

Though Clara enacts a philosophical and misogynistic idea of the female as closer to and more honest about nature's matrix of cruelty than men, her reality is more ambiguous, and her façade of control hides a more complex enslavement to cruelty as pleasure.

After taking her pleasure in the Torture Garden, she retreats into a depleted and absent state, collapsing in a paroxysm: "Leave me alone [...] Don't touch me [...] don't say anything to me [...] I'm sick" (195). The protagonist believes she is suffering, and at death's door, but the Chinese maid Ki-Pai scorns this: "Die! Her! You must be joking! It's not suffering that infects her body. It's filthiness! [...] She is still with the evil genies" (198–203). The book ends with Clara coming out of her trance, swearing "never again" whilst the protagonist watches over her sleeping, wishing she would never awaken again.

The female protagonist of "She Is Suffering" could certainly be a Clara figure, who sucks Mirbeau's male narrator into a web of sick pleasure and self-loathing and depletion. In many ways, Clara is a traditional *femme fatale,* robbing the narrator of his vitality (as is the case in Mirbeau's earlier novel *Le Calvaire,* 1886, in which the protagonist Mintié is brought low by scheming courtesan Juliette Roux). He is unable to muster the will to escape her spell. Clara remains unattainable to him: the *femme fatale* as modern reiteration of the pedestal dwelling lady of courtly love poetry, who the poet admires from afar, debasing himself below. This is a patriarchal fantasy that others and confines femininity as a victorious sexuality that must be managed through strategies of male submission. *The Holy Bible* sidesteps this well-worn and clichéd tradition by recasting femininity as weakness and suffering, for the most part shorn of any erotic power. Rejecting romance and sex, it steps into an aesthetic of asexual, or desexualized femininity, which is then worn as a proxy by a masculinity in search of depatriarchalization. *The Torture Garden* ends in paroxysms of despair as the protagonist wishes he had the strength to escape the torture that is unrequited love: Clara cannot return his love because she cannot respect him, because he cannot sever his devotion to the values of civilization that she has left behind. *The Holy Bible* short-circuits the imprisoning dynamic of the love-couple by desexualizing femininity and identifying with that paradigm. It walks a line between the radical and feminist move of desexualizing femininity in a pop music context, exploring female spaces and consciousnesses with empathy and identification, and appropriating and colonizing these very tropes to mask and re-assemble classic white male self-loathing and fragility.

CHAPTER 11

Unmanifesto: Selby and the Christing of the Miserable Self

Picking *Last Exit to Brooklyn* up again after all these years I notice that it has little quotations from the Bible before each chapter. I didn't really remember much about this book, but I must have enjoyed it enough to read two more books by Selby—*The Demon* and *The Room*—before finally stopping: those two were simply too much, too extreme and violent for me, and perhaps too lacking in redemption. Also, Darren Aronofsky's film adaption of *Requiem for a Dream* further alienated me from Selby. To me it glamorized drugs, and yes I know it ends badly for the characters, especially the one who has his arm chopped off, but in the meantime it creates a very fascinating and glamorous life for them. A glamour of misery and squalor. This is the world that Selby creates, alluring because the possibility of shocking, sexualized violence and human animal brutality is always hovering nearby.

In the introduction to the 1987 edition of *Last Exit to Brooklyn*, Anthony Burgess discusses the 1966 obscenity trial and wonders how anyone could consider the book obscene, in that it can't be obscene because it's not built for titillation, and that Selby rather "presents social horrors out of reformist zeal, not out of a desire to titillate or corrupt" (xvii). But I disagree: there is clearly pleasure in the reading of the book, even if that pleasure is a pleasure of horror and terror and fear. The reader is given glimpses of the characters' depravity and violence and then is constantly on edge that something violent is going to happen—extreme and tragic violence is always around the corner.

Selby gives you characters from the beginning that are immoral or morally dubious, protagonists who do horrible or nasty or mean or suspect things. He then leaves you with these protagonists, so you fear for their safety, because justice must surely come to them. Inevitably, the characters encounter grisly ends (Tralala and Harry), which are compounded by the reader not really knowing what happens to them next: it is unclear if these two die, but in any case they have been wounded physically, socially and psychologically beyond repair. The effect is a kind of ritual sacrifice of the outcast, but the outcast is not some pure Jesus-like figure, but rather a compromised, morally bankrupt human being, the product of a social system which is a mess, but also their own sorry choices and human weakness. As Burgess says in the introduction, the feeling the reader has for them is compassion, you want to build a world that does not produce these victims.

Both chapters "The Queen Is Dead" and "Strike" have possible bearings on *The Holy Bible,* and in particular its treatments of gendered violence and masculinity. Selby's novel is in various ways an indictment of patriarchal masculinities, perpetrators of and subject to all kinds of violence. The ever present threat of violence comes especially from the gang of hoodlums that congregates at "The Greeks," led by Vinnie. In "Tralala" the focus is on a young woman, the eponymous protagonist, who in a memorably disturbing scene beats and stomps a sailor who she has robbed, crushing his face, nose and eyes. We later learn that he needs surgery and may be blind in one eye. Her anger at men, at needing them to rob as a livelihood, is palpable: anger and contempt at their sexual needs, their insect-like sameness wells up in her. Her story then ends with her being gang raped: her body violated in graphic and horrifically violent ways and abandoned as her companions pass by and laugh. There is no redemption here, but instead a portrait of unredeemable, crushing violence from which any attempt to extract meaning will be met with jeers and more violence. Selby depicts a world gone mad, but it is our world. From this perspective it cannot be obscene, because these events are true, and happen all the time. We'd like to feel that these events happen off-stage (the etymological meaning of "obscene"): Selby's sin is that he forces us to confront them directly.

In "The Queen Is Dead" we follow transvestite Georgette, who is in love with Vinnie, and who gets stabbed by Harry and Vinnie, who are throwing a knife at her for fun. The bulk of the story is set at a party hosted by drag queens who invite over the hoodlums; they are attracted to the roughness of the men; the threat of violence and rape hangs over the scene, and in the end it happens. Intercut with this are Georgette's feelings of romantic love toward Vinnie, who treats her for the most part with contempt and humiliation. Romantic love is kind of a dream that is used to obscure the violence of her everyday life. The agonizingly long party scene draws out the feeling of dread, almost lulling you into a false sense of security that maybe, just maybe, the men will somehow not revert to violence. Georgette reads aloud Edgar Allan Poe's "The Raven," to steer the evening in the direction of poetry and beauty, yet the feeling cannot be sustained, and the scene ends with Harry and Vinnie raping Lee, one of the drag queens, and then with Georgette going down on Vinnie and tasting and smelling shit and not wanting to accept it, and still clinging to the romantic dream in spite of all the evidence to the contrary. Selby uses this story to observe how femininity and romanticism are illusions employed to paper over masculine violence yet unable to alter or transform its hate into love. The men act as if under individual and group pressure to live up to the worst expectations anyone could have of them, and disappointingly confirm the inevitability of masculinity as a living embodiment and performance of real-life horror.

"Strike" tells the story of Harry Black (many of Selby's stand-ins are called Harry: his generic white male), who is a factory worker and union man struggling with his repressed homosexuality: he suffers intense anguish, hates and assaults his wife, and whilst bigging himself up as an important organizer of the strike, reaches out to discover his homosexual side in the company of drag queens. The story opens and ends with paedophilic acts by Harry, touching his own baby's penis, and at the end, drunkenly sexually assaulting a ten-year-old boy. Vinnie and the gang then come and brutally beat him, breaking his arm in a final scene in which he is crucified by the men on an advert railing, hearing the words GOD GOD and YOU SUCK COCK in his head as he passes out of consciousness, or dies.

Harry leads a double life: as a worker he initiates fights with his bosses, prides himself on his courage to stand up to "the man," sees himself as "one of the guys," does a lot of back-slapping and homosocial grandstanding, inviting men to drink the beer that he offers, acting the local patriarch, bragging about his encounters with women, hitting his wife. He thinks he is popular, but actually nobody can really stand him, seeing him as a creep. In his double-life he hangs out with gay men and drag queens, and is characterized by being naïve and somewhat innocent: he doesn't quite know who he is, he is discovering it, and there is a kind of tenderness there.

He is an awful character, but somehow the reader is directed to feel tenderly toward him, in spite of his failings. That he is crushed mercilessly by the avenging mob that is led by Vinnie—representative of thug masculinity—but incurs the pity of the reader, can be understood as Selby's reading of Christianity. Like Cormac McCarthy's serial killer Lester Ballard, Harry Black is a "Child of God," a human being of this world that sins but is ultimately crushed and crucified by the violence of the world. The reader holds out hope that he will be saved somehow, that he will find redemption, but this is not to be and he will not be saved. In a larger sense, one of Selby's messages here is that there is not necessarily any salvation in this world or any other.

The masculinity of *Last Exit to Brooklyn* is one that is in process of becoming-woman, investigating avenues of renouncing patriarchal heterosexuality connected to violence and rape. Yet transgender does not for Selby indicate a category that somehow permits transcending violent maleness.

Masculinity, for Selby, is a system of violence, an ideology and culture of violence that is not necessarily tied to any one gender. There is a memorable scene in which the "fairy" Ginger—both gay men and drag queens are gendered "she" in the book—flirts with Harry as a form of sadistic game, having utter contempt for him, dancing with him, and crushing his hand in her elbow: Harry is hurt, and confused by the interaction, puzzled as to what just happened. Opening himself up to his homosexuality does not inure Harry from being more violent, but actually the contrary: it encourages him to hate his wife and start physically hitting her. In general, it encourages the idea of himself as a man: he wants his partners frail and weak in his arms, and builds up even further this idea of himself as a patriarchal protector. This is partly why he finds his return to work after the strike has been resolved, in which he is once again in a submissive position in a menial alienating assembly-line job, so humiliating, so he walks out, gets drunk, and tries to reassert himself by sexually assaulting the ten-year-old boy, Joey. Once the strike is over and he doesn't have a free flow of money from the union strike expense funds, he realizes with alacrity that the drag queens' interest in him depended on his money, and once he can't lavish it on them anymore, they shut him out, and he finds himself loose, hanging, with nothing to lose, plummeting towards a disaster of his own making.

In the stories of *Last Exit to Brooklyn* there is a yearning to exit from heteropatriarchal paradigms. In *The Demon* the protagonist is consumed by his violent sexuality that culminates in him pushing someone into the subway in a very gruesome and brutal scene; in *The Room* the reader is privy to the thoughts of an imprisoned man, and one fantasy of a particularly violent rape scene by the cops who framed him stands out. In the end, Harry is crucified for his sins: pathological patriarchal masculinity crushes and humiliates the most deviant version of it. Harry and Georgette yearn for other ways of being, of tenderness, and the realm of femininity, but in an idealized way which is cut off from them. Vinnie is the avenging angel that through violence brings them back or punishes them for deviating from the heteropatriarchal norm, policing the boundaries of masculinity, first and foremost in himself, as he is constantly worried about what he can and cannot do with his lads (drinking from the same glass as a "fag" is unacceptable to him).

As a whole, *The Holy Bible* replicates Selby's vision of the male body, broken, martyred, and feminized: a Christian core, though in Richey's version largely devoid of any possibility of redemption. "Yes" is the song that most visibly draws from Selby's world, reflecting both its literary style—a stream of consciousness that allows for infrequent paragraph breaks, uses sparing punctuation, rejects speech marks and apostrophes—and its content, offering a portrait of bruised, feminized masculinity in an urban location of degradation and abject commerce, masculinity trafficking in and debasing femininity, violent feminization, human relations reduced to the cash nexus

("Another Day Another Dollar" is the subtitle of *Last Exit*'s Part I), pity and suffering and degradation in an endlessly violent city world, sentiment, romance, and hope crushed by the physical materiality of misery. The song kicks off the album on a note of shimmering melancholic melodicism, yet subtly riddled with a growing rock energy, offering a shifting first-person perspective which blurringly moves between prostitute and pimp, alternating between muttered offstage abject inner monologue and the outward-looking face fronting it and offering anything you want, including that violent sexual fantasy of castration and forced feminization that so shocked and thrilled my adolescent ears. The lyrics, of whorephobic and transphobic violence channelled through self-disgust, repeat Selby's dance with obscenity: in inhabiting the degraded street level underworld, the authorial I, the writer who is describing fictional and female characters from his comfortable chair, willingly obliterates itself in an erotic act of abject self-destruction. And this is only the beginning.

Selby also gazes on middle-class life, and is no less forgiving in his analysis of uncontrolled animal rage and murder-lust festering under the thin veneer of polite society. Selby's "Song of the Silent Snow" (1986), a story which comes at the end of a collection of the same name, belongs to a later period in which he has begun to depict redemption. Another Harry, suffering from nervous exhaustion and on meds, leaves his wife and children—from whom he feels cut off and alienated—at home, to take his daily walk, today in the snow. During this walk he has an epiphanic experience, in which he feels brightness and joy, the leaving behind of "all worries and cares, all horrors of the past and future" (211) and the disappearance of his footprints in the snow: "Soon he no longer heard the crunch of his foot on the snow no matter how he strained to hear it, and it did not surprise him as his body felt so light it seemed impossible for him to even leave a print, all he knew was that he could walk forever" (212). His body begins to feel lighter and lighter and glow in the sparkle of the snow:

"He knew that he was glowing. He knew that his eyes were afire with that light. He knew that light shimmered from him even through his clothing. He felt his legs getting lighter and when he looked down there were no footprints" (212). When he comes out of this state of grace, Harry realizes and returns to the love of his family. He has been touched by grace and returns home a new man.

"4st 7lb" lifts the no footprints in the snow image from Selby, though minus the redemption. In its identification with an anorexic young woman the song performs a Selby-esque becoming-woman but, like the album's use of the Selby sample at the beginning of "Of Walking Abortion," truncates Selby's redemptive tendencies. The statement about regretting his entire life and wanting to live it over again is in answer to a question about what his defining moments have been; and there have been other interviews in which he repeats the same answer to the question of what made him become a writer—a choice he made after nearly dying of tuberculosis at age eighteen and realizing that he would regret his life if he made nothing of it (Lindbloom; Burstyn). The quote continues as follows:

> I knew that some day I was going to die, and that when I died two things would happen to me. Number one, I would regret my entire life, and number two, I would want to live my life over again, and I would die. And I was terrified, absolutely terrified. So I knew I had to do something with my life. I was terrified of living my whole life, and at the end looking at it and having blown it. I was on disability at the time, and my wife was working part-time, I think at Macy's, it was the Christmas season, so I bought a typewriter, and decided I was going to be a writer. I didn't know anything about writing. But I knew I had to do something with my life, and that was the only thing I could think to do ... So I sat there for two weeks with that typewriter and I had no idea how to write a story, I just had to do something before I died. So I wrote a letter to somebody. And that's how it

started. The long process of learning how to write.

(removables.co.uk)

"Of Whales and Dreams," the penultimate story in *Song of the Silent Snow,* dramatizes this looking backwards over one's life from the position of old age, and celebrates the path well-chosen. It begins with "Many, many years ago a man told me that to deny my dream was to sell my soul" (195), the protagonist choosing to pursue his dream of being a sailor and "teaching the whales to dance," arguably a metaphor for Selby's life as a writer, in which, through the dream he still pursues as an old man, he is dancing together with his friends "and this thing called death no longer exists, being dissolved in our oneness" (197). By preserving, isolating and looping the anxious pretext of the statement, as "Of Walking Abortion" does, whilst excluding and rejecting the redemptive component of Selby's self-preservation narrative, *The Holy Bible* demonstrates how it picks and chooses, twists its sources to suit and construct its own intransigent tales of self-destruction. "Die in the Summertime" hammers this particular nail home. Says Richey in 1994:

> "Die in the Summertime" was written before anything had happened to me, that was basically an old man looking back over his life, over his favourite period of youth. His childhood, basically. Everybody's got a perfect mental time of their life, and that's what that song is about.
>
> (qtd in Bailie, "Manic's")

In Selby's old man looking back, childhood is just the beginning: in Richey's response it is the beginning of the end.

CHAPTER 12

What a Fantastic Death Exit 2: David Bowie's Outside

[*An Outside lyric I've misheard for twenty plus years: the true version is: "What a fantastic death abyss". Obviously I prefer my version.]

The other night I was poised over the keyboard with my fingers, to write something about David Bowie's *Outside,* and compare it to *The Holy Bible.* I remember a review suggesting that *Outside* was a badly-done version of the kind of more genuine body horror done by Manic Street Preachers on *The Holy Bible.*

Then in the morning I woke up to the news that Bowie had died. The whole thing was so surreal: I was listening to his new single "Blackstar," watching the video with its weird images of worship and science fiction death. And then he dies in the middle of its release.

The idea that he had somehow stage-managed his death floated around the Internet, with *Blackstar* his final work of art: his death his final work of art. That the album dealt with his struggle with or acceptance of death, with his actual death at the middle of its release. Displaying a degree of choice, agency, will: a positive, active relation to death; embracing death rather than submitting to it passively. Did he prolong his life by force of will until the album was released? Did he time his death so that his beloved England would find out first thing Monday morning? (Yes, I actually read someone opining this.) The perfectly secular response talked of ascension and self-deification in death, its details turning into narrative. That supposed stage-managing of one's death, one's "Last Exit," as Pearl Jam put it in *Vitalogy*, their album commemorating Kurt Cobain, and the desire to see meaning, order, agency, in those details of the accounts of last hours. You can read the details of Richey Edwards' last recorded days; you can read of Kurt Cobain's last hours as a kind of ultimate or terminal performance; it becomes a performance in the telling. Cobain's "small and peaceful" (Sounes 237) room above the garage; Richey's car near the Severn, full of burger wrappings and with the flat battery suggesting that someone had been living in it for a while. What were his last thoughts about, and how can we know them? What does the desire to know these things mean?

Death, or rather, murder, as an artistic performance, is one of the themes of *Outside,* or rather *1.Outside: The Nathan Adler Diaries: A non-linear Gothic Drama Hyper-cycle,* Bowie's 1995 album which is often seen as his dabble in industrial—he was close to NIN's Trent Reznor at the time, the two collaborated and toured together. *Outside* bills itself as a murder mystery in a dystopian setting, a parallel universe sci-fi rock opera, in which Bowie "plays" various characters. Baby Grace is the victim, fourteen years of age, tortured, mutilated and dismembered; protagonist Nathan Adler, detective of art crimes; other characters are Paddy, Leon Blank, the Artist/Minotaur, the Members of the Court of Justice. The trippy booklet's Burroughsian-type text refers to contemporary body horror artists such as Ron Athey, Hermann Nitsch and Damien Hirst, and the album seems to conceptualize contemporary art as an elite obscenity, a dystopian decadence where art is a practice of Sadean oppression, serial-killing a tool wielded by power to maintain its brand. Bowie occupies the masculine presence of the private investigator, but also inhabits the victim, distorting his voice to sound like a teenage girl, serial killer victim.

The main problem for me with *Outside* is that it offers a platform for serial killer chic, for titillation which flirts with perpetrator perspective: the mystery of what is inside the mind of a serial killer is presented as erotic, necro-aesthetic fantasy. *Outside* seems to endorse serial killer logic, an amoral aesthetic of vicarious perverse enjoyment, not unlike other 90s serial killer fantasies, such as *Silence of the Lambs, Se7en,* and NIN and Marilyn

Manson's industrial shock value serial killer tropes and references to the "pigs" of the Sharon Tate murders (derived from the Beatles song "Piggies," itself an Orwell reference): "March of the Pigs"/ "Piggy"/ "Le Pig," not to mention other industrial bands Pig and Pigface. Album closer "Strangers When We Meet," a return to classic Bowie style at the end of an album of gloomy industrial rock opera experimentations, admits to "all my violence," and seems to construct a scenario in which the serial killer has got away and is free to meet new victims.

Outside uses the art world as shorthand for sick masculinity (Athey, Nitsch, Hirst), which it reifies by its performance of disaster on the body, especially with regard to the domination of animals—the case of Nitsch and Hirst, by which the brutality of the universe is used as an excuse for human, and male, supremacy. By contrast, *The Holy Bible* refuses to glamorize serial killers or apologize for their actions by elevating them to the level of art, and instead takes the listener to the perspective of victims' family ("I wonder who you think you are"). Where *Outside* romanticizes serial killers as sanctioned by society's upper echelons to carry out murder in the name of art as a form of social control, *The Holy Bible* refuses to be seduced by serial killer chic, perhaps recognizing it as a way in which pathological heteropatriarchal masculinity is reproduced through terror consumed as culture. In its cover use of Jenny Saville's *Strategy (South Face/Front Face/North Face)* it employs pain not as a matter of male bodily endurance (Athey, Nitsch, Hirst), but rather embodies suffering as a form of "brutal sincerity" (Rose 46). The subject of *Strategy* observes herself with unadorned judgment, female and crucified at the moment of self-recognition, but she also gazes outwards, out toward the world, staring down the violence of the world and of the flesh. There is active defiance in her stance, a strategy for survival.

Finally, I'd like to briefly compare both albums' booklets and their use of words, images, and intertextual allusion. *Outside*'s uses a stream-of-consciousness noir style, mentioning big-name avant artists, all amid a multicoloured swirl of glitchy computer art, sometimes grotesque images, such as one with Bowie as thug next to a body with innards, and scrambled snippets of lyrics as code. It basically resembles the bad CGI of a film like *Lawnmower Man,* the aesthetic perhaps imagining the chaos in the mind of a serial killer: jumbled, overdosing on information, where the thinker cannot really distinguish reality from fantasy. The cosmopolitan globetrotting references to Kreuzberg, Berlin, Soho, East Village, Manhattan and London, in addition to the science fictional Oxford Town, New Jersey, give the effect of a serial killer cyberpunk diary, replete with severed fingers and bodies wrapped in sack cloth strands and sleeping with the fishes. A far cry from the orderly discipline of *The Holy Bible*'s booklet, which presents us with the orderliness of officialdom as being the genuine hell, an idea common to Ballard and Foucault alike: that it is the order of our society, not its disorders, that is pathological, and in which violence and punishment alike dwell. The clarity and calm of bureaucracy, forms, white papers; the hidden violence of orderly, well-meaning texts and acts.

CHAPTER 13

Depressive Realism, Militant Depression: Lars Von Trier's Melancholia

One of the motors of "depressive realism" and its attendant belief that books are "no good [...] if you are sick, alone, and unloved" (36), according to Ben Jeffery, is the sense that art cannot keep up with the information overload era. Yet *The Holy Bible* seems to constantly make a vitalistic virtue of this impossibility to keep up, defiantly refusing to collapse under the weight of its own citationality in the same breath with which it declares that "if you stand up like nail then you will be knocked down." "Depressive realist art is unable to explain its own existence," states Jeffery (54), but *The Holy Bible* does nothing if not desperately, relentlessly try to explain its own existence via its constant referentiality and citationalism, its patchwork of intertextual quotes and allusions. In the booklet for the twentieth anniversary edition, James Dean Bradfield is still constantly recalling the musical, conceptual and literary references that make up each track, so that there is seemingly no end to the attempt to trace how each song was conceptualized and constructed, musically, textually, thematically, psychologically, socially, historically. The album is an ongoing exercise in genealogy, the process of trying to understand how we got to where we are.

The first time I saw Lars von Trier's *Melancholia* (2011), I was crushed by its misery and totally bored, but as I watch it again, I find it readable as a black comedy, or, as Sukhdev Sandhu puts it, a vision "which at times comes close to being a tragi-comic opera about the end of the world." Like *The Holy Bible, Melancholia* is no funereal dirge, but vitalistic, punchy with points of absurdity. I think of *Melancholia* primarily for the idea it puts forward that depression can be a source of strength, a survival tool, by showing you the world more clearly, as it really is: that vision that horrifies and overcomes us as teenagers, but which many of us learn in time to submerge, for survival's sake. At the end of the world, Justine (played amazingly by Kirsten Dunst) is the one who, unlike the others, is able to act with composure and dignity. There has only ever been disaster: the final one is no different.

Paul Virilio's *Negative Horizon* (1984) is a book which contains several uncanny *Holy Bible*-esque formulations: in "The Aesthetics of Disappearance," Virilio discusses the genesis of camouflage as a disguising tactic in modern warfare. The Manics were described in their youth by The Fall's bassist Steve Hanley as looking "like kids doing The Clash in a school play" (Power 67), yet their camo and military gear on *The Holy Bible* can be read as a militarization of depressive affect, like dead or undead soldiers. I would not call *The Holy Bible* a work of depressive realism, but rather one of militant depression: where depression is weaponized as shock tactic for knowledge over complacency, avowal over passive spectatorship, action over apathy, even if that action is self-harm. In the midst of its shudderings there is a steely resolve, a serenity, a stoic and regimented calm that is a source of comfort and strength.

CHAPTER 14

Ballads of the Sad Young Man: Richey Haunts

Richey haunts the Manics and their fans in several literary ways. By way of his canon—the Richey reading lists, of which are there many floating around the internet; by way of the texts and books written about and inspired by him; and by way of the writing he did not get to produce. The "b-movie-fication of Richey's myth" (qtd in Carpenter), as James puts it, a process which he objects to but in which the Manics themselves cannot help but also participate, includes imagining where he'd go from where he was when he went missing. In Nicky Wire's mind he would have become a writer: "Richey wasn't looking for an Ivor Novello [Award], he wanted a Pulitzer Prize":

I love the idea of Richey's ambition. It goes back to 'Faster' – *"I am stronger than Mensa, Miller and Mailer..."* – the insane ambition of his intellect. That's what I meant about the Pulitzer Prize. He was taking lyric writing really seriously, he reached the apex of creativity with this record. For me, after this, he would have started writing novels, would have been the logical conclusion. He could still have written lyrics, still been in the band but he would definitely have started writing ... serious fiction.

(qtd in Davies)

What kind of novels would he have written? Why fiction, and not poetry, for example? To what degree are Richey's literary talents fictional rather than poetic, or dramatic? All this is academic of course: his literary legacy is the lyrics the Manics put to music, above all *The Holy Bible*.

Richey haunts also by way of the books he didn't get to read or recommend: what would he be into if he were around to read and share literary recommendations? One of the consequences of his body not having been found is that we can more freely imagine what he'd be into, should he be still alive. We can picture him in his monastery, keeping up with current authors and literary trends: which books would he enjoy, published after 1995? Did he ever read Joan Didion in the end?

There's a little bit of this in Wire's speculations about what Richey would enjoy. *The Machinist,* for example: such alternate history—imagining what Richey would be into now isn't just a game for fans, or obsessives, but for the Manics themselves. In a 2009 *Drowned in Sound* interview, we see Nicky Wire indulging this, wondering what he'd think of *The Virgin Suicides* film (he loved the book), and thinking of *The Machinist* through the figure of Richey: the machinist, who is anorexic, paranoid and delusional (and is called Trevor Reznick—a clear pun on the name Trent Reznor) as a Richey figure. Nicky Wire:

> Well, obviously, Richey never saw *The Machinist,* but with the things on there, we thought either

he did like it, or he would have liked it. *The Virgin Suicides* ... in "Doors Closing Slowly." He never saw the film but he loved the book so it seemed to fit. With *The Machinist* ... he would have liked the film ... I think he would have loved Christian Bale. He's the only person who could play Richey in a film [...] I think [Christian Bale] would do it justice. His ability to morph into things.

(qtd in Davies)

Richey lives on as Christian Bale, as that archetypal literary figure he can never escape from: the troubled young man. That same troubled young man in a lineage we can trace from Oedipus to Dante and Petrarch's courtly love sufferers, to Hamlet and his angsty indecisions, Byron and Shelley and Keats and Werther and the poetry of doomed young male Romanticism, nineteenth-century decadents, Rimbaud and Baudelaire and Flaubert and Stendhal, modernist antiheroes Eliot, Conrad, Pound, Hemingway, Fitzgerald, Joyce, Svevo, Tozzi, Gadda, angry young men and Beats of the mid-twentieth century, Orton and Ginsberg and Kerouac and Miller, his contemporary manifestation as the doomed rock musician, Morrison, Curtis, Cobain. This figure of the troubled young man, which *Richard* author Ben Myers in an interview with *The Quietus* describes thus:

> I think the literary comparisons are maybe easier to draw: Thomas Chatterton, Arthur Rimbaud and maybe some literary creations, like the brilliant, tormented young men in the writing of people like Céline, Hamsun or Mishima – men who are either so highly sensitive or have such a wider view of the world that they cannot exist in it easily.
> (qtd in Acharya)

Unlike, say, James Joyce, who wrote the at times bitter and intransigent and priggish *A Portrait of The Artist As A Young Man,* and then moved on to *Ulysses,* a book that exudes a warmth, the warmth of compromise and making peace with life, Richey's canon remains that of the angst-ridden young man;

fundamental, even life-saving when you are young and despairing; limiting and oppressive and inadequate when you grow beyond that stage. Part of the reason writing this section has been so traumatic for me is that I've had to immerse myself in a canon I didn't know how gladly I had left behind: that genre of books about self-obsessed and miserable young men. I don't know if Richey ever read *Ulysses* (or that he even read *A Portrait*). I remember reading *Ulysses* in college and it made me see the world in a new light; for the weeks I was reading it and afterwards, I was seeing the world through *Ulysses*. Basically it told me that there was a life after the cold intransigence of those "young man" texts—*A Portrait,* "Prufrock" and *The Waste Land,* etc.—there was a light at the end of the tunnel. These writers had been there, grown up, and could testify. Sadly, Richey's canon gets stuck at the young man stage. One idea I keep seeing in interviews with Richey is the notion that after childhood life is continually worse, a series of continually diminishing returns. From a literary point of view also, his canon never really gets to open up to books that embrace hope as a way out.

After *Everything Must Go* I basically forgot about the Manics, didn't seek them out, wrote them off as having joined the enemy, the Britpop hordes which I saw as characterized by an I'm-alright-Jack attitude I wanted nothing to do with. I grew into my twenties and thirties without the Manics. But the 2010 video for "Postcards From a Young Man" really grabbed me, galvanized me on some level. It encapsulated feelings about Richey that I'd sort of forgotten and was suddenly happy to remember: Richey stuck in the past, but calling out to you nonetheless, with missives, sharp missives, notes that you don't want to forget because they meant so much to you back then, they meant everything. Of course Kurt Cobain was in the video, in photographic form. But so is Will Self: did Richey ever read Will Self? He doesn't appear on manics.nl, a site which documents the band's literary and cultural references. Would Richey have enjoyed his Ballardisms, his Ovidian sex-switching tale *Cock and Bull,* in which sexual difference is reduced to a cruel joke? Or would he have hated his smarmy nihilism, his often cruel enjoyment of senseless violence, his constant refusal to be pinned down in terms of meaning, in terms of what the fuck he is actually saying. When I got the album the picture of a young Tim Roth with the camera and bared skinny torso in black and white on the front makes perfect sense. And look, T.S. Eliot is in there too, of course. Thus, the young man is frozen, but what happens *after* the young man?

Richey's canon remains frozen on some level: the canon of the young man. Or, as online poster TheSilentMan puts it "Books for generic disaffected 16–18 year olds." We might get more serious biographic work which records more precisely what Richey read and didn't read; in any case his canon is crystallized at that age, a reading list of a young man, a reading list for a young person, in many ways as generic as all of ours. The pointless yet alluring question is where would it have gone next—we can sit around the fire all night and talk about what authors of today he would have liked. Would he enjoy Michel Houellebecq? Would he dismiss him as yet another masculinity-obsessed male, or would he take delight in man's liberation from his own masculinity through becoming female that occurs at the end of *Atomised/The Elementary Particles?* In which directions would Richey's reading have moved?

For my part, I at some point moved beyond the angst-ridden white man canon to discover different genres and voices. Richey's canon is very white and very male. After my fill of that stuff, one direction I moved into, in grad school, was science fiction. There is SF in Richey's canon, of the dystopian or inner space kind: Ballard, Orwell, and the *2000AD* comic he loved as a child (Richey had a drawing of Ace Garp published in the magazine, for which he won £3 [Jet Simian]). What would he have made of mind-bending psychedelic science fiction: Philip K. Dick, for example. Or Octavia Butler's defamiliarizing Afrofuturistic explorations of race and slavery and alien genders? Questions, questions.

Richey haunts the Manics post-*Bible* output, of course: you can look all over Manics lyrics post 1995 and scour them for references to Richey, seeing the "you" of various songs as being directed toward Richey, and interpret the songs as being "about Richey," or not. Nicky Wire himself seems to have developed a kind of strategy for deflecting and pre-empting Richey-readings by saying that the song is about something else: that's me on the bridge, and it's another bridge anyway.

James is tired of the B-movie-fication of Richey, yet the band has used this very technique as a coping mechanism. Price quotes them doing just that:

> "It's only a matter of time before some film-maker does the Richey biopic," Nicky Wire told *Q* in 1998. "An Agatha Christie-type mystery. John Hurt as Richey, Leonardo DiCaprio as Sean ... no one tall enough to play me." James Dean Bradfield, warming to the theme, continued: "I'll be the simple

diamond geezer. Richey'll be in the corner cutting himself and I'll be going: 'Don't think too much, man. Let's just go and have a pint.' And it'll end up in Goa. Sunset. And Richey busking, smiling, happy."

(qtd in *Everything* 197)

Manics records have become the most appropriate place for Richey-grieving, but Richey lives on in other literary materials, the various Manics biographies, the best and most exhaustive of which is of course Simon Price's 1999 *Everything (A Book About Manic Street Preachers)*.

CHAPTER 15

Books about Richey
I

Rob Jovanovic's *A Version of Reason: In Search of Richey Edwards* (2009), is set up a bit like a detective investigation into what happened to Richey. The topic of "clues" comes up quite a bit, as if this were a mystery to be solved. Jovanovic dutifully pores over Richey's book collection as a source of potential information about his life and his disappearance, finding some books more interesting than others. *The Bell Jar* "caused my cup of tea to grow cold while I turned page after page" (42), he writes. M. Ageyev's *Novel With Cocaine,* and the story of author's mysterious disappearance, which Richey alluded to before disappearing, get his attention, as does Mishima's ritualized suicide. *A Version of Reason* contains interesting passages about T.S. Eliot and *The Waste Land* and sections on Richey reading *The*

Atrocity Exhibition, in hospital, as well as his obsession with Dante's *Inferno,* having a map of the ninth circle and a hell diagram tattooed on his arms.

However, as if following Nicky Wire's assertion that you could look over the whole flat (read all the books?) and still not have a clue, Jovanovic dismisses the book collection as a part of the whole, that likely does not tell us much we didn't already know:

> What do all these books tell us? Edwards was intelligent, he was interested in mental health, suicide, disappearing, existentialism, outsiders, rebels and revolutionaries. In the end, it might be that – even after close research – we confirm only what we already knew: any life is merely the sum of the tiny interactions that build up a picture. So and so was born here, he went there, he read this book, he watched this film, then he was gone. (43)

But he wasn't just a reader: he was a writer, a divulger, a popularizer, his act of reading not just inward-looking but an outward-facing gesture of empowerment, exposing young people to a passion for literature via the band and his lyrics, a political act in favour of the freedoms of literacy: not for nothing were slaves in the USA forbidden to read and write.

CHAPTER 16

Books about Richey II

There are two novels inspired by Richey's disappearance: *How I Left the National Grid: A Post-Punk Novel* (2015) by Guy Mankowski, and *Sympathy for the Devil* (2011) by Howard Marks. Paul Outhwaite's *The Preachers on Manic Street* (2005), a pink square book in the colour tones of *Generation Terrorists* and shaped like a 7" vinyl, is a self-published novel inspired by the Manics, covering a group of friends from a Welsh mining town over the course of several decades, starting with Thatcherism. Jenny Watkins-Isnardi's *In the Beginning: My Life with the Manic Street Preachers* (2000) is a novelization of the writer's early days with and stint as a singer for the Manics: it includes some scenes which describe an encounter with Richey in a college canteen, and an appendix consisting of some letters Richey sent to a friend.

Ben Myers' 2010 novel *Richard* has been standing on my shelf for a while now, so I pick it up and devour it between last night and this morning. There is something off about it: mainly that the voice does not sound like Richey, doesn't sound like his lyrics. One Amazon commenter mentions that the gender politics are off, and that Richey would not refer to himself as a "pussy." A conversation ensues in which his being a Valerie Solanas reader is discussed as precluding him from using such a derogatory term. Sexually, Myers constructs Richard as being bi-curious, but essentially straight; homosexuality is flirted with, wielded as a critique of patriarchal straightness. The homoerotic bond with Wire is explored, with at one point Richey tantalizing Wire over the phone about the time they spent in Philip Hall's London flat sharing a bed, then confessing it was nothing, just that Wire's feet stank, and that he'd come to enjoy and feel reassured by the smell. Richard fantasizes about Brad Pitt, and recalls sexual encounters with amorphous females, all through a drunken haze.

Richard splices timelines, and uses the second person singular, as used by Jay McInerney in *Bright Lights, Big City*, in the present tense part—when Richard has left the hotel and is returning to Wales, Myers splits him into two characters, making him talk to himself. The result is jarring, not fully convincing, but the dialogue allows Myers to illustrate some of the dilemmas the protagonist might have been going through. His abandonment is also seen as a rejection of the USA, refusing to want to sell the band in "America." The Manics started off so fascinated by the USA, and ended up on *The Holy Bible* denouncing it as a corrupt force in the world. Ultimately though, *Richard* enthralls as we hurtle toward the end, and we picture young Richard, on his way up the mountain.

It also does a good job of giving insight into the books Richey was reading and quoting: we hear of Camus, Mishima, Sartre throughout the text, and the book itself is framed through *Hamlet* quotes (Hamlet being one of the key templates for this confused young man literary protagonist), and a reading list at the end, that has "verified facts, provided inspiration or helped in the writing of this book" (Myers 395) featuring Jun' ichirō Tanizaki and Knut Hamsun. Did Richey read these authors? I did. And there's plenty more to explore. Richey set a ball rolling, and it keeps going in terms of what writerly connections you can make next. And you think, well, he could have been a writer, left the Manics, and become a full-time writer.

But—

CHAPTER 17

Interview with Richard Author Ben Myers

For a few years in the early 2000s Ben Myers and I were both colleague freelancers at *Kerrang!*. We didn't interact much. Since then he's made a career as a novelist and writer of rock books. His first novel, *The Book of Fuck,* came out in 2004. His second novel, *Richard,* was published in 2010. Despite my trepidation and reluctance, in the end I was moved by the book. I reached out to Ben, who was gracious enough to answer some questions about *Richard* via email.

Daniel Lukes: What exactly do you think that the Manics were reacting to, and trying to achieve, with their overt intellectualism and bookishness in the early days? One thing I think they have achieved is to

foster a community of people tied together not only by being fans of the band and music, but also via a shared set of texts: they have in that sense established a literary and cultural canon in many ways, more so than a strictly musical legacy.

Ben Myers: I think you've possibly answered the question yourself here. I'd say they were reacting against the consensus that says rock 'n' roll has to be dumb, hedonistic, clichéd and therefore, by extension, conformist. My attraction to them early on was for exactly the reason you mention—because they bridged the gap between literature/poetry and music at a time when few bands came anywhere close to doing this. Others had done it before, of course—most notably and, at the time, most recently, The Smiths—but I think the Manics were bolder and brighter than Morrissey. There was humour there too, whereas Morrissey only had wit and bitterness. I think they were inherently aware that intelligence is not something to be hidden away, suppressed or embarrassed by and that, in fact, throughout the ages there have been so many writers who are far more exciting than any rock stars. They constructed their own canon, and then invited fans to explore it. For those of us out there seeking guidance beyond what the music press had to offer, or were living in the provinces, suburbs or countryside away from easy access to an abundance of culture that the bigger cities had to offer, they were a godsend. A guiding light, so to speak. Beacons of good taste.

DL: To me the literariness of *The Holy Bible* was important: not only did the album interpret my angst to me and make some sense of it, making me feel less alone in it, but it also pointed me in the direction of further reading, helping me form an identity in the light of this sense of literary continuity that their

quotations provided. What function did that album perform for you back in the day, and what books and writers did the band point you towards that were significant to you?

BM: I had been a fan of the band since around about early 1991, so I was more than ready for *The Holy Bible*. Thanks to elder siblings I had grown up a fan of Hanoi Rocks and Guns N' Roses, The Clash, Public Enemy and Iggy Pop—and was aware of contemporaries of theirs such as Birdland—so I got where they were coming from right away. We shared the same sources. In fact, the album came out the month that I left home and moved away to study English Literature at university in a home counties town I had never visited and knew nothing about. It was autumn. Dark. The album struck a chord and became my soundtrack for the coming months, a strange time of new beginnings, new people. There was a lot of drinking, drug experimentations, a different life. I remember it seeming cold all the time and I wasn't eating well—was it the tones of the album that has shaped these memories? Each night I would buy a can of Special Brew and a can of cheap lager to wash it down with and would drink them in my little room while listening to *The Holy Bible* and reading books. Sonically it was claustrophobic and energising, and lyrically it was puzzling, over-ambitious, insane and brilliant. It wasn't entirely original either—I don't think musical originality has ever really been their strength—but then they really never made any bold claims to be pioneers.

The Holy Bible also helped forge links too. Manics fans gravitated to one another and I made friends as a result of that band, that album, who are still there today. 1994–1995 was entirely comprised of literature, amphetamines, jumping the train into London to spend the day wandering Soho with a bottle of vodka, fleeting sexual encounters, dawn comedowns—and *The Holy Bible,* which seemed to narrate events: "In these plagued streets..."

I was already a big reader by my teenage years, but this album encouraged me to dig deeper into the university library—I read anything I could get my hands on by Camille Paglia and Andrea Dworkin, William Burroughs and Henry Miller. Also Zola, Bukowski, Orton, Camus, Plath, Bret Easton Ellis, Mishima. All the books that *weren't* on my syllabus, which is possibly why my academic standing wasn't particularly strong, but higher education is about learning, and I was certainly doing that. I was reading some of these authors before I went to university, so wasn't entirely indoctrinated by the band. It was more of a parallel discovery, but the Manics got me more interested in feminism, gender politics, American trash culture. Ultimately they made me aware that I didn't have to hide my interests in literature and poetry, that intelligence was something to aspire to rather than retreat from. I've wondered how many people have discovered (the wildly different) Miller, Mailer, Plath and Pinter as a result of that one line on "Faster." A highly influential reference.

DL: Which novels specifically were you reading before or at the time of writing *Richard*, in order to get into Richey's headspace?

BM: In researching the novel I certainly concentrated my literary intake towards those texts Richey Edwards had read or cited as influence. I also read around the subject of the non-fiction novel—those works which feature a real life person in a setting in which a creative leap is required and artistic licence may be exercised. A couple of prime examples would be *Alma Cogan* by Gordon Burn and *Hellfire* by Nick Tosches, two very different but near-perfect non-fiction novels. I think this was the point that critics of *Richard* missed: I wasn't attempting to write a Richey Edwards biography, but rather a novel that captured the era and its prevailing themes: anxiety, depression and I suppose what could crassly be termed "(pre)millennial male crises." I wanted something rooted in 1980s and 1990s Conservative Britain, but which expanded out into the wider world as the band found themselves experiencing a degree of success.

And, of course, I wanted to try and get somewhere close to Richey's state of mind during his final weeks, which is not only an arrogant conceit, but an impossible task to undertake. Aside from sifting through all the music press cuttings, a number of books that I read during the writing of the novel, or inspired it in different ways (tonally, thematically, linguistically)—or were simply used for research purposes—would include:

Confessions of A Mask by Yukio Mishima

The Thief's Journal by Jean Genet

Our Lady of the Flowers by Jean Genet
The Road by Cormac McCarthy
Novel with Cocaine by M. Ageyev
Hunger by Knut Hamsun
The Eden Express by Mark Vonnegut
Bad Vibes: Britpop and My Part in Its Downfall by Luke Haines
The Heart of a Dog by Mikhail Bulgakov
Diary of a Rock 'n' Roll Star by Ian Hunter
Head-On/Repossessed by Julian Cope
The Damned United by David Peace
Notebooks of a Naked Youth by Billy Childish
Residues by R.S. Thomas
Nausea by Jean-Paul Sartre
Everything by Simon Price
GB84 by David Peace
The 90s: What The Fuck Was That All About? by John Robb
Ariel by Sylvia Plath
The Bell Jar by Sylvia Plath
The Rules of Attraction by Bret Easton Ellis
Under Milk Wood by Dylan Thomas

City of Night by John Rechy
Some Prefer Nettles by Jun' ichirō Tanizaki.
One Day in the Life of Ivan Denisovich by Alexander Solzhenitsyn

DL: Can you tell me in more detail about the reading list that appears at the end of *Richard?* Some of the books are documented to have been read by Richey, others are books somehow about MSP, but what about the rest? Do you know if Richey ever read *Hunger?* I ask because back in the late 1990s I also read Knut Hamsun's *Hunger,* in the Sverre Lyngstad translation: and it seems like a very "Richey" book. I also ask because in writing about the literariness of *The Holy Bible* I am not restricting myself to books it references directly, but am following various trails, so to speak, indicated by more tenuous literary suggestions,

including books Richey never read but might have enjoyed.

BM: The reason I listed *Hunger* is because it is at the very genesis of *Richard.* Back in 2008 I had a conversation with my now-wife—who herself had grown up listening to The Smiths, Suede and, yes, the Manics and is now an English Literature academic—about what a modern re-write of *Hunger* might entail; I'd actually given up on it once when I was younger but when I re-read it became something of an obsession.

That lead to us talking about intense young men, starved and half-mad with lust, desire, despair, which then led to a deeper discussion about what Richey might be doing were he still alive. But I didn't want to write a book that speculated too wildly beyond the point of his last known sighting, which is why the ending is ambiguous, and not so much a conclusion as simply the last page in my telling of the story. It's open ended—and very sad, of course—but hopefully captures something of the person, the charisma and the era.

It was at this point—before I put pen to paper—that I saw Richey as part of a wider tradition of the existential European male, adrift in time and place. There are dozens of novels and films which cover such similar ground—think of Dostoevsky or Genet, for example. Or Céline. And of course Hamsun. So I set out with these writers and their protagonists in mind, locating Richey to a contemporary, almost Ballardian world of service stations, hotel rooms, newly-built dock-side apartments and so forth. And then, ultimately, he moves onwards into the great question mark of his future.

DL: In *Richard* you emphasize the protagonist's very personal sense of letting go—of everything; he is as if letting himself get carried away by his own rejection of or weariness of life. To what degree do you think he consciously staged his exit partly as a form of entering

the rock/literary pantheon? He'd seen it done by countless others (Mishima, Plath, Curtis, more recently Cobain), and so would have to assume a similar path would await him once gone. The mystery of disappearance would also provide a different kind of twist, which might go toward explaining why he did not kill himself in a visible manner. I guess my question is: to what extent do you concede his own agency in his own disappearance? Or do you feel he did eventually cave to forces larger than his own will? I ask because we tend to see suicide in the contemporary West as a kind of surrender, a loss, a failure, rather than an assertive or creative or positive act. Must we believe that Richey ended his own life out of despair? Or might we see it also as a form of bestowing canonical status on his masterpiece? I don't mean to either romanticize suicide or be cynical about it

here, but—as is also the case of Kurt Cobain (see the Neil Young quote about not fading away)—I can't help seeing this move as having aesthetic intentions too.

BM: I really don't know. I originally thought it could have been a slightly staged move, but the older I get the more I think that assumption is wrong. Clearly he was aware of the mythological potency of the "doomed rock 'n' roll star"—live fast, die young and leave a good-looking corpse and all that rubbish—but Richey Edwards had real problems, and was clearly consumed by despair. I don't think he wanted to create a mystery for his family and friends, or mythologise himself. I think he just wanted out.

DL: Writing about Richey/*The Holy Bible* can be depressing and stressful at times: how did you, whilst writing *Richard,* counteract or resist this sense of being sucked into a despairing state of mind? What did it feel like to dwell in

Richey's mind and how did you keep a sense of balance throughout the experience?

BM: I'm beginning to realise that I possibly wrote the novel because I already had some awareness or understanding of anxiety or depression—or perhaps just plain sensitivity. I think the modern world punishes the sensitive one way or another. If you watch TV or read a newspaper or go online and have a sensitive disposition, how can you not be effected? But, yes, writing it was not easy, but I at least felt like I, as much as anyone else who didn't actually know Richey Edwards, was qualified.

This book was written in London and I seem to recall taking up jogging while working on it. A few times a week I would run round Nunhead cemetery, a vast and wildly overgrown Victorian place. Or else I would go swimming at lunch time; physical exercise seems to slow the whirring mind a little. But I definitely had to put myself into his state of mind, by absorbing all the same cultural references as Richey Edwards. Also my work as a music journalist meant I was more than familiar with the music business and life on the road too, as I have been on tour with many bands, played in them, and seen the indie/rock/whatever worlds at closer quarters during that same time period: I have seen people embrace excess, fame, exhaustion, failure. It's an unreality, a strange sphere in which to exist.

I have to take care monitoring my own mental well-being because writing novels is such an intense and introverted experience. For the most part I enjoy it but when a project is completed is usually when I am hit by a wave of mental exhaustion. I have to re-integrate myself into society and watch out for the signs that might suggest I have been over-doing it; writing *Richard* taught me this. Also I don't drink, which is a common outlet for writers, so it's not like I cut loose and drink myself into oblivion after a hard week's writing.

About two months after *Richard* was finished—but before it had found a publisher—myself and my wife left London after over a decade of living there and moved to a small eighteenth-century weaver's cottage that was surrounded by fields in the Pennines. It was probably the right thing to do at the time and certainly helped me decompress from the experience. Suffice to say I've found it very difficult to listen the Manics ever since. Now and again I'll listen to the Richey-era albums, and still appreciate them, but as the experience was so immersive I had to step back. I've barely listened to the band's past few albums.

DL: You put Stephen King's *Insomnia* in *Richard*, and you have the protagonist reading it: do you know of Richey ever reading Stephen King, or was this more of a joke perhaps?

BM: The *Insomnia* thing ... I actually have no recollection of that, but I'm almost certain he will have been reading it at the time. I'm pretty sure it must have been mentioned otherwise I wouldn't have put it in. I certainly wouldn't have had the "fictional Richey" reading it for no reason...

CHAPTER 18

Dying in the Summertime: Purity's Doomed Romance

Yukio Mishima's 1953 short story "Death in Midsummer" narrates the story of a family that loses two children and an aunt to drowning and a heart attack at the beach one summer. Focusing primarily on the mother, Tomoko, and how she copes with her grief, the story traces a full circle of a year, from the summer death of Tomoko's son and daughter and sister-in-law, to the family's return to the beach, a year later, with a new baby. There are four children total, which makes one think of the four photos of the Manics as children that accompany the lyrics of "Die in the Summertime" in the booklet. The story opens with a quote by Baudelaire:

"Death ... affects us more deeply under the pompous reign of summer." This sets the tone for how the story negotiates between two poles: the shimmering dreamlike world of the beach, with its light of the summer, its brightness, the death, the world of emotions that engulfs Tomoko ("If only summer would end. The very word 'summer' carried with it festering thoughts of death" [*Confessions* 14]), and on the other side the realm of the practical activities that the three deaths oblige, the trip to the cemetery to see the burial plot. At one point the narrator clinically notes: "A death is always a problem in administration. They were frantically busy administering. One might say that Masaru, in particular, as head of the family, had almost no time for sorrow" (12). This sentence makes me think of Richey, and the paperwork side of his disappearance, the bank accounts, the 2008 legal declaration of death.

Mishima's story explores its title's oxymoron, that of death in summer (similar to Henry Miller's *Black Spring*), as an investigation into the of cruelty of being, which turns up no meaningful answers or moral lesson beyond the natural ebb and flow of life, the tides of the beach, the return of life after death: "Not that Masaru and his wife had sacrificed two children and a sister to teach a lesson. The loss of the three had served no other purpose, however; and many a heroic death produces as little" (25–26). What lingers for the protagonist is a kind of yearning, a looking out to sea, an unnamable and unnamed emotional pull, almost a seduction of "the Far Shore," that world beyond into which the once smiling children have entered forever, a guilt at being still alive, still here: "In the very cruelty of life was a deep peace, as of falling into a faint" (20). Death operates a fascinating seduction. In Mishima's works death, especially by violent means, is erotic and beautiful. The coming-of-age protagonist in *Confessions of a Mask* has his first ejaculation to a picture of Guido Reni's *St. Sebastian*. In the painting, the figure cowers in pain from the arrow that has entered his torso, and gazes upwards in melancholic expectation, perhaps searching the heavens for a god whose presence he cannot feel. *Confessions'* protagonist lives in a world of his own corrupt purity, which extends to his incipient romantic predilections: "of all the kinds of decay in this world, decadent purity is the most malignant" (72).

Mishima's works feature violent penetrations of the body by blades, and it is the short story "Patriotism," that anticipates the author's own suicide. It graphically describes the ritual *seppuku* suicide of a young lieutenant and his wife Reiko, following a mutiny by several of the lieutenant's colleagues. I would assume a story called "Patriotism" would be using the word ironically, but that is not the case here. Mishima's narrative, primarily seen through Reiko's eyes, eroticizes and elevates the double suicide to a pact of perfect love. The husband and wife explore each other's bodies, gaze into each other's souls, and ascend, through a shower of blood and guts, into an afterlife which will see them reunited with the conspirators: Shinji jokes at one point that they will mock him for having brought his wife along.

Paul Schrader's 1985 film *Mishima: A Life in Four Chapters* centres around the writer and now militant's last day. Early on in the film actor Ken Ogata, playing Mishima, makes the point that "words are not enough," not enough to transmit his message. He needs a stronger medium, and that medium will be his suicide. The film's four dramatizations of Mishima texts illustrate how he had idolized suicide over the course of his career: as an act of strength, an affirmative act, a choice. Not a caving into defeat of circumstance, nor a tragic collapse, but the ultimate affirmation of the will. Shinji's choice is a refutation of "the premise of the democratic age—that it is best to live as long as possible" (Williams). A rejection of the dominant Western idea that life is above all worth living, that living is always better than not living, that human life is the ultimate good. Yet living involves compromise, which is antithetical to that purity Mishima's characters cling to.

In discussing the suicide of hacktivist Aaron Swartz, Eileen Joy asks:

But what if the suicide has thought everything through with gorgeously elegant logic? What if the suicide knows exactly what they are doing, what the actual/real alternatives are, and exactly what the (dead) future holds? What if the suicide is opting out of what is, actually, unbearable, unlivable, and "too much"?

Suicide can be read here as a conscious answer to the unlivability of the world, its "too much." Words will not be enough of an answer, and so suicide, which perversely transforms the body into words, speaks louder, makes the words speak louder. There is nothing left of the bodies of Mishima, Richey, Swartz, but their words remain, fortified, underscored by the sacrifice of their bodies. Mishima's suicide is a political act, yes, but also an artistic one in that it coronates and culminates his work as a writer. Suicide canonizes his work—the artist and his work, like Shinji and Reiko, become one, crystallized, locked up tight together, in ways that the messy business of living and its inertia would never allow.

There is little discussion of Richey's agency in his own disappearance, perhaps correctly: he is often presented, as biographer Ian Thomson presents Primo Levi in his last days, as a victim of overbearing circumstances. (Martin Amis counters this thus: "perhaps we can see Levi's suicide as an act of ironic heroism [...] My life is mine and mine alone to take" [*Time's* 176]). Richey is not Mishima, who idolized masculinity, the cult of the body and politics of violence; Richey did not make his disappearance an explicit performative declaration of choosing death. But reading "Die in the Summertime" through Mishima certainly makes you want to see some of that agency, some of that power-taking worship of beautiful immortality, into Richey's disappearance. Makes you, in spite of yourself, want to read it as in part a ritual suicide: the last objects placed where they were, the final missives sealed and sent, the business of picking everything up and making a story out of it left to everybody else.

CHAPTER 19

Literal Castrations: Valerie Solanas

If you'd asked me ten years ago, I would have had a lot to say about Valerie Solanas. In grad school I wrote a paper called "Manics to Mitochondria: Searching for Man in the Third Millennium," in which I wondered whether the "so tear off his cock" image in "Yes" was to blame "for triggering an obsession that I would somehow end up being castrated" and how Richey's disappearance, following Kurt Cobain's suicide "did nothing but cement the certainty of my own impending doom."

I can't remember whether the Manics introduced me to *SCUM Manifesto* (1967), which I read in college, or not. Her name is misspelled in the cover of *Generation Terrorists,* which happens quite often. Solanas totally informs Richey's rejection of patriarchal masculinity as central to human structures of power, violence and oppression. Richey is asked what message he would leave for the next inhabitants of the planet, in the last minutes of a nuclear war. "I'd cut off my cock, nail it to the wall with a message. 'If you can learn to live without this you might do a better job than humanity'" (qtd in Bailie 78).

In *SCUM Manifesto* Solanas expresses her complete rejection of masculinity by way of a gender science fiction narrative bolstered by real-world reproductive technological advance: "we now have sperm banks" (47). Humanity does not need men any more to survive: women can be impregnated by men's frozen sperm for a potentially infinite future. Out of love for humanity, we must feminize, as a species. Monique Wittig's *Les Guérillères* (1969) can be read as imagining, in lyrical écriture féminine prose and incantations, Solanas' postmasculine world, where women have violently overthrown and eliminated men, and now live free to cultivate and enjoy life.

I wonder how hard the Manics could have embraced Solanas, in spite of Richey and Nicky's status as "feminised males" (Price, "Return") and rejection of manhood ("I don't wanna be a man")—unless of course, you read Richey's own self-annihilation as in part a form of adherence to Solanas' project. Out of Solanas comes the graphic level of verbal and literal castratory violence advocated against the male body, necessary to the ultimate overthrow of masculinity. *The Holy Bible* certainly seeks to foreground femininity, to castrate and erase the male and hypermasculine subject in favour of a suffering female one. James' vocals perform a kind of sonic femininity, with their sweet and dulcet high pitches, soft enunciations, and aching tenderness at times. Solanas offers a stance of self-styled bitchiness as part of her strategy to defeat men, and a rejection of imposed ideas of sweetness on women. *SCUM Manifesto* is a revolutionary tract to rewire female (and male) psychology in favour of female assertion and male submissiveness: Solanas' unapologetic stance of aggression is a political act of defiance, one that is literarily scandalous. In her future world, women "groove" off one another: women learn to enjoy themselves and each other again. *The Holy Bible* provides glimpses into female homosocial worlds or spaces, in which men are absent or marginalized: "4st 7lb"'s panoply of Kate and Emma and Kristin and Kit Kat (and Twiggy), "She Is Suffering"'s all-consuming, narcissistic femininity, Saville's cover art of three female forms.

And yet *The Holy Bible* arguably lacks *SCUM Manifesto*'s *pars construens,* its constructive part, the part which imagines a positive future for women now free of patriarchy, the part which celebrates female strength and laughter and sexuality and agency and joy, as Solanas does. The bitchiness. The speaker of "4st 7lb" is bitchy and assertive, but in the midst of her downward spiral, finding glory only in terminal self-destruction. *The Holy Bible* options the strength of self-destructive femininity in order to drag it downwards.

SCUM Manifesto's biological essentialism has also increasingly begun to be seen as transphobic, and "Yes," with its lyric "he's a boy, you want a girl so tear off his cock · tie his hair in bunches, fuck him, call him Rita if you want" problematically re-iterates feminization as a violent reduction or humiliation of masculinity, a brutality which is further trivialized by interview remarks by the band presenting the song as a metaphor for selling out. "Whore" is an old-school misogynistic insult, which seeks to reduce femininity to prostitution, and masculinity to femininity. Applying it to your band of men doesn't change that. Becoming-woman in *The Holy Bible* is not an act of agency or self-empowerment, but feminization as an act of violence done to someone in the name of the violence of capitalist desire, a tableau involving de-masculinization via castration and rape, which then, with a touch of David Cronenberg, is captured and broadcast on video. Masculinity is split between violently fucking and being fucked as female. Solanas inverts Aristotle, and his millennia-long shadow justifying violence against women, when she states "the male is an incomplete female, a walking abortion, aborted at the gene stage" (35), yet "Yes" appears to invert Solanas by imagining femininity as castrated masculinity. "Yes" seeks to establish a portrait of heteropatriarchal capitalism oppressing women through sexual violence, yet appropriates it as a metaphor for male self-loathing, a problematic use of Solanas' diatribe.

The Holy Bible here demonstrates the limits of empathy and appropriation, showcasing not affirmative images of transgender, but a darker, more troubling androgyny than their drag outfits of their earlier glam days, employed politically as a statement of hate toward patriarchy. The album's journey of transition, from male to female, is a metamorphosis that fails: masculinity and its violence can never fully be transcended or left behind; they may be abhorred, indicted, gathered, as fragmented images, documented as evidence of the evil that masculinity and its toxic hyper-mutations have wrought. But they cannot be transcended, especially not through femininity. The phallus now crawls as a worm and that worm is the Hitler of the soul, demented personification of twentieth century inflated masculinity gone wrong, seemingly impossible to fully dig out.

CHAPTER 20

Art: Site of the Body-Disaster: J.G. Ballard

I've had a more hate than love relationship with Ballard ever since as a teenager I flipped through the RE/Search illustrated edition of *The Atrocity Exhibition,* with Phoebe Gloeckner's illustration of a severed penis. And it horrified me, making me physically feel sick. I've read *Crash* a few times and never enjoyed it. David Cronenberg's film, I got bored with immediately. I'm trying to read *The Atrocity Exhibition,* but it's hard work, I keep getting stuck.

I've decided to read the book in weekly instalments, at ballet, in the half hour I wait for my daughter with all the other parents, in the theatre's bunker-like backstage area. I keep having to hide the book's title with my hand, or hold it at an angle: I don't want any of these fellow parents peeking onto the page, seeing what I'm reading. I've also been reading about Richey's *Journal for Plague Lovers* lyrics, and thinking about that line about ballet dancers getting their feet chopped off, which was pilfered by Bloc Party, and not used by the Manics after all.

I am thinking of Richey reading this book in hospital, as he supposedly did: an appropriately morbid setting for the novel's exploding carnage of bodies and shattered images, words placed next to each other in obscene order: for it is the orderliness of the novel that sears and scars, or rather prods and irritates, mainly with a ghastly boredom punctuated by the odd chuckle. The novel has none of that empathy, that human warmth that you expect and demand from a work of fiction. No, *The Atrocity Exhibition* has mannequins for protagonists, empty soul blanks, screens against which you buckle and kick. The body, so mutilated in Ballard, is reduced to the word.

In *Saville* (2005), an oversize collection of Jenny Saville's paintings, John Gray compares Ballard with Saville in a fascinating essay, arguing that what both have in common is a statement on how "humans are the sport of chance and no special significance can be discerned in their suffering" (9). Gray argues that unlike Francis Bacon, in whose art religious impulses remain at the level of form, Saville presents a new order of art, one which engages with human bestiality, that "region of experience in which meaning is absent" (10). But that can't be right: *Strategy*, with the triptych's origins in and associations to Christian art, is still religion at the level of form, a female crucifixion, for the living world. And in Ballard religion lives on at the level of shock horror media performance art: "Christ's crucifixion could be regarded as the first traffic accident" (*Atrocity* 29).

Ballard's world is a world devoid of emotion ("The Death of Affect"): filled with words, choked with spurious meaning, words that cannot but slide down the surface of things, always failing to correctly encapsulate the meaning of matter, the tragic solidity of flesh, its "contours," to use a word that Ballard employs, over and again, obscenely, pornographically. For Ballard pornography is an idea, an abject weapon against good taste and the idea of human decency. The word is to be brandished ironically, as a punishment, for its failure to signify. Saville's world is one that has largely given up on words, except when they are used in abstracted, allusive, Ballardian fashion—her painting titles. Saville's world is committed to knowledge of the body as true and only, and thus tragic canvas.

Ballard, Saville, *The Holy Bible* all use shock tactics, aesthetics of gorgeous abjection to assault the viewer. Ballard does it with crashed bodies and psychologies smashed to shards; Saville with bloated bodies out of control, tragic flesh of saints, sanctified for their suffering with no meaning, of no purpose beyond the physical carrying-through of their existence. *The Holy Bible* does it with its ruptured squabbles, soul sores leaking pus of humanity's capitulation to the dark side, rotten missives, accusations, breakdowns and weaknesses, as if it can't stop shaking anymore.

All three want to make their mark on you, perceive their own mission as one of violence upon the spectator: a moral mission because amidst all the white noise and static of the information-entertainment world, the jeering is too loud, and the crying is all but drowned out. In the service of truth, the artist must lacerate, and the profound abjection of the body, the scarification of the self, the breaking of the taboo of the illusion of sanctity of the body as self-contained whole, is a perfectly acceptable way for encroaching on the complacency that allows us to live complicit lives. Aesthetic butchery is thus a moral enterprise. Obscenity, critically modulated, pulls you out of your comfort zone and makes you confront yourself, or at least the parts you hide daily in order to live in polite society and in good conscience with yourself.

I'm still in the bunker, my Atrocity Ballet. Reading Ballard's noxious dreams of ash surrounded by pink tutus seems incongruously appropriate. I think of

Ballard writing these books, surrounded by his three kids whom he brought up as a single dad after his wife died on holiday in Spain. Reading *The Atrocity Exhibition* is surely to approach feeling what it is like to be dead. But I'm grinding through it to get to "Why I Want to Fuck Ronald Reagan," a section written as mock sex study paper, which had an afterlife as a practical joke, distributed by ex-Situationists at the 1980 Republican National Convention in Detroit, replete with the Republican Party seal. "Revol" does not mention Reagan, but the song is constructed around the same joke, which in Freudian terms uses obscenity and caricature to "bring about the degradation of the sublime" (Freud 194), employing humour for desacratory purposes, reducing political leaders to their sexual foibles. Ballard's point, furthermore, is that politicians exert upon us a fascination of eroticized violence: the violence of power, and violent power, exert an erotic fascination on us. We are turned on by brutality against humans, against ourselves even. The "boot on the face" from Plath's

"Daddy." Politicians' brutality and murder is a fuck fantasy we outsource to them. We elect them to do our bidding and sexually enjoy the murder and brutality of people near and far.

Ballard is closely concerned with the fascism of everyday life, the one we disavow. Ballard's last novel, *Kingdom Come,* is about a white supremacist fascist revolution that quietly occurs in the suburbs, via sports fan clubs and centred around a shopping mall where a former TV personality struggles to fill the hollow role of a local dictator. With its bilious descriptions of the crowds of sports fans milling and gathering, *Kingdom Come* is also hilariously funny, a great example of late Ballard's comic voice. I cannot look at sports fans the same way again now. "Revol" is also one of the funnier songs on *The Holy Bible:* a puerile joke, imagining the sex lives of politicians; a very British genteel puritanical sport, that of the politician's sex scandal, that dangerous moralistic equation of sexual conformity with moral probity.

I am downstairs, on the last day of ballet, on the final day before the recital, sat on the corridor floor of a bigger bunker, backstage, a kind of brutalism that reminds me of a slicker version of the Barbican Centre, finishing *The Atrocity Exhibition.* It's been a long slog. Probably one of the most horrible books I have read. The text is wickedly boring: it reads like a manual for an undefined state of mind that is caught in a kind of flattening deadness, where the "contours" of life are reduced to an idea, an irritable fever dream that the mind keeps returning to in a guise of endless rationality. The body meets Ballard's text in a sort of reduction: "pornography" is one of its guiding concepts, where pornography has become a metaphor for horror. Ballard is on the surface a satirist of language; he reproduces the flat affect and dry tone of official writing—manuals, reports, studies, memos—using the style's truthfulness to show us parts of material and psychological reality that we forget are there.

I just don't think *The Holy Bible* is as Ballardian as it thinks it is. Yes, there is the body as the canvas for the art of disaster. "Faster" explodes with a poetry of Ballardian abruptness. "Ifwhiteamerica"'s "Zapruder the first to masturbate" is a Ballard tribute; but as a whole there is not that flatness, that ironic distance, that inhumanity of the real; there's too much emotion, too much tenderness, too much humanity, too many tears and too much self-pity. Does anyone ever cry in a Ballard novel? Does anyone ever laugh?

I also wonder if the RE/Search editions of Ballard and Mirbeau's *The Torture Garden,* with their interplay of image and text, are an influence on *The Holy Bible*'s booklet.

CHAPTER 21

The Hokey Bible: Laughter in The Holy Bible

I keep coming back to the idea of finding comedy and humour in *The Holy Bible,* and coming up short. It's riveting to read a reference to *The Producers* in the twentieth anniversary liner notes, with Keith Cameron writing about "Revol" "there's a definite air of Mel Brooks' *The Producers* about this, possibly the strangest of all Manics songs." That line in "Faster"—"man kills everything"—now that I re-watch *The Producers,* recalls for me LSD (Lorenzo St. DuBois)'S song "Love Power" and its ending: "Hey, man, a flower/A flower/What you do to my flower, man?/Hurt it, like everything else/Everything else/Flowers." Of course, the "man" in "man kills everything" is not a gender-neutral hu*man,* but very much a Solanasian "man." In *The*

Producers, in the words of LSD, it is "hey man," a humorous hippy affectation. *The Holy Bible* has that tendency to take a joke and hollow out its punch line. And it does similar things to my mind with *Monty Python's Life of Brian.* I've often wondered if the band name comes from those manic street preachers, one of whom Brian pretends to be when he's evading the Romans and is first mistaken for a messiah. I also wonder if *The Holy Bible* itself is not some extended, bitter inversion of Eric Idle's "Always Look on the Bright Side of Life."

There is musical comedy in *The Holy Bible:* the rat-a-tat martial drums and mock marching band in "Ifwhiteamerica" ... *and* I'm coming up short again. "Tipper Gore was a friend of mine" is certainly a joke. The album has witty word play aplenty, scattin 'n' beboppin' cut 'n' paste juxtapositions and puns, generating much of the album's comedic content. That breathtaking unexpectedness—you could listen to "Faster" twenty-seven times and still marvel at the brutality of the transitions: meat, architecture, butchery, literature. Abrupt shifts of register worthy of Eliot or Larkin from the mundane and the local to the sublime and the universal, working-class voices, abstract philosophical modernisms, placed side by side, together. There is the absurdism of "P.C.P." with its mutated *Alice in Wonderland* "king cigarette snuffed out by her midgets." And the album's cover is also on some level a sick joke, on those who want a sexy young woman on the cover of their pop album or maybe yet another hot male torso like the first two albums. Yet though its lyrics may read, as Bradfield remarks, like "a set of sarcastic commandments" (qtd in Quantick), *The Holy Bible,* where it deploys laughter, seemingly does so to extinguish laughter. At best its laughter is nervous and involuntary, the laughter of panic and despair, in the end smothered by the brutal sincerity of it all that perhaps precludes laughter entirely.

Journal for Plague Lovers, by contrast, comparatively abounds with jokes and silliness, displaying a different level of comfort with making light of one's despair: "Oh mummy what's a sex pistol" is a joke about a joke, and sex is a "joke sport severed." "Me and Stephen Hawking" is populated with cartoony characters treated with deceptive levity and "spins an entire song out of one old joke—'what did the anorexic say to the paraplegic?'" argues Amy Britton: "The punchline here forms the chorus of the song, with Edwards imagining it as a conversation between him and Stephen Hawking" (393). *Journal for Plague Lovers* reminds me of the hospital and psych ward world of *The Bell Jar,* a bitterly funny book.

CHAPTER 22

If Bible America

In some ways *The Holy Bible,* or parts of it, belong to that genre of the European or British observer of the USA. Alexis de Tocqueville has a great early one, and some of his observations, such as on the cheapness and bad quality of mass-produced goods for sale in the US, ring true today. Angela Carter's 1977 novel *The Passion of New Eve* tells the story of young British man, Evelyn, who travels to the USA and gets kidnapped by a desert feminist cult who surgically transform him into a woman, Eve, to be impregnated with a new messiah. Eve escapes, and on her journey encounters an army of Christian child soldiers. Using not satirical science fiction but reportage, Martin Amis charts moments in the political rise of the US Christian right in his strongly-titled *The Moronic Inferno and Other Visits to America* (1986), a collection of previously published newspaper articles. There are pages dedicated to Reagan's presidential campaign, and, in "Too Much Monkey Business: The New Evangelical Right" (1980), he recounts a trip to televangelist Jerry Falwell's headquarters in Lynchburg, Virginia. Amis betrays a sense of amazement at the apparent religious sincerity of the born-again Christians he encounters: you can't be serious, he seems to be asking himself. He can barely keep a straight face, but beneath the laughter, lies a conceited confidence that they do not represent a genuine threat. Yes, this movement "will have to be heeded" but "I don't think the Evangelicals will soon be running the country" (*Moronic* 118) he says, with what now looks like a depressing lack of foresight.

In many regards it has come to pass, they do run the country. The Republican Party, over the past thirty years, has become the political arm of Christian conservatism. At time of writing Republicans rule thirty-one of the fifty states. They pass theologically-inspired laws across a range of areas: education, abortion restriction, anti-LGBTQ, ecological deregulation. Openly theocratic discourse dominates domestic and foreign US policy, from George W. Bush's neo-medievalist "crusade" on terror and his conversations with God, to recent homophobic "religious freedom" laws. In the US, the words of Christ, a man who socialized with lepers, pariahs and prostitutes, is used to sanction and justify war, the death penalty, vast accumulation of wealth, homophobia. It's no surprise *The Holy Bible* and the Manics never caught on there.

In BBC documentary *Factory: Manchester from Joy Division to Happy Mondays,* Paul Morley mentions a small influential Sex Pistols gig in Manchester, discussing Jonny Rotten lecturing to the crowd: "You know, like Darwin, the world has changed, this is what it is now, evolution is the truth, the Bible is dead, and so we all believed it." But this has proved not to be the case. We now live in an era some are calling post-secular. The atheistic Eden that Nietzsche prophesized has not come to occur; religion not only endures, but rises up once more emboldened, and theocratic states abound. Even on the left, secularist or atheistic positions are increasingly regarded as problematic. The idea of a post-religious society has been overly optimistic at best, and it is through religious extremism and ethnic identity based on religion that global conflicts today flare.

CHAPTER 23

The Bible as Literature

The literal meaning of the Bible is τὰβιβλία, the books. Primo Levi asks whether the stories that came out of Auschwitz might not constitute a new Bible:

> He told me his story, and today I have forgotten it, but it was certainly a sorrowful, cruel and moving story; because so are all our stories, hundreds of thousands of stories, all different and all full of a tragic, disturbing necessity. We tell them to each other in the evening, and they take place in Norway, Italy, Algeria, the Ukraine, and are simple and incomprehensible like the stories in the Bible. But are they not themselves stories of a new Bible? (*If* 72)

This is not so much to sacralize the Holocaust, as others have done, but rather to desacralize the idea of a Bible. Richey makes a similar point in his last TV interview, when he puts forward the notion that if a Bible is to be truthful, then it should address contemporary reality. Taking issue with the Catholic Church's misogyny, he says:

> If the Holy Bible is true, it should be about the way the world is, and that's what I think my lyrics are about – you know, they speak about the world as it actually is, don't ignore things, don't pretend things don't exist; I don't think that's any way to live your life, really. ("Richey's")

Both of these statements challenge the status of the Bible, seeking to replace it with a secular, living anthology of stories. In Levi, stories are told in the evening, and they reveal a common, shared humanity, comfort and bulwark against disaster. In both cases we may discern a protestant move, in the manner of Martin Luther, but more radical, in that it no longer seeks a truer interpretation of the Bible within the Bible itself in order to displace the Bible with a truer version of what it should be. "Archives of Pain" directly references Luther's ninety-five Theses, and in this light one may read *The Holy Bible* as an act of heresy, a reclamation of that which is holy, according to a contemporary paradigm, from those who have forgotten and perverted holiness by replacing truth with dogma. *The Holy Bible* arguably pushes documentary hypothesis to its logical conclusion: namely that the Bible is a human document, and must not be mistaken for anything else. No word of God, but a bunch of texts stitched and edited together by human hand, not divinely-ordained or dictated by God himself, but an imperfect human work. *The Holy Bible* thus belongs to a genre of unbibles, para-bibles, or would-be-bibles that question, wittingly or not, the very difference between the Bible, and any other work of literature: from Dante's *Divine Comedy* and Milton's *Paradise Lost* to Russell Hoban's *Riddley Walker* and Will Self's *The Book of Dave*.

Boswell writes that "the central irony of the album is that there is nothing holy about" it (126), yet I find myself disagreeing both with this, and with the notion that *The Holy Bible* is a fundamentally impious text. *The Holy Bible* does not reject the idea of bibles; it is not a satanic anti-Bible; instead it propositions itself as a truer Bible. It rejects biblical transcendence, seeking to replace the distraction of ineffability with a secular and realist notion of holiness. As Allen Ginsberg's "Footnote to Howl" chants "Holy! Holy! Holy! [...] The world is holy! The soul is holy! The skin is holy! The nose is holy! The tongue and cock and hand and asshole holy!" (27), this is not a desecration, but a rightful, outrageous and outraged reclaiming of life's right to holiness and respect. All life, the whole body of it, not just the sanctioned parts. *The Holy Bible* may well be a middle finger to God, but it is also an extended hand to fellow humanity, a work of secular, secularizing comradeship.

CHAPTER 24

The Unbearable Whiteness of The Holy Bible

The Manics may have started out wanting to combine Guns N' Roses with Public Enemy, but *The Holy Bible* was their whitest album yet. Paul Gilroy's book *"There Ain't No Black in the Union Jack": The Cultural Politics of Race and Nation* (1987), which takes its title from a skinhead chant, and which "Ifwhiteamerica" references, explains how anti-racist movements themselves often end up unwittingly reifying more subtle forms of racism. *The Holy Bible* produces and is haunted by a whiteness of horror, a horror of whiteness; it reifies and fetishizes a monstrous, terminally self-critical whiteness. Visually, the album and its booklet set white on white: the whiteness of the artwork, especially the band of white on the album cover between the title and band name, and *Strategy*'s white flesh and white underwear, and the booklet's centre pages also dominated by a white band above the band member photos. The whiteness of the snow in "4st 7lb" unstained by human footprint, its purity unsoiled, and "Mausoleum"'s "lamb-like winter, winter," link the anorexic girl's body with the Holocaust body. Like many white musicians and writers, Richey idolized and othered black anger as more authentic. "Black people have got a far more genuine rage than a white man could ever have. White people feel repressed, but black people are completely oppressed – so you get a real militancy" (qtd in Heatley 57), he remarks, whilst also addressing the specificity of white malaise as being one not of material circumstances, but of spiritual and ideological poverty, another iteration of Blur's *Modern Life Is Rubbish:* "There's an awful lot of white British kids who have never really gone hungry, always had a roof to live under but at the same time are desperately unhappy. It's not total poverty, just a poverty of ideas" (qtd in Heatley 75).

The Holy Bible's critique of whiteness extends to and constructs a terminal whiteness of death, a *memento mori* for embattled whiteness, whose claim on hegemony is long out of date.

CHAPTER 25

A Portrait of the Artist as an Old Man: The Dresser

The last line of *The Holy Bible* goes to Albert Finney as Sir in the 1983 Peter Yates film of Ronald Harwood's 1980 play *The Dresser.* Sir is the fading star actor-manager of a Shakespearean theatre company trying to act its way through WWII England. His dresser, Norman, played by Tom Courtenay, is his assistant, who enables him to struggle through his last performance of *King Lear.* The film is largely a sequence of exchanges between the two men, who exemplify a Hegelian master-and-servant relationship of mutual dependency: Sir is lost without his dresser, and Norman anticipates having no role once Sir has died. In the midst of his panicked preparations, Sir laments that he cannot remember how the play begins, seeking a prompt from

Norman then flying into a rage at having to be walked through it: "Take me through it?" he yells, "Nobody takes you through it, you're put through it, night after night after night. I haven't the strength." Ever on the verge of collapse, Sir is repeatedly brought back from the brink by Norman, who chastises him in this circumstance on the ugliness of self-pity:

> I must say, you of all people, you disappoint me, if you don't mind my saying so. You, who always say that self-pity is the most unattractive quality on stage or off [...] Struggle and survival, you say, that's all that matters. The whole world's struggling for bloody survival, so why can't you?

Struggle and survival, and self-pity are the two poles that Sir stumbles between, lurching from one to the other. What illuminates and inspires him is a dedication to art, to drama, to performance, as indicators of human civilization, decency even, in the face of barbarity. Nazi bombs are literally falling on the city of Bradford around them as they act out that last performance of *King Lear,* with Sir frequently shaking his fist at the Nazis: "Bomb, bomb, bomb us into submission if you dare! But each word I speak will be a shield against your savagery, each line I utter a protection against your terror." Norman, with comic punctuality, brings Sir's self-centred grandiloquence back down to Earth with witty commentary: "I shouldn't take it too personally, Sir [...] I don't think they can hear you, Sir."

What permeates *The Dresser* is a sense of being out of time, of being at the end of things, of coming to the end of your rope and finding it frayed, of there being not enough time, to stop Nazi bombs with the words of William Shakespeare or to prevent or stay your own unravelling. With "La Tristesse Durera," the Manics had played with the perspective of an elderly person, an old man and war veteran, coming to the end, and looking backwards in disappointment and bitterness. The song didn't really work, due to its extreme corniness, but they get it right with "This is Yesterday," a desultory take on the McCartney classic, perhaps the most vacant and soothing, and out-of-place song on *The Holy Bible*—the calm after the storm and before you hurtle into the maelstrom of the final three songs of the album, ending on the adrenalized note of "P.C.P.," which once more reprises the theme of old age looking backwards: when I was young.

A young man identifying with old age as a way to express his sense of despondency or despair is something I can relate to. I remember doing it myself, as a teenager; my elementary school teacher, a kind old man, explained to me that what I was going through was not old age, but *life.* If I was feeling all this turmoil that meant I was living. T.S. Eliot does it too, with "Gerontion," where he imagines himself "an old man in a dry month/Being read to by a boy, waiting for rain," crushed by history but absent any redemption of wisdom or revelation, a fantasy of getting to the end without the solace of understanding.

But imagining old age to be devoid of wisdom is a limited position, a product of selective reading, and that self-destructive worship of youthful purity that inhibits choosing the world of adult compromise. The young man cannot know how he will change, how his ideas will grow and mutate, expanding to embrace a life that to him now seems bitterly corrupt, but might, once he gets there, not seem that bad. The tendency to respond to this position with anger and frustration is strong, as is to judge this vision of adulthood and old age as a terminal decline, as impatient, short-sighted, fatally so. I'm in general happier and better adjusted at thirty-nine than I was at twenty-seven. It's hard not to think of Bradfield's comment: "Richey, if you could just have held on a little longer, things might have been a lot different. Maybe then you could have had all these things you wanted. You might have been happy" (qtd in Heatley). But perhaps, it is not so much a matter of thought, but endurance. And it being so damn easy to cave in. *The Dresser*'s Sir is impatient to be done with it, be done with it all: "I am being crushed, the lifeblood is draining out of me. The load is too much [...] I cannot give any more. I have nothing more to give. I want a tranquil senility [...] I cannot move that which cannot be moved."

CHAPTER 26

Why I Hated the Wildhearts (and the Boo Radleys)

Once I had embraced the idea of rock music as articulate and intelligent and literate, I could not stand rock that acted stupid. I also hated rock music that sounded like it was having a good time, that was happy: no, it had to be about misery and pain. Music that was jolly, I despised. Male rockstars who sounded confident with girls, I abhorred. So I avoided The Wildhearts because they were all of those things: big, loud, drunken, fun-loving tomfoolery. As I research this section, I have gone back and listened to a lot of 90s music, especially bands I avoided the first time around. I am finding The Wildhearts somewhat enjoyable. Ginger has a Lennon-esque knack for the occasional catchy anthem. I am strangely touched by his reference to Richey on the 1996 version of "29 X The Pain," where he replaces the line "Oh God I miss Kurt Cobain" with "So where you hiding, Richey James?" The bands toured together in 1992. It's strange to see barriers I thought were so important dissolving.

The Boo Radleys I knew from "Wake Up Boo!"—one of the most horribly happy-sounding songs ever. I deeply hated it. To my complete surprise, I discover that The Boo Radleys did an acoustic radio show cover of none other than "4st 7lb" in 1995. One of the saddest songs ever. It's a heartbreaking listen, totally capturing the pain and sadness of the original, even refining it.

Everything Must Go felt like a betrayal. I remember staying in Cambridge that summer, buying the singles: I loved the B-Side "Mr. Carbohydrate." But I could not tolerate the album: how could they go on without Richey, and with basically indie music? I felt they had become an indie band and gone and joined the Blurs and the Oases and the Pulps. I almost couldn't bear it, but part of me had moved on already. Yet part of me stayed, and I did love the album, its wistful melancholia. I liked but also cringed at "A Design for Life": I didn't really understand the album, it seemed bland, and looks a bit like an IKEA catalogue to me now, the band members dressed as clothes shop mannequins. I didn't get what they were aiming at, but I accepted it: I felt that without the pain I couldn't really relate to the Manics anymore, that they'd gone over to the other side and they weren't really mine anymore. Something had gone with Richey and so had my love for the band. I loved "Removables," because it was like a Nirvana song with its bouncy acoustic guitars and it was kind of in a spirit that I recognized, of sadness and loss: that which is removed, that has been removed, from the band. I had a similar feeling when listening to the first Foo Fighters album, especially the song "This is a Call": an almost overwhelming sadness. The music lives on, but different. The spirit of Kurt Cobain is in *Foo Fighters* in a similar way to how the spirit of Richey is in *Everything Must*

Go: both albums are haunted by them and their loss. The ache of what is not there anymore animates the music somehow, imbuing it with a melancholic and overwhelming tug at your innards. When I listened to "This is a Call" on headphones, in Tower Records in Piccadilly Square, I felt overcome by this heart aching beautiful sadness.

There are living albums haunted by the dead and missing, and there are ghost albums that never were: that "Pantera meets Nine Inch Nails meets *Screamadelica*" follow-up to *The Holy Bible* that didn't happen and that Nirvana album with Michael Stipe and strings.

I fell out of love with the Manics and they sort of faded from my world, and one of my favourite parts of writing this section has been discovering their post-Richey output: *Journal for Plague Lovers,* which I bought excited, then recoiled from and filed away for years, is now my second favourite Manics album; *Send Away the Tigers,* which I had never even heard of, and now love its big warm pop sound. But on the whole it has been kind of a nightmare:

if *The Holy Bible* was meaningful to you I wouldn't recommend spending six months thinking and writing about it, inevitably trying to put yourself in some kind of Richey headspace, if you can avoid it.

CHAPTER 27

"Dancing in the Moonlight"

It was an unusually warm day in late winter, here in Bloomington, Indiana, where I now live. The Chocolate Moose was open for business, and as we waited in line for ice cream, two girls from the family in front were dancing to Toploader's version of "Dancing in the Moonlight". It crossed my mind that never would anyone dance in Middle America to a song on the PA from *The Holy Bible* whilst standing in line to get ice cream. In the UK perhaps, to "A Design for Life." But that's a different story.

CHAPTER 28

Hopelessness

The books are piling up around me and I am running out of time and space. Twenty odd years have passed, and the world is in considerably worse shape than it was in 1994. Wealth inequality, austerity, climate change, geopolitical instability, the rise of the extreme right in mainstream politics, the vanishing of the idea of peace in the Middle East. I write this in the aftermath of the Brexit referendum victory and under the shadow of Donald Trump's presidential campaign. African-Americans are being murdered by US police officers, and I'm reading articles on the racism of the Second Amendment and the National Rifle Association, and thinking of "Fuck the Brady Bill." The Manics never regained their handle on contemporary events, and became something of an inward-looking nostalgia act after Richey disappeared. If *The Holy Bible* does seem in retrospect a bit of an album out of key with its time, to paraphrase Ezra Pound's *Hugh Selwyn Mauberley*, it certainly would become so for the time immediately following it. The "post-Richey Edwards pop world is the Robbie Williams era" (160), writes Mick Middles: Britpop and Cool Britannia. But today Tony Blair falls humbled by the Chilcot report on the Iraq War, and music that speaks truth to power is needed more than ever. Who carries on *The Holy Bible*'s legacy? Radiohead and Massive Attack have to some degree, with their biopolitical glitchy dystopias and filtering of political outrage through a sense of militant melancholia, as if sadness and despair were a way into action.

Whilst writing this section these last few months I have been devouring Anohni's *Hopelessness,* an album which breathes renewed hope and beauty into protest music, an apocalyptic global vision that luxuriously and with bitter sarcasm bathes in the end of the world, invoking catastrophe with death-embracing torch songs that submit with daring masochism to power's killing lust. "Drone Bomb Me" begs to be annihilated, "4 Degrees" wants to see the creatures burn, "Watch Me" submits to surveillance as an erotic act—"I know you love me/'Cause you're always watching me – Daddy," "Execution" implores to be given the death penalty with no mercy, in a global "American dream." The album's centrepiece is "Obama," which Anohni intones in a lugubrious voice, spiritual like that of a biblical patriarch from beyond the grave—channelling to my mind the ghost of Osama Bin Laden, executed "without trial"—to decry the truth-telling whistle-blowers punished: a *j' accuse* of thrilling potency, a demonstration of how pop music can be an act of aesthetic and moral terrorism.

Works Cited

Acharya, Kiran. "*Richard:* An Extract & Interview with Author Ben Myers". *The Quietus.* 14 Jan. 2011. Web.

Adorno, Theodor. *Aesthetic Theory.* Trans. Robert Hullot-Kentor. London: Athlone, 1997. Print.

Agamben, Giorgio. *Homo Sacer: Sovereign Power and Bare Life.* Trans. Daniel Heller-Roazen. Stanford: Stanford UP, 1998. Print.

Amis, Martin. *The Moronic Inferno and Other Visits to America.* Harmondsworth: Penguin, 1987. Print.

———. *Time's Arrow.* London: Jonathan Cape, 1991. Print.

Anohni. *Hopelessness.* Secretly Canadian, 2016. CD,

Antony and the Johnsons. *Antony and the Johnsons.* Durtro, 2000. CD.

Arendt, Hannah. *Between Past and Future: Six Exercises in Political Thought.* New York: Viking, 1968. Print.

Ballard, J.G. *The Atrocity Exhibition.* London: Fourth Estate, 2014. Print.

_____. *The Atrocity Exhibition – Revised, Expanded, Annotated, Illustrated Edition.* San Francisco: RE/Search, 1990. Print.

Bailie, Stuart. "The Art of Falling Apart." *Mojo* (February 2002): 74–86. Print.

_____. "Manic's Depressive." *New Musical Express* (October 1, 1994): 32–34, 61. Print.

Barker, Clive. *Books of Blood: Volume One.* London: Sphere, 1984. Print.

Boswell, Matthew. *Holocaust Impiety in Literature, Popular Music and Film.* Basingstoke: Palgrave Macmillan, 2012. Print.

Bowie, David. *Outside.* Virgin, 1995. CD.

Brennan, Claire, ed. *The Poetry of Sylvia Plath.* Cambridge: Icon Books, 1999. Print.

Britton, Amy. *Revolution Rock: The Albums Which Defined Two Ages.* Bloomington: AuthorHouse, 2011. Print.

Burstyn, Ellen. "Hubert Selby Jr. Interview Transcript." *Glamour and Discourse.* Nd. Web.

Cameron, Keith. "Chapter and Verse: 13 Reasons to Believe in The Holy Bible." Liner notes. Manic Street Preachers. *The Holy Bible: 20th Anniversary Deluxe Edition.* Columbia Records, 2014. CD.

Carpenter, Lorraine. "Manic Street Preachers: Betrothed Lyrics and Existential Questions". *Under the Radar.* 15 Jul. 2016. Web.

Chapman, Jake and Dinos. *The End of Fun.* London: White Cube and FUEL, 2013. Print.

Clarke, Martin. *Manic Street Preachers: Sweet Venom.* London: Plexus, 2009. Print.

Daiches, David. *A Critical History of English Literature: Volume II.* London: Mandarin Paperbacks, 1994. Print.

Davies, Catherine Anne. "Nicky Wire on Richey and the Manic Street Preachers' Return". *Drowned in Sound.* 17 Jun. 2009. Web.

Deller, Jeremy. *The Uses of Literacy.* London: Book Works, 1999. Print.

The Dresser. Dir. Peter Yates. Columbia, 1983. DVD.

Eliot, T.S. *Collected Poems 1909–1962.* London: Faber and Faber, 1974. Print.

Factory: Manchester from Joy Division to Happy Mondays. Dir. Chris Rodley. BBC, 2007. Film.

Foucault, Michel. *Discipline and Punish: The Birth of the Prison.* Trans. Alan

Sheridan. New York: Vintage, 1995. Print.

Freud, Sigmund. *The Joke and its Relation to the Unconscious.* Trans. John Carey and Joyce Crick. New York: Penguin Classics, 2003. Print.

Gilroy, Paul. *"There Ain't No Black in the Union Jack" – The Cultural Politics of Race and Nation.* Chicago: The U of Chicago P, 1987.

Ginsberg, Allen. *Howl and Other Poems.* San Francisco: City Lights, 1959. Print.

Heatley, Michael. *Manic Street Preachers: In Their Own Words.* London: Omnibus, 1998.

The Holy Bible. Grand Rapids: Zondervan, 2011. Print.

Houellebecq, Michel. *The Elementary Particles.* Trans. Frank Wynne. New York: Vintage, 2000. Print.

Jeffery, Ben. *Anti-Matter: Michel Houellebecq and Depressive Realism.* Winchester: Zer0 Books, 2011. Print.

Jet Simian. "Comic Strip Reachers?" *Jetsam.* 16 Jul. 2014. Web.

Jovanovic, Rob. *A Version of Reason: In Search of Richey Edwards.* London: Orion, 2010. Print.

Joy, Eileen A. *Facebook.* 1 May 2013. Web.

Levi, Primo. *If This Is a Man.* Trans. Stuart Woolf. New York: Orion, 1959. Print.

_____. *Opere II.* Torino: Einaudi, 1997. Print.

Lindbloom, James. "The Tao of the Willow Tree: An Interview with Hubert Selby, Jr." *Gadfly Online.* Aug.1999. Web.

Lynskey, Dorian. *33 Revolutions Per Minute: A History of Protest Songs, from Billie Holiday to Green Day.* New York: Ecco, 2011. Print.

Macey, David. *The Lives of Michel Foucault.* London: Hutchinson, 1993. Print.

Maconie, Stuart. "Smile, It Might Never Happen." *Q Magazine* (October 1994): 34–35. Print.

Mankowski, Guy. *How I Left the National Grid.* Alresford: Roundfire Books, 2015. Print.

_____. "How to Make Comrades and Alienate People." *Repeat Fanzine.* Nd. Web.

Marks, Howard. *Sympathy for the Devil.* London: Vintage, 2011. Print.

Melancholia. Dir. Lars Von Trier. Nordisk Film, 2011. DVD.

Middles, Mick. *Manic Street Preachers.* London: Omnibus, 1999. Print.

Miller, Henry. *Black Spring.* London: Flamingo, 1993. Print.

Mirbeau, Octave. *Le Calvaire.* Trans. Christine Donougher. Sawtry: Dedalus/Hippocrene, 1995. Print.

_____. *The Torture Garden.* Trans. Michael Richardson. Sawtry: Dedalus, 1997. Print.

_____. *The Torture Garden.* Trans. Alvah C. Bessie. San Francisco: RE/Search Publications, 1989. Print.

Mishima, Yukio. *Confessions of a Mask.* Trans. Meredith Weatherby. New York: New Directions, 1958. Print.

_____. *Death in Midsummer and Other Stories.* New York: New Directions, 1966. Print.

Mishima: A Life in Four Chapters. Dir. Paul Schrader. Warner Bros., 1985. DVD.

Myers, Ben. *Richard.* London: Picador, 2010. Print.

Nine Inch Nails. *The Downward Spiral.* Nothing/Interscope, 1994. CD.

Outhwaite, Paul. *The Preachers of Manic Street.* Middlesbrough: D.M. Productions, 2005. Print.

Parkes, Taylor. "There Are No Horizons: *The Holy Bible* at 20." *The Quietus.* 9 Dec. 2014. Web.

Plath, Sylvia. *Ariel: The Restored Edition.* New York: HarperCollins, 2004. Print.

_____. *The Bell Jar.* New York: Harper Perennial, 2005. Print.

_____. *Johnny Panic and The Bible of Dreams and Other Prose Writings.* London: Faber and Faber, 1979. Print.

Power, Martin. *The Story of Manic Street Preachers: Nailed to History.* London: Omnibus, 2010. Print.

Price, Simon. *Everything (A Book About Manic Street Preachers).* London: Virgin Books, 1999. Print.

———. "The Return of the Manics." *Melody Maker* (January 13, 1996): 24–27. Print.

Quantick, David. "Manic Street Preachers: 'There's just so much hate within this band. Why are we still like this?'" *Uncut.* Time Inc., 2 July 2014. Web.

Reed, Simon. *Assimilate: A Critical History of Industrial Music.* New York: Oxford UP, 2013. Print.

"Richey's Last TV interview." thisisyesterday.com, Tom Hatfield. 1994. Web.

Rose, Gillian. *Mourning Becomes the Law: Philosophy and Representation.* Cambridge: Cambridge UP, 1996.

Sandhu, Sukhdev. "Melancholia." *The Telegraph,* May 18, 2011. Print.

Saville, Jenny. *Saville.* New York: Rizzoli International Publications, 2005. Print.

Selby, Jr., Hubert. *The Demon.* Chicago: Playboy Press, 1976. Print.

_____. *Last Exit to Brooklyn.* London: Flamingo, 1993. Print.

_____. *The Room.* New York: Grove Press, 1971. Print.

_____. *Song of the Silent Snow.* New York: Marion Boyars, 1986. Print.

TheSilentMan. Comment on "Manic's favourite books..." *Forever Delayed Forum.* 30 Jun. 2007. Web.

Solanas, Valerie. *SCUM Manifesto.* London: Verso, 2004. Print.

Sontag, Susan. *Against Interpretation and Other Essays.* New York: Picador, 1966.

Sounes, Howard. *27: A History of the 27 Club through the Lives of Brian Jones, Jimi Hendrix, Janis Joplin, Jim Morrison, Kurt Cobain, and Amy Winehouse.* Boston: Da Capo, 2015. Print.

The Third Man. Dir. Carol Reed. British Lion, 1949. DVD.

Thomson, Ian. *Primo Levi*. London: Hutchinson, 2002. Print.

Virilio, Paul. *Negative Horizon*. Trans. Michael Degener. London: Continuum, 2008. Print.

Watkins-Isnardi, Jenny. *In the Beginning: My Life with the Manic Street Preachers*. London: Blake, 2000. Print.

Williams, Hywel. "Blood and Guts." *The Guardian*. Guardian News and Media Limited, 24 Jun. 2001. Web.

PART III

Architecture of Memory: The Holy Bible and the Archive

LARISSA WODTKE

CHAPTER 1

Past Presence, or Forever Delayed

"...the pressures of the transitory affect the monumental itself: the only monument that counts is the one already imagined as a ruin."
– Andreas Huyssen, *Past Presents*

Many claim that *The Holy Bible* is Manic Street Preachers' masterpiece. I argue that it's their *Gesamtkunstwerk*. It is the beginning and the end, the moment the Manics split their identity into two, the watershed at which the shadow of memory flows in different directions. It condensed and intensified everything the Manics were up to that point and became the touchstone for what they could ever be. It finally made them authentic, but it also made them impossible. The Manics are polarizing, even amongst fans. Fans speak of the *Generation Terrorists* era, the *Holy Bible* era, the *Everything Must Go* era, and they often rally behind one of them. For better, and sometimes worse, memory and the archive came to define Manic Street Preachers.

The Holy Bible has been called the sound of intolerance and body horror, bleak, pressurized, contorted, nihilist, vile. To me, it is the sound of a monument being built for the sole purpose of its wreckage and ruin, endlessly perpetuating the significance of its own archive. It sounds monolithic and monochrome, beautiful and frightful in its symmetry. It is the cover art of Jenny Saville's *Strategy (South Face/Front Face/North Face)* made sonic. The music has the intensity of a silent scream, throwing razor-sharp, post-punk angles and white noise around a dark distillation of trauma. There are few reprieves, and when they come, they are funereal and just as damning. The grind and knell of the low register and the metallic clang and scratch of the guitar and percussion create a claustrophobic anxiety and relentless, righteous fury. The lyrics range over totalitarianism, genocide, serial killers, prostitution, anorexia, self-harm, racial violence, class war, discipline, censorship and self-obsession; they have been broken and malformed into a scansion that James Dean Bradfield somehow manages to sing in twisted tongues. In the irony of a bible with verses that defy memorization, this album exemplifies the impossibility of language to bear witness, not by taking a reverent posture of abstention, but by challenging the silence with verbosity, or a glossolalia of excess meaning. Just as *The Holy Bible* confronts you with everything humanity would like to forget, it also desires its own annihilation. It's hard not to make comparisons between the album and the band itself. With Richey Edwards having written seventy percent of the lyrics for *The Holy Bible* and having lived through a highly public breakdown in the year leading up to the record's release, this 1994 album will always be inextricably bound to his disappearance the following year.

The Manics have built an identity around an intensely present absence and acts of memorialization. Their position is unique: a band that had lost a member who was simultaneously nothing and everything. As a guitarist who couldn't really play guitar and thus had only played a couple of small parts on recordings, and as a prominent lyricist who had the ability to generate intelligent and provocative soundbites and thus had most often been the public face of the band, Richey Edwards was an odd entity. The consecrated space at stage right where Edwards once stood is like Rachel Whiteread's *Fourth Plinth* in Trafalgar Square. An absence made present. A negative index.

The self-memorialization began well before *The Holy Bible*. It is well-known that the

Manics plotted their ascendancy with researched precision and strategy; they were planners, especially Edwards, who became their "Minister of Information," a role borrowed from one of the Manics' favourite bands, Public Enemy. With self-consciously "iconic" photos and outrageous soundbites, the Manics were intent on devising their own celebrity myth. The death drive of vowing to break up after selling sixteen million copies of their debut album is a case in point. Their idolization of those defined by the Pop Art death drive, such as James Dean and Marilyn Monroe, reaffirmed their desire to become legendary, but also ephemeral. They revelled in the idea of short-lived glamour and immortality through the media archive. This conflict between wanting to live on in memory and to completely destroy that which made you famous has an interesting precedent recounted in Andreas Huyssen's book *Present Pasts.* Huyssen writes of Richard Wagner's first thoughts about a performance of his opera *Siegfried* to be mounted near Zurich. Wagner intended for the theatre to be dismantled three days after the performance and for the score to be burned. At the same time, Wagner's work is inherently Romantic and has become bound up with the fascist tendency towards epic monumentalism. This tension between Wagner's wish to be hugely memorable and everlasting, and his consciousness of the transitory, which may, too, contribute to monumentalism, creates a friction at the heart of memory studies.

A comparison between Wagner's incongruous, yet somehow compatible, attitudes and those of Manic Street Preachers is striking, and can begin to explain the contentious composition of the band's identity and of *The Holy Bible* itself. Derision of and desire for nostalgia were also already a part of the Manic Street Preachers' repertoire before *The Holy Bible*. Songs like "New Art Riot," "Motown Junk," "Methadone Pretty," and "Nostalgic Pushead" condemned society's inclination to immerse itself in complacent, comfortable nostalgia, to anesthetize with the familiar and shallow. They often pledged to destroy history and the art that came before them, and if they destroyed themselves in the process, so much the better. In spite of these denials of the past and accusations against history itself, the Manics also longed for youth and childhood. In "Life Becoming a Landslide" and "From Despair to Where," the assumption is that childhood was a more innocent time, now corrupted by age and the passing of time into adulthood. These ideas of modern, swift self-destruction and Romantic, nostalgic myths of childhood innocence then tumbled into the event horizon that is *The Holy Bible.*

Manic Street Preachers' grand narrative is tempting. Hindsight provides the best foreshadowing, and as Simon Price has noted, their story begs to be narrativized. *The Holy Bible* became the apotheosis of their memory work by intensifying the private made public, the personal made political. Edwards' disappearance, crucially not a visible suicide, heightened its effect. Perhaps due to the self-memorializing that had already been intrinsic to the Manics' presentation of themselves, the sense of impending drastic change was already being taken up by the media before Edwards went missing. At the time of *The Holy Bible*'s release, the music press was heralding the end of a chapter. Many regard *The Holy Bible* to be the Manics' truly authentic moment, the critically acclaimed cult success. People will persist in comparing everything that follows to the myth of that album. The Manics have also used it in a myriad of ways, including kicking against it to produce their next most acclaimed album, *Everything Must Go,* and returning to it to make *Journal for Plague Lovers.* As the band who pronounced "Libraries gave us power," their strength and worth seemed to keep springing from the archive. Their story and music are palimpsests, inscribed and reinscribed, self-referential and self-reverential. Furthermore, *The Holy Bible* crystallized the postmodern preoccupation with discourses of memory and the representation of difficult knowledge, affecting not only the band's future memory work, but that of other artists and fans to follow, including artist/curator Jeremy Deller's *The Uses of Literacy* (1997) and *Unconvention* (1999) exhibitions, and Kieron Gillen and Jamie McKelvie's comic-book series Phonogram: Rue Britannia (2006). The Manics' use of cultural archives and iconography throughout their work, as well as the histories of working-class Wales, not only act as a gateway to culture for their fans (see Part II of this volume), but make them of particular interest to artists and fans who create art to interrogate memory and its connection to identity. In this respect, they were the most appropriate band to appear in actor Michael Sheen's *The Passion of Port Talbot,* a town-wide piece of memory-based performance art created in 2011, and later released as the film *The Gospel of Us.*

The band's past is inescapable, and the way they work with it and within it time after time is fascinating. Repeat after me, death sentence heritage. The combination of an extraordinary album with an extraordinary act of self-mythologization has irrevocably shaped Manic Street Preachers. The band haunted their own future, and their past continues to bleed into their present; time has been particularly malleable for them. The phrase "forever delayed" first appeared in the Manics' history as a lyric on "Roses in the Hospital," a song from their second album *Gold Against the Soul,* and then it became the title for their first greatest hits collection in 2002. A single called "4 Ever Delayed," which was originally planned for this greatest hits collection but then scrapped, resurfaced on the b-side collection *Lipstick Traces* the following year. The phrase implies infinite stasis. And there have been times when the Manics could be accused of stagnating or becoming stultified by their own nostalgia. But another way of looking at "forever delayed" is "always becoming." The Manics will never reach a real completion, nor will they lose sight of the potential in their own traces.

The Holy Bible proved that their eyes were set on a memorable ruin, born to end before they began. And it put them in the perfect position to be the band that meant everything and nothing.

CHAPTER 2

Archive of Pain

> *"Of course, it is always precarious to predict the future, but looking at the state of the world in 1994, it seems unlikely that the 1990s will be remembered as another belle époque, and given what followed only a few years after the last fin de siècle, the whole comparison is not very comforting to begin with."*
> – Andreas Huyssen, *Twilight Memories: Marking Time in a Culture of Amnesia*

> *"In a very simple way, self-mutilation, like self-starvation, is a plea to be witnessed."*
> – Kim Hewitt, *Mutilating the Body: Identity in Blood and Ink*

> *"But I am from a distance."*
> – Richey Edwards, in reply to music journalist Simon Price's comment that it was easy to applaud strict moral attitudes from a distance

According to religion scholar Brian Britt, Walter Benjamin viewed the Bible as an "archive of pure language." In this context, "pure language" means the state of language before the dispersion of communication at the metaphorical episode of the Tower of Babel, before the interventions of translation and their inadequacies in conveying true meaning. This archive of pure language is a seeking of origins despite the inability to reach them. In a sense, *The Holy Bible* by Manic Street Preachers is an archive of pure origins for the band, a record of a particular identity—often thought of as the definitive meaning—of the Manics as well as the recognition of its untenable position. It could not be successfully repeated or returned to, but persisted in defining the band through endless recapitulations, reversals and translations, which were always going to remain impossible and incomplete—in other words, impure. *The Holy Bible* is an album of instability and overripe signification, the sound of a centre on the verge of losing hold. Even as this album represents an archive of the band, it is also profoundly concerned with the archive of history, culture, and knowledge, and the structures of power which determine, delineate, and deny it. *The Holy Bible* is obsessed with memory and its failures.

Writing in 1994, the same year in which *The Holy Bible* was released, Andreas Huyssen posited that "the current obsession with memory is [...] a sign of the crisis of that structure of temporality that marked the age of modernity with its celebration of the new as utopian, as radically and irreducibly other" (6). He goes on to observe that preoccupations with memory could be a strategy to cope with information overload and a speeding world (7). Though *The Holy Bible* contains the song "Faster," which could be interpreted as an embodiment of this kind of information overload, it does not attempt to arrest the pace of this potential excess; in fact, the album accelerates it. This exacerbation of chaos serves as a confrontation and memorialization of failure. The upheavals and revolutionary thinking of the turn of the twentieth century are parts of the same totality, and the atrocities of the former were often results, inadvertent and otherwise, of the latter. The exciting, creative dreams of the avant-garde ushered in a century of fascism and totalitarianism, and in many ways failed, just as the post-war utopianism of the West eventually failed in the 70s and 80s. In the final years before neoliberalism hit its stride, there was a brief reworking and resuscitation of earlier avant-garde movements in a perhaps unlikely place: popular music.

Post-punk, as its name indicates, grew from the fertile ashes of punk, and used intertextuality and modernist influences to produce an avant-garde music milieu that maintained an "out-of-sync relationship with the broader culture" (Reynolds 7). In fact, this eclectic group of musicians, which created the sounds of early industrial, synthpop, no-wave, experimental jazz, self-aware funk, politicized art rock and race-blurring ska, also maintained a modernist outlook in a postmodern era, dreaming of and innovating futures that had been discarded in the post-war years. Music critic Simon Reynolds compares post-punk with its brief, nihilist predecessor by observing that "[d]estroying is always more dramatic than building. But post-punk was constructive and forward looking. The very prefix 'post-' implied faith in a future that punk said didn't exist" (11). Bands of the period often took their names and lyrical content from critical theory, intellectual literature and the leftist, radical movements of the early twentieth century and '68: for example, Scritti Politti, Gang of Four, Pere Ubu, Cabaret Voltaire, Clock DVA, The Birthday Party and The Durutti Column. Many of the post-punk bands were DIY products of the British art school system, and the visual imagery of these groups was often grounded in modernist art, including constructivism and minimalism, and vague idealizations of the Eastern Bloc (likely an echo of the fascination with the exoticism of life behind the Iron Curtain that appeared in David Bowie's Berlin trilogy). One such group was Simple Minds, a Scottish band that blended expansive synth sounds with driving bass lines. Their third album, *Empires and Dance,* which contained music of austere and ambitious proportions, was housed in cover art featuring what looked to be a chipped statue of a soldier/air force officer in an eastern European landscape and the album title in stark Cyrillic font on a white background. The "n's" and the "r" were mirror images of themselves. The Manics adopted the same typeface and reversal of "r's" for *The Holy Bible* album cover, which not only gives the album a monumental and modern aesthetic, but also hints at the music contained within. With its heavily politicized and intellectual content, which can veer into the abstract, *The Holy Bible* can definitely be described as post-punk. The music itself references the metallic, jagged sounds of Public Image Ltd., Magazine, Wire, Joy Division, and at its harshest and most sonically abject, The Birthday Party (the clanging five-note guitar figure in "The Intense Humming of Evil" bears a similarity to the nauseating descent of Rowland S. Howard's guitar in "Nick the Stripper"). In describing *The Holy Bible*, the Manics' biographer Simon Price writes, "message and medium are inseparable: the music discordant and irregular, is onomatopoeic for the content" (143). Nevertheless, the album is hardly as wilfully difficult and alienating to listen to as the avant-garde and industrial sounds of Throbbing Gristle, Einstürzende Neubauten, or *The Drift/Tilt/Bish Bosch* trilogy by Scott Walker; it is still certainly attempting to communicate and maintain a melodic through-line, a nod to the Manics' populist aims. The promise of this kind of avant-garde is of no use to the Manics. In as much as *The Holy Bible* is a post-punk album, it is also a post-post-punk album, a remembering of the failure of the first remembering. This is the record where post-punk eats itself and throws up.

Beyond the memorial use of a musical style, *The Holy Bible* is very obviously composed of content that has either been consigned to the archive, and thus forgotten, or has been filtered out of the archive by those in positions of power in order to narrativize a sanctioned past or a particular history, disallowing multiple less comfortable "truths." In his seminal work on the archive, *Archive Fever,* Jacques Derrida theorizes the death and destruction as impetus and as innate to the archive itself:

> right on that which permits and conditions archivization, we will never find anything other than that which exposes to destruction, and in truth menaces with destruction, introducing, *a priori,* forgetfulness and the archiviolithic into the heart of the monument. [...] The archive always works, *a priori,* against itself. (12)

Without the threat of forgetfulness and limits of human memory, there would be no need to create an archive, but at the same time, the creation of an archive allows forgetting by placing memory somewhere outside of everyday life. The drive to memorialize and make monuments, or what Derrida calls "archive fever," functions through its own violence and imagining of eventual ruins, and is intimately linked with the Freudian death drive (*Archive Fever* 19).

The Manics' *Holy Bible* produces an archive on two levels: it provides a record of historical events, as well as contemporary realities and conditions, which most would like to forget, and it builds a monument to itself, which ostensibly imagines the band's own need to forge a truthful identity for posterity. After what the band perceived as a straying from their original purpose in the form of their second album *Gold Against the Soul,* they needed to rebuild and enforce a strong statement about what they meant as a band, and ultimately, as a cultural text. This sense of futurity is essential to the concept of the archive, and contrary to the oft-held belief that the archive is primarily about preserving the past, the archive and memory itself are actually future-oriented. Derrida describes the question of the archive as one of the future, a query which can only receive a response and reveal its full meaning in the future; in this way, the archive haunts and promises with "spectral messianicity" (*Archive Fever* 36). In other words, the true meaning of *The Holy Bible* and Manic Street Preachers would be discovered in the years following its release. With its extremely uncomfortable and confrontational stance, *The Holy Bible* didn't seem to be operating in relation to its own present, or even within its own discourse of popular music, and in doing so, it bequeathed itself to the band's future.

The tension between memory and forgetting, as well as the erasure of traces and the inability to leave a trace, dominate *The Holy Bible.* Despite the demands to "remember victims" in "Archives of Pain," to "come and walk down memory lane" in "Mausoleum," and the relentless implicit demand to hear truths that are unbearable throughout the entire record, in "This is Yesterday," James gently sings, "I repent, I'm sorry, everything is falling apart · houses as ruins and gardens as weeds · why do anything when you can forget everything." It is in moments like these that *The Holy Bible* breaks, and shows the price it must pay for remembering. At times, the body itself is willed to be forgotten, or more tellingly, obliterated. In "4st 7lb" the anorexic narrator says, "I wanna be so skinny that I rot from view · I want to walk in the snow · and not leave a footprint · I want to walk in the snow · and not soil its purity"; the very index of her materiality will have disappeared, and she will have become too insubstantial to even be an empty signifier. The desire to be forgotten becomes tied to the yearning to return to a supposedly less troubled past. "She is Suffering" features the lyric "no thoughts to forget when we were children," "Mausoleum" uses the metaphor "the world lances youth's lamb-like winter," and in "Die in the Summertime" the narrator is locked in a futile battle to arrest maturation and change, linking such development with failure and ruin. This last song begins with ominous, lumbering guitar and bass before expanding into full-blown miasma, at which point James sings, "Scratch my leg with a rusty nail, sadly it heals · colour my hair but the dye grows out · I can't seem to stay a fixed ideal · childhood pictures redeem, clean and so serene · see myself without ruining lines · whole days throwing sticks in streams." The culturally manufactured trope of childhood innocence, with its ties to the natural world and childhood as a "natural" state, has appeared before in the Manics' work: in "Life Becoming a Landslide," the narrator repeatedly insists "I don't wanna be a man" and declares "my idea of love comes from a childhood glimpse of pornography," and in "From Despair to Where," James sings, "there's nothing nice in my head/the adult world took it all away." In a rather biblical fashion, *The Holy Bible* continues the preoccupation with an Edenic fall into knowledge. It follows, then, that knowledge stands in for both corruption and truth, producing the noted contention between remembering and forgetting. To remember is the more moral and intellectual action, but it is also fraught with violence and trauma. The last line of the final song on *The Holy Bible,* "P.C.P.," "Pass the prozac, designer amnesiac," is followed by the unsteady voice of Albert Finney saying, "227 'Lears' and I can't remember the first line." This finale could be read as a taunt to the masses who would rather anesthetize than analyse, a denunciation prevalent on the album, but it could also be the final admission of failure and weakness, a need to halt and dissociate from the chaos and impossible memory work preceding it. *The Holy Bible* embodies the violence committed *a priori* by the archive, which obsessively preserves in order to combat mortality, but in turn, encourages the relief of forgetting, and in some cases, begs to be quarantined from interior memory entirely.

Distance and Disjuncture: Difficult Knowledge, Allegory and Irony in The Holy Bible

Difficult knowledge, as defined by Deborah Britzman and Alice Pitt, is knowledge that remains incommensurable and cannot be assimilated into one's existing worldview. Difficult knowledge works in opposition to lovely knowledge, which confirms and affirms one's beliefs. Examples of difficult knowledge abound: living as a colonizer on the lands of the colonized; the falsity of a post-racial society; the reality that history is not a linear progression that sees humanity improving; the fact that democratic societies do not actually practice democracy; and of course, the unprecedented horrors of the Holocaust. Pitt and Britzman contend that there is a "kernel of trauma in the very capacity to know" (756), and learning from difficult knowledge is significantly more challenging than merely perceiving such knowledge. The pedagogy of difficult knowledge is a learning process without closure, stability or mastery; instead it is about "provoking, not representing, knowledge" (Pitt and Britzman 769). The content of Manic Street Preachers' *The Holy Bible* is dominated by provocative difficult knowledge, and whilst some is more obvious, and dare I say slightly more lovely in its less controversial confirmations of human atrocity, there are many more moments in which the knowledge is incommensurate with common views of supposed morality. In "The Intense Humming of Evil," one of the two songs about the Holocaust on the album, the chorus goes: "6 million screaming souls · maybe misery – maybe nothing at all

· lives that wouldn't have changed a thing · never counted – never mattered – never be." These stark statements describing the victims of the Holocaust could be read as from the perspective of the perpetrator or Holocaust denier, or a mixture of both. Or it could also be a deliberate evasion of a moral position because it is impossible to take one in the face of such incommensurability, especially as non-witnesses. In *Testimony: Crises of Witnessing in Literature, Psychoanalysis, and History,* Shoshana Felman and Dori Laub identify this quandary by claiming that "[t]o talk about the Holocaust from a position of self-righteousness and rightness is to deny the very essence of the Holocaust, which was to render this position unavailable" (123). The difficult knowledge of the Holocaust itself disallows an authentic engagement with morality. At the end of the same song, the Manics explode the ostensibly indisputable fact that the Allies were the moral heroes of World War II with "Churchill no different · wished the workers bled to a machine." These last lines reference British domestic policy regarding the working classes, discarding the lovely knowledge of Britain's "victory" and Churchill's heroism as so much soiled bunting. *The Holy Bible* also takes aim at American foreign and domestic policy, especially as manifested in its institutionalized racism. In "Ifwhiteam ericatoldthetruthf oronedayit'sworldwouldfallapart," the Manics mock the hypocrisy of American morality and their governing bodies' belief that they could be the world's saviour. Despite having written this song at the time of a Democratic President in the US, it is a track steeped in the bitter dregs of the neoconservative 80s in which principles of decency were declaring war on drugs and being applied to the lyrics of popular music. The line "Tipper Gore was a friend of mine" alludes to Tipper Gore's co-founding of the Parents Music Resource Center, which began applying parental warning stickers on albums that were deemed inappropriate for young people. This song particularly lambastes the Brady Bill, an American piece of gun legislation that Richey saw as further disenfranchisement of African

Americans; hence, the deconstruction of America's claim to being a free, godly country whilst allowing particular kinds of citizens the right to bear arms in two brief lines: "if God made man the same Sam Colt made him equal." James has explained that the inspiration for the music for "Ifwhiteamerica" came from *West Side Story,* which is apparent in the rather frenzied back and forth of the verses and exaggerated upbeat tone that has been pushed to its limit; the music reflects a Broadway smile that's frozen into a grimace.

Not confined to larger societal ills, difficult knowledge is illustrated at a more individualistic level in songs like "4st 7lb" and "Faster." "4st 7lb" begins with a jagged barrage of guitar akin to Adam and the Ants' "Zerox," along with an audio clip of an anorexic female declaring that her weight places her in a liminal position of existence, before descending into a wobbly, disorienting rhythm that seems to parallel the manic mental state of someone who is wilfully starving her body but gorging her mind. The murky music emphasizes the narrator's precarious balance at the threshold of life and death, as well as the eventual slowing in the latter half of the song. Amongst this almost oneiric dragging and falling, James sings:

> too weak to fuss too weak to die · choice is skeletal in everybody's life · I choose, my choice, I starve to frenzy · hunger soon passes and sickness soon tires · legs bend, stockinged I am Twiggy · and I don't mind the horror that surrounds me · self-worth scatters, self-esteem's a bore · I long since moved to a higher plateau · this discipline's so rare so please applaud · just look at the fat scum who pamper me so · yeh 4st. 7, an epilogue of youth · such beautiful dignity in self-abuse ...

These are powerfully articulate, lucid, and poetic words, which challenge a common, perhaps more comprehensible, view held by those who pathologize people with eating disorders, the belief that these people are helpless victims of low self-esteem who have unthinkingly fallen prey to media images of thinness. "4st 7lb" counters this lovely knowledge by demonstrating the agency and intelligence of those who are engaging in a deliberate act of control, and perhaps even sublimity (see Lintott). Similarly in "Faster," the self-harming narrator declares a strong sense of agency by voicing an identity that contrasts with what others believe to be true: "I am an architect, they call me a butcher · I am a pioneer, they call me primitive · I am purity, they call me perverted." This antithetic parallelism is rhetorically powerful in its echo of Biblical style as well as in its reinforcement of difference between the solid subject and the unspecific, amorphous opposition. There is a comparable self-awareness, superiority and deliberateness in lines like "self-disgust is self-obsession honey and I do as I please" and "I am stronger than Mensa, Miller and Mailer · I spat out Plath and Pinter." The troubling aspects of self-harm are shown to be something more problematic to absorb: they are under a profound self-control that can account for its "butchery" more effectively than murderous and torturous acts committed by nation states and their ideologies. Both "4st 7lb" and

"Faster" force listeners to confront their preconceived views, generating an irreconcilable dis-ease with what was originally thought to be merely disease.

How do these confrontations with difficult knowledge in *The Holy Bible* relate to the album's potentiality as an archive? By looking at *The Holy Bible* through the lens of Walter Benjamin and Paul de Man's conceptions of allegory and irony and their relationship to temporality, it becomes apparent that *The Holy Bible* represents what film studies scholar Jaimie Baron calls "one of the paradoxes of the archive: it is constituted by both absence and excess" (109). This description of the archive points to the overabundance, both literally and figurally, of the memories and knowledge contained by the archive, whilst also acknowledging that there will always be gaps in the material and in our understanding of it. Allegory, which is often defined as an extended metaphor, has been theorized as a major feature of postmodernism, particularly in its capacity to contain a multiplicity of meanings. In his two-part formulation of a theory of post-modernism, "The Allegorical Impulse," Craig Owens asserts that "[a]llegory *is* extravagant, an expenditure of surplus value; it is always *in excess*" (84). Fredric Jameson expands on this argument by observing that allegory is "the opening up of the text to multiple meaning, to successive rewriting and overwritings which are generated as so many levels and as so many supplementary interpretations" (29–30). The archive itself—as well as *The Holy Bible,* which itself is an allegory of the archive—engenders an excess and ongoing instability of meaning.

The sheer excess of *The Holy Bible* is readily apparent, from its aural sensory overload, to its numerous allusions and intertextualities, to the very surfeit of lyrics. There are so many lyrics to be fit into each song that they have been broken and malformed into a scansion that James somehow manages to sing, often sounding like an alternate unholy language. The awkward enjambments reveal a contorted straddling, a posture of evident discomfort for both performer and listener. For many songs, without the aid of the lyric sheet, which famously was printed as a double-spread advert in the music papers prior to the album's release,[2] they are incomprehensible. For example, the torrent of serial killers, mass murderers, right-wingers and dictators in "Archives of Pain"—"kill Yeltsin, who's saying? Zhirinovsky, Le Pen, Hindley and Brady, Ireland, Allit, Sutcliffe, Dahmer, Nielson, Yoshinori Ueda, Blanche and Pickles, Amin, Milosovic [*sic*]"—is delivered in a blur of odd syllabic emphases and ligature. Not only are many of these referenced names possibly unfamiliar to the Manics' audience, but they are rendered in such a quick, breathless fashion that there can be no instant recognition or connection between them. In some cases, the flood of lyrics in *The Holy*

---

[2] In these two-page adverts, several "offensive" words of the lyrics were blacked out, producing an ironic effect whereby the remaining onslaught of words expressing difficult knowledge were deemed as not needing censorship.

Bible are forced into a liturgical rhythm, as in "Mausoleum":

> regained your self-control · and regained your self-esteem · and blind your success inspires · and analyse, despise and scrutinise · never knowing what you hoped for · and safe and warm but life is so silent · for the victims who have no speech · in their shapeless guilty remorse · obliterates your meaning · obliterates your meaning · obliterates your meaning · your meaning, your meaning ...

This particular group of lyrics provides some armature for James to hang on to as he hammers the downbeats into place. Despite these footholds, the listener is still confronted with a linguistic deluge that can only be deciphered through repeated listening.

Not only is *The Holy Bible* allegorical in its excesses, but its expression of history, temporality and representation through language places it in line with Walter Benjamin's theory of allegory. In his discussion and definition of allegory, Benjamin uses the device of the symbol as viewed by the Romantics to contrast with the allegory of the Baroque in their engagement with time and history. He writes of the symbol's totalized connection to nature and the resulting possibility of redemption in the face of destruction, whereas allegory expresses the stilted and less progressive version of history, which is often "untimely, sorrowful, unsuccessful" (166). Following Benjamin, literary theorist Paul de Man argues that:

> Whereas the symbol postulates the possibility of an identity or identification, allegory designates primarily a distance in relation to its own origin, and, renouncing the nostalgia and the desire to coincide, it establishes its language in the void of this temporal difference. In so doing, it prevents the self from an illusory identification with the non-self, which is now fully, though painfully, recognized as a non-self. (207)

Both Benjamin and de Man identify the temporal difference between symbol and allegory, the latter as bearing a more distant relationship to its original text, enforcing a break in direct correspondence between the signifier and the signified and exposing the misleading coherence of a symbolic representation. The allegory, then, comes to embody a more authentic relationship between language and meaning. This conception of allegory, with its lack of totality of meaning and preponderance of fragmentation, can be related to the experience of difficult knowledge. For Pitt and Britzman, "representation is a compromise, an attempt to ward off crisis, because constructions are made from an argument between the wish for coherence and the anxiety over what coherence excludes" (759); thus, allegory, in its fractured representation and resistance to total coherence, is more conducive to conveying difficult knowledge.

Because of this desire to produce a coherent meaning in the face of trauma that cannot be totalized, difficult knowledge poses a seemingly impossible challenge to learning and understanding; this incapacity to master trauma so significantly outside of one's own frame of reference in turn leads to what Britzman terms a "time of otherness," or an always already belated witnessing; it's the "ambulance at the bottom of the cliff" in "Yes." In learning from difficult knowledge, Britzman argues that "we are given too little and too much, too early and too late" (134); in other words, the absence and excess confounds the temporal position of the witness. This alternate temporality contained in both allegory and the confrontation with difficult knowledge is also present in Felman and Laub's work on the incommensurability of witnessing. They observe that traumatic events exceed the limits of "normal" reality, placing them outside of a coherent, linear time structure that privileges cause and effect, thereby making them difficult to understand or communicate (69). For these traumatic events, history itself becomes fraught with temporal dislocation and stasis.

In his critique of historical materialism, Benjamin addresses this dissolution of linearity and dialectic progression in history by conceiving of a "dialectic at a standstill"

("Paralipomena" 403). Britt describes Benjamin's dialectical image as epistemologically creating a pause in this progressive, linear history to allow for some critical distance and an awareness of the contradictions and oppositional forces acting on each other within history (128). He goes on to explain that this dialectic image is connected to Benjamin's formation of the allegory in that the former is both the "modern counterpart to the allegorical emblem" and the "historiographic archive of pure language," reaching for a fleeting insight via "disjoined, aphoristic statements and quotations" (128), and furthermore, this methodology of montage can extend to the writing of history "to recover repressed history and to oppose the ideology of progress" (125). In reference to his unfinished opus of historical observation, *The Arcades Project,* Benjamin himself stated that "I have nothing to say, only to show" (73) and demonstrated this method of collage and montage not only in *The Arcades Project,* but also in *One-Way Street* with its seemingly disconnected catalogue of observations and aphorisms. This disjunctive style parallels what Benjamin refers to as "'*schöne eingemengte Sprüche*' [beautiful, interspersed apophthegms]" that are "conjured up from allegorical constellations" throughout the Baroque *Trauerspiel* (196), and it also describes Manic Street Preachers' Style from the beginning of their career, progressing from the cut-up sloganeering in their early interviews to the epitome of their parataxis of pithy lyrics in *The Holy Bible.* In many ways, the Manics have utilized the same aphoristic and citational style, selecting quotations to adorn their records and singles and communicating in succinct soundbites to the music press. Their lyrical work also draws on this disjunctive demonstration instead of attempting a tidy, totalizing whole. *The Holy Bible,* if anything, heightens the unsettling effect by producing so much of it. As Pitt and Britzman contend, though the traumatic event can be felt, it is often untranslatable into meaning (758), leading to breakages and aporia, moments in which language can no longer create holistic arguments or sustained statements. There is a feeling that the album, like the band, was hurtling toward a spectacular ruin even whilst declaring its grandiosity and revelling in its own ugliness. At times, *The Holy Bible* resembles the allegory employed in Baroque *Trauerspiel,* which is "characterized by its accumulation of atomized linguistic, sound, or image ruins as dislocated signs, brought together [...] as the staccato-like commentaries that abandon any pretence to dialogue" (Day 152). As already discussed, James' vocals often become awkwardly staccato in order to permeate the deluge of thought rushing through the songs, and many of the lyrics are dislocated references that are brought together in spectacular fashion to draw attention to themselves and prompt the listener to think more deeply about the content. In his own aphoristic mode, Benjamin states: "Allegory [...] declares itself to be beyond beauty. Allegories are, in the realm of thoughts, what ruins are in the realm of things" (178). As an allegory of difficult knowledge and archival confrontation,

The Holy Bible, too, moves beyond beauty—in the words of "She is Suffering," "beauty is such a terrible thing"—and reinforces the death drive that Derrida argues is inherent in the archive and memory itself. The album exists in a temporal void that cannot operate within the logic of chronological, progressive history, but instead repeating fragments of trauma and atrocity to underscore that "never again" ultimately has no meaning. Echoing Britzman's "time of otherness," Benjamin's version of allegory "sanctions no idea of an originary Garden of Eden, or record of unity. Instead of timeless truths, there is the 'untimely,' the history that stands outside the chronological narrative or progress that makes up 'official' history" (Tambling 117). Similarly, in Derrida's conception of the archive, there is also no origin to which to return, manifesting in a compulsive archive fever to attempt to reach such origin in a search for understanding and meaning. Like a snake eating its own tail, *The Holy Bible* sees no beginning or end to human cruelty, suffering and injustice.

Dorian Lynskey identifies *The Holy Bible,* and more specifically the song "Of Walking Abortion," as the moment when the protest song eats itself (*33 Revolutions*). Put differently, this record places the blame of humanity's atrocities and inhumane actions on everyone's doorstep, annihilating the idea of protest and any sense of political agency in the process. Within "Of Walking Abortion," there are several strong condemnations of innate human cruelty and hypocrisy, including, "Hitler reprised in the worm of your soul," "loser – liar – fake – phoney · no one cares, everyone is guilty" and "a moral conscience – you've no wounds to show · so wash your car in your 'X' baseball shoes." In one of the most famous lyrics from the song, perhaps from the whole album, James ends by half-screaming, "who's responsible · you fucking are · who's responsible · you fucking are · who's responsible · you fucking are · who's responsible · you fucking are · who's responsible," the final "responsible" a strangulated distortion of human communication. These accusations of delusional mendacity abound in the album. "The Intense Humming of Evil" disdainfully tells the listener to "drink it away, every tear is false" and on "Faster" the narrator declares, "I've been too honest with myself I should have lied like everybody else." This implication of all people includes the Manics themselves. Not only are they "the band that likes to say 'yes'"—the ultimately unused slogan for "Yes," the unreleased single recounting the experience of prostitution—but in the second iteration of the chorus for "Archives of Pain," James slips "Manic Street Preachers" in the place of "Milosovic [sic]," a barely perceptible acknowledgment of the right-wing views the song is endorsing in its demand for merciless violence to seek justice.

As already observed by others, some post-punk bands, such as Devo, Throbbing Gristle, and Joy Division, flirted with the far-right (Boswell 126; Reynolds 82). I propose that difficult knowledge, in its incommensurability with hope and a linear, rational narrative of history as progress, could lead to a critique of rationalism and humanism altogether, a deconstruction that bears a similarity to Counter-Enlightenment philosophies, including post-structuralism and its probing of the failure of liberalism and language itself. In turn, these philosophical movements that question empirical truths and realities can often slide into right-wing tendencies and fascism, creating what seem to be odd bedfellows (Wolin). Nevertheless, in the face of unstable truths and meanings, coping strategies can embrace the choice to either seize or submit to control. The ostensibly surprising right-wing views on capital punishment expressed in "Archives of Pain" and the critique of the politically correct language of liberalism in "P.C.P." could be viewed in light of this impasse at the confluence of deconstruction and critique of rationality, which can be traced through Nietzsche, Bataille, and even Derrida. Another reaction could be the recognition that (a)temporal distance from the witnessing of trauma can only make the memory of difficult knowledge available through irony.

In his study of Holocaust impiety in popular culture, Matthew Boswell describes "The Intense Humming of Evil" as a "full-on assault on some of the central pieties of the Holocaust: namely, that suffering ennobled the victims and that the historical memory of this suffering is inherently meaningful" (128), and quotes Susan Gubar's *Poetry After Auschwitz* to account for the "ironic friction" between "voicing subjectivity" and a "history that assaulted [...] the very idea of sovereign selfhoods" (129). This impossibility of true comprehension, mimetic representation, and belated recuperation is expressed in Paul de Man's discussion of irony in relation to allegory:

> Irony divides the flow of temporal experience into a past that is pure mystification and a future that remains harassed forever by a relapse with the inauthentic. It can know this inauthenticity but can never overcome it. It can only restate and repeat it on an increasingly conscious level, but it remains endlessly caught in the impossibility of making this knowledge applicable to the empirical world. It dissolves in the

narrowing spiral of a linguistic sign that becomes more and more remote from its meaning, and it can find no escape from this spiral. The temporal void that it reveals is the same void we encountered when we found allegory always implying an unreachable anteriority. Allegory and irony are thus linked in their common discovery of a truly temporal predicament. (222)

The detached position taken in "The Intense Humming of Evil" is indicative of this temporal void and the distance that it creates. Additional irony is apparent in the tone of alienation from desire, whether as a prostitute in "Yes," or "nature's lukewarm pleasure" in "She is Suffering." Throughout the album there's a friction between knowing and feeling too much, and refusing both engagement and emotion. This disruption of meaning and real comprehension creates instability, which can be related to allegorical and ironic language. de Man also describes irony as "unrelieved *vertige,* dizziness to the point of madness. Sanity can exist only because we are willing to function within the conventions of duplicity and dissimulation, just as social language dissimulates the inherent violence of the actual relationships between human beings" (216); or in the words of "Faster," "if you stand up like a nail then you will be knocked down · I've been too honest with myself I should have lied like everybody else." Much of the music of *The Holy Bible* is built on vertiginous guitar figures, which seem to fall and spin in ever tighter circles of purgatorial claustrophobia. This unsettling effect appears in the choruses of "Revol" and "Yes," in the slower section that concludes "4st 7lb," and throughout "Faster," embodying a spinning time of otherness without beginning or closure, or de Man's semiotic spiral. The motion of *The Holy Bible* also bears a similarity to that of Albert Camus' *The Fall* as described by Felman and Laub:

> The movement of the plot has a pronounced, repetitive, *concentric* thrust, as though searching for a silent center that remains, however, absent from the circles and *excentric* to their *concentration* [...]

an effort at—but also, paradoxically, an impossibility of—getting at the center. (187)

Moreover, this concentrated and concentric movement can be compared to what Felman and Laub identify as a "concentration-camp universe," or the twentieth-century realities of fascism and totalitarianism that delimit any human progress.

Just as the use of Jenny Saville's *Strategy (South Face/Front Face/North Face)* for the album cover rearticulates the abject reality of remembering and confronting difficult knowledge, the use of Martin Kippenberger's art for the covers of *The Holy Bible*'s singles complements the aphoristic and fragmented nature of irony and a disordered archive. Kippenberger's style is one of ambiguity and often unexplained juxtapositions; his works' captions and titles frequently don't make sense to viewers, and thus, his work can be construed as apolitical. The art used for the singles of "Faster," "Revol," and "She is Suffering," *Fliegender Tanga, Sympathische Kommunistin,* and *Des tètons, des tours, des tortellinis,* respectively, is possibly ironic, but one can't be certain. All of these artworks appear to show happy subjects of totalitarian regimes, albeit the young Chinese communist in *Fliegender Tanga* is also drinking liquid capitalism in the form of Coca-Cola. An example of this kind of ambiguity in the content of *The Holy Bible* resides in "Revol," a track that places Russian leaders next to sexual acts with no apparent correlation to reality: "Mr. Lenin – awaken the boy · Mr. Stalin – bisexual epoch · Kruschev [*sic*] – self love in his mirrors · Brezhnev – married into group sex · Gorbachev – celibate self importance · Yeltsin – failure is his own impotence." One possible interpretation is to see political power as related to the personal power struggles within sexual relationships—one aspect of being human connected to another—but it's tempting to try to read more into the song. The ironic and allegorical nature of the album makes this a particularly troubled action; as cultural studies scholar Gail Day observes, "allegories involve complex webs of meaning spun across 'horizontal verbal surfaces.'

Disjunctions and juxtapositions encountered on these surfaces, then, must be treated with caution. They tempt the reader to make translations in an act of resolution" (148). The tension between leaving fragments unresolved and the desire to make connections for meaning is indicative of a struggle with confronting and learning from difficult knowledge, a fever to keep returning to the archive and make sense of it. In his update to Craig Owens' "Allegorical Impulse," art critic Hal Foster writes of an "archival impulse" and posits that archival art might arise from a "sense of a failure in cultural memory, of a default in productive traditions [...] For why else connect so feverishly if things did not appear so frightfully disconnected in the first place?" (21–22). *The Holy Bible* is such archival art, serving as a reaction to the failure of cultural memory and the morsellated meaning in its wake. At the same time, the Manics use particular allegories of the body in order to demonstrate that, where difficult knowledge is concerned, we can never get past the first morsel.

Body Index: Anorexia, Self-Harm and the Inability to Digest and Witness

The Holy Bible is intensely concerned with the body and disordered eating. In addition to "4st 7lb," which is explicitly about anorexia, the title of "Faster" can be read in terms of the refusal of food, and hunger and starvation are equated with language in "The Intense Humming of Evil" and "P.C.P." Vomit is mentioned in "Yes" and "Mausoleum." A thin, wiry sound pervades the music, along with a Spartan discipline and control of rhythm; the Manics' musical approach feels hallowed and hollowed. *Anorexia nervosa* is most often found amongst females and thus linked to problematic gender roles and bodily norms imposed by society and its culture at large; however, it can also be read as reflective of the "central ills of our culture—from our historical heritage of disdain for the body, to our modern fear of loss of control over our futures" (Bordo 29), and as part of coping with "contemporary bourgeois anxiety" (36).

Whilst there is definitely a theme of control dominating *The Holy Bible,* another facet of this control is refusal and rejection, and this rejection can easily slip into abjection. In her psychoanalytic study of horror, Julia Kristeva relates abjection to the inability to tolerate:

> There looms, within abjection, one of those violent, dark revolts of being, directed against a threat that seems to emanate from an exorbitant outside or inside, ejected beyond the scope of the possible, the tolerable, the thinkable. It lies there, quite close, but it cannot be assimilated. [...] like an inescapable boomerang, a vortex of summons and repulsion places the one haunted by it literally beside himself. (1)

She specifically calls attention to the revulsion toward food, which she describes as "perhaps the most elementary and most archaic form of abjection" (2). Food and language are often interchangeable in *The Holy Bible,* a characteristic that opens up another avenue of inquiry related to difficult knowledge and confrontation of the archive.

Not only is the refusal of food an exercise in discipline and control, but it can also be read as a metaphorical refusal, and ultimately an inability, to assimilate difficult knowledge, to make it so unpalatable as to draw attention to itself. The radical otherness of difficult knowledge is always in danger of being replaced by lovely knowledge; as Derrida notes, there is a human need to assimilate and make otherness knowable and acceptable within a preconceived framework, and "[w]hat is radically alien in the other doesn't have a chance—it will be digested, melted down in the great tradition, wolfed down mercilessly" (qtd in Birnbaum and Olsson). Flying in the face of this tendency, *The Holy Bible* takes its strategy of confrontation and abjection from the J.G. Ballard audio clip included in "Mausoleum": "I wanted to rub the human face in its own vomit and force it to look in the mirror." When it comes to difficult knowledge, it's better out than in. Alternatively, difficult knowledge is not digestible or assimilable, but instead, leads to an alternate temporality of "deferred action" (Pitt and Britzman 769). This deferral, which relates to the aforementioned time of otherness, precludes consumption of traumatic truths, and instead highlights the impossibility of real comprehension. For Derrida, this is "respect for that which cannot be eaten—respect for that in a text which cannot be assimilated. My thoughts on the limits of eating follow in their entirety the same schema as my theories on the indeterminate or untranslatable in a text. There is always a remainder that cannot be read, that must remain alien. This residue can never be interrogated as the same, but must be constantly sought out anew, and must continue to be written" (qtd in Birnbaum and Olsson). These remnants, or ruins, must be returned to repeatedly to acknowledge the incommensurability of difficult knowledge, and the impossibility of ever fully assimilating it.

Perhaps paradoxically, Manic Street Preachers succeed in putting the listener in an anorexic position by overfeeding her/him. As already noted, the lyrics of

The Holy Bible are in excess, in terms of literal number and allegorical meanings. The "diet's not a big enough word" lyric from "4st 7lb" finds its parallel in "hunger's a word" in "The Intense Humming of Evil." There is an implication that words are not enough to express meaning, or that they fall short of the meaning and acts behind them, as well as a sense that traumas can be easily dismissed through language. "P.C.P." begins with "Teacher starve your child, P.C. approved · as long as the right words are used," and then goes on to a series of lyrics that are equivalent to a linguistic binge: "P.C. she speaks impotent, sterile, naïve, blind, atheist, sadist, stiff-upper lip, first principles of her silence, of her silence"; "P.C. she says inoculate, hallucinate, beware Shakespeare, bring fresh air, king cigarette snuffed out by her midgets, by her midgets"; and "P.C. caresses bigots and big brother, read Liviticus [*sic*], learnt censorship, pro-life equals anti-choice, to be scared of, of feathers." In all of these examples, words, which communicate knowledge with insufficient, lost, sublimated, trite, and overwhelming meaning, are related to food. The narrator of "4st 7lb" may be "choked with roast beef" but the listener of *The Holy Bible* is choked with language and ideological indigestion.

Additionally, this logorrhea that suffuses the record speaks to the phenomenon of prolific writing taking the place of eating. In the case of hunger artists and hunger strikers, there is a "link between starving and writing, between the hunger of the flesh and the gluttonous proliferation of the signifier" (Ellmann 24), and "it is as if the lilliputian diminution of the flesh entailed a corresponding brobdingnagian inflation of the word" (22). *The Holy Bible* functions within this ostensible contradiction between bodily and intellectual needs. As one anorexic described her experience, it was one of "absolute purity, hyperintellectuality and transcendence of the flesh. My soul seemed to grow as my body waned; I felt like one of those early Christian saints who starved themselves in the desert sun. I felt invulnerable, clean and hard as the bones etched into my silhouette" (qtd in Bordo 35). There are many parts of *The Holy Bible* that boast this sense of purity and transcendence, particularly in "Faster" and "4st 7lb." The album, too, is corpulent with verbiage, but on the verge of shrinking into the compression of a black hole, forever ensuring the unassimilated distancing of self and other. For Maud Ellmann, "[a]ll eating is force-feeding: and it is through the wound of feeding that the other is instated at the very center of the self" (36), therefore, by referring back to the metaphor of food and knowledge, it can be argued that knowledge, difficult and otherwise, is always invasive and has the potential to become abject.

It would be remiss not to discuss the significance of the use of Jenny Saville's *Strategy (South Face/Front Face/North Face)* on the cover of *The Holy Bible* in terms of this inability to digest knowledge. Saville's triptych is immediately striking in its filling of the frame with flesh, its excess. Three different views of the same woman, who is dressed only in underwear that seems to meld with her flesh, loom from above; her eyes directly confront the onlooker, not allowing the woman to be passively consumed, but instead, making a demand of those looking. In her article on Jenny Saville's paintings of obese women, Michelle Meagher observes that "[i]n a cultural climate that encourages women to conceal, if not excise, those parts of their bodies considered fat, jiggly, out of control, and excessive, Saville insists upon revealing precisely these features" (24), and in so doing, her art embodies what Meagher calls an "aesthetics of disgust." Drawing upon Kristeva's theory of the abject, Meagher relates disgust to bodily reaction and the forceful recognition of the borders between the self and that which is external to the self. As Kristeva argues, abjection is "what disturbs identity, system, order. What does not respect borders, positions, rules. The in-between, the ambiguous, the composite" (4). It is both the disordered bodies of Saville's work and the disordered eating that place them outside of control and totalities. Derrida relates Kantian aesthetics to digestion by asserting that a concept of economy acquired from digestion governs the view of the beautiful in Kantian aesthetics. While the beautiful is a name for the balanced and harmonious metabolism, the closed economy remains threatened from within by disgust, and this analytic of the beautiful falls apart when it reaches the point of disgust and vomiting—a point at which the economy reaches its limit in terms of what is absolutely inassimilable.

(qtd in Birnbaum and Olsson)

In contrast to Kantian aesthetics, Meagher argues that an aesthetics of disgust "offers an opportunity to both acknowledge and interrupt disgust reactions—which is to say that it allows us to feel disgust in order to interrogate its sources" (30). Put differently, the provocation of disgust can actually ensure that the consumer of the painting cannot politely dismiss and digest the piece of art, and thereby becomes aware of her/his own reaction and the discourse that shaped this reaction in the first place. This confrontation with difficulty in Saville's paintings not only draws attention to the spectator's disgust, but breaks through the normative political correctness that usually prevents its expression, "disgust itself has been rendered disgusting and shameful" (Meagher 29). Looking at Saville's work, as well as the album that it adorns, through an aesthetics of disgust, it becomes apparent that both works of art are employing a repulsion untempered by the dilution and economy of political correctness (so castigated by "P.C.P.") to ensure the receiver of their messages cannot digest and assimilate difficulty, nor heal breakages that cannot be sutured and ignore the difficulty altogether by externalizing it in an archive. Of course, some incommensurable truths and traumas do manifest externally to demonstrate the impossibility of witnessing.

In addition to the preoccupation with disordered eating, *The Holy Bible* is rife with references to skin, whether in a state of decay, disease or mutilation. "She is Suffering" views the personification of beauty as leprous and pale; in "Mausoleum" everything has become "rotting flesh"; the narrator of "4st 7lb" has skin that is "cling-film on bone"; racialized skin appears in the counter-refrain of "there's not enough black in the union jack · there's too much white in the stars and stripes" in "Ifwhiteamerica," and of course, the most remarked upon theme that appears in "Yes," "Die in the Summertime" and "Faster" is self-harm. In the interview for the tenth anniversary edition of *The Holy Bible*, James Dean Bradfield admits that wearing a balaclava during the performance of some of the more personal and voyeuristic *Holy Bible* songs was likely his subconscious way of dealing with "inhabiting someone else's skin."

It is readily available knowledge that Richey Edwards not only experienced anorexia himself, but also engaged in self-harm, the most visceral and public instances being the time he cut "4-REAL" into his forearm with a razor blade to make a point about authenticity to journalist Steve Lamacq, and the time he lacerated his chest with knives gifted to him by a fan before going on stage in Thailand in 1994. The song "Yes," which describes literal and figurative prostitution, features the lines: "I eat and I dress and I wash and I can still say thank you · puking – shaking – sinking I still stand for old ladies · can't shout can't scream, I hurt myself to get pain out." "Faster," arguably the most famous track from *The Holy Bibl*e, is an Übermenschian declaration of a strong mind over a weak body that obliquely references self-harm. James blasts through the staccato opening lyrics, which of course commences with "I am an architect, they call me a butcher." Yet another instance of self-harm appears in "Die in the Summertime": "Scratch my leg with a rusty nail, sadly it heals." These three songs engage with self-harm in various registers: as an outlet for psychic pain; as a position of agency and control beyond the comprehension of others; and as a need to produce a trace that "reinstates the boundary between the existence and nonexistence of self" (McLane 112). On some level, all of these ways of representing self-harm speak to a border between self and other similar to that of the one between body and food (tellingly, the lines preceding the admission of self-harm in "Yes" commence with eating and then puking); of contending with difficult knowledge; and of remembering trauma and preserving identity.

Skin, which has been theorized through psychoanalysis as an extension of the ego or as a psychic envelope (Anzieu; Anzieu et al.; Lafrance), is often perceived as a psychic border between the self and the other and a way of forming subjectivity. In some cases, skin can be seen as a cultural border or a symbolic surface upon which identity is written (Benthien), and through its relationship to embodiment, skin can also function as a text of gender politics (Ahmed and Stacey). Evidently, skin can come to represent a canvas for individual inner states and the sublimated state of culture at large. Humanities scholar Jay Prosser argues that one of the functions of skin is to record: "[s]kin re-members, both literally in its material surface and metaphorically in resignifying on this surface, not only race, sex and age, but the quite detailed specificities of life histories" (52). If the skin remembers, can self-harm be viewed as a self-recording, leading to strata of a bodily archive? Relating typographical print to the rite of circumcision, Derrida notes that the latter is an incision on the skin that also functions as an archival document and trace, beginning a process of archival layering on both the physical body and the exteriorized archive of memory whilst simultaneously remaining slightly open like wounds (*Archive Fever* 20). Self-harm, in its deliberate inscription of the body, then, can be read as a multi-layered recording of memory, made visible but remaining largely subliminal, and thus containing excess meaning.

As a visible act and a visual trace, self-harm can then be read as a type of testimony (Kilby 124). In her study of self-harm as a testimony in need of a witness, Jane Kilby explores the impossibility and excess related to this form of testimony. She notes that the harm of one's own skin "speaks with a 'voice' so sheer that it is virtually impossible for anyone to bear witness to it. Arguably, then, there is something about this 'voice' that defies witnessing, even as it insistently demands it" (124). Notably, Kilby relates self-harm to speech and language, asserting that skin cutting is its own language that repeats and expresses previous trauma with a difference, highlighting the insufficiency of verbal language (125). The sheer scream of the self-harmer's inner voice, in combination with the fracturing and absence of language, exceeds understanding and thus complicates witnessing. Much like the distancing achieved through an aesthetics of disgust, self-harm produces a gap between the viewer and the difficult knowledge of trauma (Kilby 136). And again, like the effect of visceral self-awareness generated by the aesthetics of disgust and the unassimilated/undigested, self-harm can force the reader into a comparable feeling of disjuncture and critical engagement with her/his own incomprehension and assumptions. In this way, self-harm can become a pedagogy for difficult knowledge by revealing the "fragility and permeability of the reader's own skin boundary" (Kilby 130). Kilby goes on to explain the constructive potentiality of witnessing self-harm in terms of encountering trauma and testimony where "the loss of all comprehension becomes the condition of possibility for testimony, since this acute disorientation forces the reader to make a social and political context for both herself and the testimony" (130). When Richey writes, "I am an architect," he is building this structure of critical engagement and calling attention to the limits of witnessing including thoughts that he cannot communicate in any other way. In fact, the self-harm in *The Holy Bible* could be seen as a "means of protection against further emotional rupture following a devastating event, or even (paradoxically) as a means of caring for oneself in the face of ongoing emotional turmoil" (Failler 169). This care for the self could perhaps be extended to "caring for difficult knowledge" (Lehrer, Milton, and Patterson); the linguistic connection between care and curation further links *The Holy Bible*'s theme of self-harm to that of the curated archive.

The initial refusal and then the impossibility of bearing witness are demonstrated throughout *The Holy Bible.* In "Mausoleum," James sneeringly sings,

> come and walk down memory lane · no one sees a thing but they can pretend [...] and blind your success inspires · and analyse, despise, and scrutinise · never knowing what you hoped for · and safe and warm but life is so silent · for the victims who have no speech · in their shapeless guilty remorse · obliterates your meaning ...

This set of lyrics is complex in its accusation of forgetting atrocity and the implication that no one saw what was happening, a common defence from bystander perpetrators of the Holocaust and other inhumanities. Nevertheless, it exhorts listeners to attempt to use language to justify their position of distance despite its futility and ultimate failure, erasing their own senses of self in trying to account for alterity.

Language remains inadequate to describe and bear witness to the atrocity, and as Felman and Laub argue, there aren't really any true witnesses to the Holocaust since any who experienced the full enormity of the cruelty perished before the liberation of the camps. Instead, the Manics fill up the linguistic abyss with an indigestible glossolalia, in recognition that too much can mean at least as much as nothing. The enactors of self-harm in *The Holy Bible* are not only silently screaming their own testimonies, but also those of silenced victims and the memories that have been consigned to the archive.

The Pre-Emptive End of an Era

It is a well-trod path through the history of the Manics to discuss the downward spiral experienced by the band throughout 1994: the amoral quagmire of the band's trip to Thailand as documented by Barbara Ellen, Richey's hospitalization, the doomed European tour with Suede, the increasing malaise and stress permeating the entire band, and the foreboding, yet intensely cathartic, three gigs at the London Astoria in December, replete with suspicious nosebleeds and the utter destruction of the band's equipment on the final night. Nicky would later describe the Astoria gigs as a "full-stop in our career [...] something's stopped, something's changed." Then in February 1995, Richey Edwards disappeared, changing the full-stop to a question mark.

The Holy Bible took the extremities of the twentieth century and combined modernism's "negativism and antitraditionalism, defiance of authority and convention, its antagonism or indifference to the expectations of its audience, and, on occasion, its rage for chaos" (Sass 29) with the postmodern fragmentation of subjectivity and preoccupation with its own pre-emptive deconstruction. In his study of the similarities between modernism and schizophrenia, psychology scholar Louis A. Sass asks, "What if madness [...] were to derive from a heightening rather than a dimming of conscious awareness, and an alienation not from reason but from the emotions, instincts, and the body?" (4). In Sass' view, schizoidal personalities are often either hyperaware of themselves to the point of questioning everything they say and do in their interactions with others, or they are hyperaware of their own superiority, seeing societal mores as the artificialities that they are and perceiving most people as not using the full capacity of their intellects. I would say that *The Holy Bible* and its creators find themselves in both camps; though they sing "I am stronger than Mensa, Miller and Mailer," they also add, "I've been too honest with myself I should have lied like everybody else." In relation to the disorderly eating and self-harm portrayed in *The Holy Bible,* there appears to be a rational hyperawareness within the band, but a detachment from emotional externalities and appetite that could potentially place them back into a less disoriented, but acetic state, a state that Sass describes as "a sort of corpse with insomnia" (Sass 7–8).

According to Simon Price, one of the most striking, and perhaps most disturbing, aspect of Richey's psyche at the time of *The Holy Bible* was his ability to be both patient and analyst of his own condition. When viewed through a modernist, schizoidal prism, this hyper-self-awareness and reflexivity seems more natural. With Richey's disappearance in 1995, the band itself had to work through their own self-reflexivity, opting not to split in actual terms, but to separate themselves in a more conceptual way.

CHAPTER 3

Archive Fever

"...freed from the memory, escape from our history. And I just hope that you can forgive us but everything must go."
– Manic Street Preachers, "Everything Must Go"

"...archivization produces as much as it records the event." – Jacques Derrida, *Archive Fever*

"That's the gift of schizo."

– Scritti Politti, "Wood Beez (Pray Like Aretha Franklin)"

In the aftermath of Richey's disappearance, Manic Street Preachers created *Everything Must Go,* gently absorbing remaining fragments of Richey's lyrics into an album that functioned as the band's own *sous rature*. This absorption, or assimilation, is in many ways a liquidation of *The*

Holy Bible. The music of *Everything Must Go* is a radical departure from the dizzying claustrophobia and disjuncture of *The Holy Bible;* rather, it is dominated by sweeping anthems and breathing room. For *Everything Must Go,* the Manics opted to use the production skills of Mike Hedges, who had worked with Everything But The Girl, the Beautiful South, and McAlmont & Butler, and traded the failed promise of post-punk for a Spector-esque wind of change. Absence took the place of excess; it was as though the band's lack of knowledge about what had happened to their friend and bandmate had extended to the style of their art and lyricism. The band's image also experienced an erasure, adopting non-descript clothing and album artwork composed of stark photography, including a void between the parentheses in the album's title that emulated a lifespan with uncertain dates of beginning and end. William Shaw describes their look at this juncture as "aggressively ordinary" (84). The blankness offered both freedom and potentiality. At the same time, like *The*

Holy Bible, Everything Must Go became an allegory of memory, difficult knowledge and the archive, and in so doing, didn't quite fulfil the album's title. As Derrida observes, allegory and irony often "say something quite different from and even contrary to what seems to be intended through it" (*Memoires* 74). Understandably, the Manics sought distance from the turmoil of *The Holy Bible* and the subsequent trauma of Richey's disappearance. However, in consigning part of their identity to the archive to move on, they produced a spectral trace, a schizoid identity.

The Internal Split: The Schizophrenia and Vicissitude of Being Manic Street Preachers

Though the Manics have described their band identity facetiously as schizophrenic, usually in reference to the seemingly opposite musical styles they have adopted since *The Holy Bible,* or to the oscillation between being a tight machine and a hot mess onstage, I think it's worth probing the idea of schizophrenia in relation to the band's identity. In the reverberations of the traumatic touring of *The Holy Bible*, Richey's disappearance, and the making and promotion of *Everything Must Go*, the band reinforced the break between *The Holy Bible* and the history held behind its bulk and their present incarnation. Talking about *Everything Must Go*, James said, "I think we realised there should be an end and we've either got to start again, which I think we have on this album, or end with dignity" (qtd in Cameron 74). Music journalists appeared to agree:

> They need to find another ideal for living, one that allows them to see that being the Manics isn't a life or death thing after all. [...] The Manics—again, more than anyone else—will be aware of the frightening parallels between that monumental fuck-up and their own paranoia-riddled position. (Williams 76)

This declaration of detachment and a fresh start dominated the representation of the Manics in the public eye throughout the rest of the 90s, but the very separation that was so necessary also became the source of a seemingly overdeveloped self-reflection, that could be read through the lens of schizophrenia. Louis A. Sass describes schizophrenia as "imbued with hesitation and detachment, a division or doubling in which the ego disengages from normal forms of involvement with nature and society, often taking itself, or its own experiences, as its own object" (37). This type of compulsive self-evaluation, and even self-obsession, becomes apparent in the Manics' artistic output and public face from this point on, as they negotiate what the band's identity should be, perhaps even feverishly attempting to reach an "archive of pure language," or an origin that can never be attained.

Talking to Stuart Maconie in 1998, James said, "If you think *The Holy Bible* was gratuitous and hard-going, imagine what The New Testament would have been like. It probably would have been a dead end ultimately" (qtd in

"Everything" 99). This denial of a plausible and artistically fulfilling future for the band that made *The Holy Bible*, a future that crucially never came to pass, is reminiscent of the strategies utilized in dealing with difficult knowledge. Britzman observes that "strategies such as the discounting of an experience as having anything to do with the self and the freezing of events in a history that has no present" and "mechanisms of defense—undoing what has already happened and isolating the event in a time that has long past—are key ways the ego attempts to console itself" (119). Similarly, the schizophrenic "has severed bonds not only with reality but also with the entire content of his or her personal history" (De Bolle 23), living in an overly present present. This severance as a tactic of survival can also make way for something new via abjection; as Kristeva argues, abjection can also function as a form of resurrection that gives new life to the death drive, thereby transforming it (15). For *Everything Must Go*, the abject wasn't the excess of difficult knowledge in the broader context of the world; the abject was the band itself.

The titular track is emblematic of the splitting strategy used throughout the album. Against production that has been blown out beyond its limits and oversaturated—the aural equivalent of staring at the sun—James sings, "freed from the memory, escape from our history, history/And I just hope that you can forgive us but everything must go/And if you need an explanation, then everything must go." It is a plea to be released from the archive that has come to form the Manics' identity. The music video for the song sees the destruction, rather than the dislocation, of time itself as clocks are smashed, audio tapes unspool, and cherry blossom trees shed their ephemeral beauty. In the documentary that accompanies the tenth anniversary edition of *Everything Must Go,* Nicky Wire describes the song as a "preemptive strike." From a band that had always planned and anticipated its future in the present until there wasn't a difference between the two, this action made sense.

In an alternate way, the biggest hit from *Everything Must Go* and the Manics' biggest commercial hit overall, "A Design for Life," a song which dispenses with reflections on personal memory and the current history of the band, acted as *the* cathartic release from *The Holy Bible.* Though less obviously a declaration of letting go of the past, this soaring paean to the working classes was actually the most decisive severing of ties to the previous incarnation of the band. Nicky's use of language is succinct and fluid, and James and Sean's music is correspondingly confident and full-bodied; it is the antithesis of *The Holy Bible.* The track's declaration that "Libraries gave us power" was ironic in light of the rest of the song, but it was a tribute to the strength of the archive despite the problems that knowing too much can entail. Nevertheless, ambiguity and doubt did find their way into the rest of the record.

Aside from "Everything Must Go," the lyrics of "Australia" are perhaps the next most explicit expression of the desire to escape the band's history whilst simultaneously reclaiming it differently and under less challenging terms: "I've been here for much too long/This is the past that's mine/I want to fly and run till it hurts/Sleep for a while and speak no words in Australia." The silence of sleep and not speaking is telling; after the indigestible overload of *The Holy Bible,* the most effective way to move on was to cease with words altogether. There is a sense that words were once again inadequate, this time to testify to the trauma of losing Richey and the uncertainties bound up in consigning so much of themselves to the archive. These lyrics from "Australia" also gesture to ownership of the past, reinstating the need to remember and continually reclaim these personal memories. This ambivalence complicates the Manics' manoeuvres in deciding how much should actually be remembered. The fear of the instability and loss of memory is evident in "Interiors (Song for Willem De Kooning)," which tells the story of the abstract artist's experience of Alzheimer's: "Who sees the interiors like young Willem once did/Your beautiful triangle of distortion/Now you seem to forget it so much." One must also contend with the context of de Kooning's painting process, which involved applying turpentine to his paintings and repeatedly sanding down the surface to reveal lost images of previous paintings (Leader 91). Taking all of these factors into account, "Interiors" is a song of loss, and the repetition and mourning of that loss. Likewise, "No Surface All Feeling," a song already in progress before Richey disappeared, is less clear about the value of the past: "It makes me angry ashamed but really alive/It may have worked but at what price/What's the point in looking back/When all you see is more and more junk." This final track leaves the album on a note of introspection and re-evaluation that never really answers the question of whether there is a point in looking back.

The schizoidal attributes developed by the Manics, conceivably to provide escape from the "hyperconsciousness and self-control" of *The Holy Bible*, "may, in fact, be an extreme manifestation of what is in essence a very similar condition" (Sass 10). The split in their identity, as read through Derrida's theory of the archive and consignation of knowledge to the archive, is rife with various pressures, including repression and suppression (*Archive Fever* 78). These kinds of pressures, though necessary for moving on, end up producing more meaning and signifiers than they compartmentalize. In fact, "[w]e might say that schizophrenia is a disease of adaptation and one that adapts; it is the failure of semiotics and the remaking of semiotics" and possibly the inspiration for deconstruction itself (Herr 136). Apparently, the Manics couldn't entirely leave *The Holy Bible* and its deconstructive methods behind.

Spectral Traces: Sublimated Returns

In the liner notes for the tenth anniversary edition of *Everything Must Go,* John Harris writes that at the core of the album "there lies a reminder that though cutting loose from the past is sometimes necessary, it is never nearly as easy as some people would have you believe." No matter how much you split the subject, traces remain. The introduction to *Everything Must Go*, "Elvis Impersonator: Blackpool Promenade," is a somewhat difficult entry into the record, with its lyrics a combination of those left by Richey and new ones written by Nicky after he disappeared. The track becomes an allegory of the position in which the Manics now found themselves, and the ongoing struggle they would experience for the rest of their career. The belatedness of part of the lyrics echoes the time of otherness related to difficult knowledge. Despite the escape velocity into the future and the will to forget displayed in much of the rest of the album, the belated witnessing and dislocation of temporality that results from their trauma still haunts it. The archival promise built into the monumental ruin that is *The Holy Bible* lingers in both present and future, resisting closure. Derrida characterizes the archive as "*spectral*" and argues that it is "spectral *a priori:* neither present nor absent 'in the flesh,' neither visible nor invisible, a trace always referring to another whose eyes can never be met" (*Archive Fever* 84). This ambiguity of the archive is not a simple haunting; the archive exists in a strange temporality that can never fully be sought after or responded to. Any exchange or dialogue with the archive is fraught with gaps in visibility and understanding, as well as unexpected connections and dissociations. Though "Further Away" is ostensibly about Nicky's loneliness when he's on tour and away from his wife, it features the lyrics "feel it fade away into your childhood further away. [...] The circular landscape comes back only with regret, only with regret/The more estranged I feel from my youth further away." These lines complicate what would otherwise be a "love song," a genre so avoided by the Manics. The cyclical movement of regret contradicts the spatiality of "further away," even as the song repeats the tropes of childhood innocence and the loss thereof that are found on *The Holy Bible*, and on the albums that preceded it. There is a sense of repetition embedded in linearity; the spectrality of the Manics' archive is both referential and dissociative.

Despite much of their work in distancing themselves from their past, the Manics cannot stop preservation and memory work from occurring in *Everything Must Go.* In "Enola/Alone," which refers back to the palindromic doubleness of "Revol," Nicky writes, "I'll take a picture of you/to remember how good you looked/Like memory it had disappeared/naked and lonely within my fears." He later explained to Stuart Maconie that "Enola/Alone" "stems from [...] me looking at my wedding photos and seeing two people [manager Philip Hall and Richey Edwards] standing right by me who are not around anymore" (qtd in "We Shall Overcome" 85). "Enola/Alone" is preceded by "Kevin Carter," penned by Richey, which tells the story of photographer Kevin Carter, his Pulitzer Prize-winning photograph of a vulture stalking a dying child in Africa, and Carter's subsequent suicide. In juxtaposition, these two songs speak to the desires to preserve and reproduce time, and the unexpected consequences of such interventions, albeit in different ways. They both describe the haunting traces of photography, but the resolve to survive dominates "Enola/Alone," whilst "Kevin Carter" embodies a foregone conclusion. The rest of Richey's lyrics, "Small Black Flowers That Grow in the Sky," "The Girl Who Wanted to Be God" and "Removables," are evidence of the more compressed pockets buried throughout the otherwise open vistas of *Everything Must Go*. Accompanied by acoustic guitar and harp, "Small Black Flowers" is notable for its subtlety and quiet bleakness as it expands upon the abject, trapped position of prostitution in "Yes," and applies it to the spectacle of incarcerated animals. In "Small Black Flowers," reproduction is to be avoided in order to stop a torturous cycle: "wanna get out here you're bred dead quick/for the outside [...] harvest your ovaries dead mothers crawl." Anteriority is enforced against one's will. "The Girl Who Wanted to Be God," apparently about Sylvia Plath, is performed against a backdrop of a manic, exaggerated anthem, the contemplative guitar arpeggios of "Motorcycle Emptiness" reappearing as rushes of sound that can barely hold together. It doesn't have the assured pacing of other songs on the album, such as "A Design for Life," "Everything Must Go" and "Australia," and thus feels like an attempt to assimilate the unassimilable into the new framework. Similarly, "Removables" stands out from the rest of the album in its grunge aesthetic, which seems to drag somewhere below the surface. Its broken, stilted lines ("Killed God blood soiled unclean again/Killed God blood soiled skin dead again") reflect the refracted style of *The Holy Bible,* and notes the same futility in attempting to stay in a fixed temporal position ("a bronze moth dies easily") that appears in songs like "Die in the Summertime." These seemingly less congruous songs written by Richey become a crucial memorial site within the schizoid consignment of identity, preserved even as they must be sublimated. Therefore, they form a sort of cryptic trace underlying *Everything Must Go.* Such a crypt "can be built as a monument or niche of a lost object preserved within the split ego" (Ihanus 123). The Manics' defensive split produced as much as it jettisoned, and as much as the band continued to cope with the ramifications of their own schizophrenia, their fans, too, experienced a splitting of sorts, and in some cases, came into conflict with the band over what Manic Street Preachers should be. Due to the gaps in the difficult knowledge of Richey's disappearance, bearing witness became an impossibility for both the band and their audience, leading to an ongoing identity debate and the interrogation of what kinds of lovely knowledge might have been created in its wake.

Belated and Indirect Witnessing: Memory Work and the Manics

The present absence of Richey endured even through the years immediately following his disappearance, when the band was most vociferously separating from their past. Speaking in 1996, Nicky stated, "We'll never fill that gap. We'll never get another guitarist. James will never go over to that side of the stage" (qtd in Maconie, "We Shall Overcome" 88); the space of stage right became a sacred site of remembrance for the band, but also a heightened, present absence for fans. In the documentary for the tenth anniversary edition of *The Holy Bible,* James describes his discomfort whilst playing Reading Festival in 1994 as a three-piece (at this time, Richey was hospitalized), which included the fact that some of the fans "were staring at the space of the stage where Richey should be, refusing to look at me." This desire to look at the empty space usually occupied by an object perceived as valuable is arguably an expression of the connection between emptiness as an index of a sign that holds symbolic meaning; the absence ironically brings more meaning to the surface than was originally recognized in the object itself. In his discussion of the spectators who flocked to see the empty space in the Louvre from which the *Mona Lisa* had been stolen in 1911, Darian Leader posits that this incident makes manifest the split between art and the space it usually occupies, thereby prompting an interrogation of the usually unseen or hidden meaning in the artwork that typically isn't in question. In becoming a signifier of totemic mythologies of tortured genius and martyred rock stars, Richey's absence became an index for that signifier, whereby spectators intuit meaning even by staring into the void of the lost signifier. These mythologies then perpetuate a kind of lovely knowledge because they fit into an already established perspective and narrative of popular culture. Within the last twenty years, the proliferation of music magazine covers featuring Richey have played into this lovely knowledge, rather than confront the difficult knowledge his disappearance evokes.

Conversely, Kieron Gillen and Jamie McKelvie's comic-book series Phonogram: Rue Britannia dissects this lovely knowledge in a loving fashion, using the context of the tensions and connections between cultural and personal memory and identity. Described by musician Luke Haines as a "meta romp through nostalgia," Rue Britannia critiques the nostalgia industry of 90s

Britpop along with the supposed mythologies about pop music that sustain it. One such mythology is that popular music can change your life in a magical or religious fashion. Protagonist David Kohl is a cynical former fan of Britpop, which is represented in the series by a goddess named Britannia who is said to have died over seven years ago. David is a phonomancer, a musical magician of sorts, who spends much of the series philosophizing about the Britpop genre, memory, and the indie snobbery that goes with it, or as he describes it, "I do intricate vivisection rituals on pop songs to better understand their totemic powers."

One of the key sub-plots involves David and Manic Street Preachers fan Beth, a girl from his past. In the series, he first encounters her as an eyeliner-smeared, boa-wearing apparition standing on an overpass stubbornly waiting for Richey Edwards. She embodies the fans known as the Cult of Richey, a faction of fans that offends the Manics and other fans in equal measure. In Chapter 3, "Faster," David meets the present Beth, who refuses to discuss the Manics and denies any past fandom, a sentiment which is further reflected in the disavowal and dismissal of Manics fandom by phonomancer Emily Aster several panels later. The fact that Beth is still alive implies that her ghost in the previous chapter is more of a consignment of memories, an exterior archive that allows her to forget and split her identity.

The final chapter, "Live Forever," opens with a visual parody of the album cover for *The Holy Bible,* and concludes with David donning the garb of a Manics fan and returning to Beth's exiled memory. In speaking with the apparition, David says: "Want me to take you after Richey?" She agrees, and they end up at the Severn Bridge, where Richey's car was found abandoned. She becomes angry, saying, "Where is he? You said you'd take me to him." David corrects her: "No, I said I'd take you after him. This is as far as I can go. And Richey's not here." After she insists that she feels Richey's presence, David explains, "It's a toll bridge. Entry point to Wales. Richey used it as an entry point into myth. That's what you're feeling." He continues, "Richey's defining aspect now is that he's gone. If he came back, he wouldn't be Richey anymore. Waiting for a man whose main characteristic is his absence is a stupid waste of time. And Manics fans are anything but stupid." David then encourages Beth to follow Richey, and she thanks him before plummeting from the bridge.

As he begins to shed his Manics fan garb, David enters into a lengthy monologue over several pages:

> I've tricked something like a ghost into committing suicide because I think that'll help Beth. [...] Richey's not dead. Richey's not alive. Richey's **gone.** Different thing altogether. Rock immortality. How do you obtain it? By being memorable. An untimely death just doesn't cut it anymore. You need something a little more unprecedented to become ever-living narrative. Did he do it deliberately? Doesn't matter. All that matters is the act was enough to make the idea of Richey into a god. The price

was suicide without a note or a disappearance without saying he was alive. The price was being a shit. He didn't owe us anything—and vice versa. That's how pop works. Pop is for **you.** But his ascension put the people who loved him—really loved him—through a living hell. Belief is all-important in what we do. You believe, it burns, flickers and dies. The ashes mix with the soil and we call them memories. What do you do with a memory? The retromancers huddled around theirs as their world grew cold. [...] And yeah, even I worked out that no matter how bad it objectively was ... It's how I was made.

Returning to Beth and her relationship with the past, he says,

All Beth did was fill her mouth with it until she couldn't taste anything else. To enjoy the memory would be to betray it. No one can live like that, so that bundle of belief was exiled. All her ghost did was feed Richey's myth. With her ghost gone, the memories should return. I hope it does her some good.

The final panels of the series show Beth waking up to "Motorcycle Emptiness" on the radio and finally being able to sing along with the song and go back to sleep with a satisfied look on her face. The "bundle of belief" that was exiled is Beth's archival consignment, her schizophrenic act, which resulted in a literal spectral trace that remained even after its repression. This entire passage deconstructs the lovely knowledge surrounding Richey's disappearance and refracts it through critical distance. As in *The Holy Bible,* eating becomes a metaphor for memory, but rather than a starving refusal and inability to assimilate difficult knowledge, Beth fills her mouth with the lovely knowledge of Richey's mythology, and in so doing, feeds into it. Moreover, the Rue Britannia series analyses the concept of an unbridgeable gap of signification. Richey's main characteristic of absence becomes the pre-emptive separation that makes the figurative and literal bridge in the series impossible to cross, leaving only a belatedness, or an "after" rather than a "to." To find meaning, Beth's spectre waits and looks for Richey, but it is only ever a looking *at* an absence, rather than engaging in actual witnessing. In the end, she is performing an assimilative, "imaginative sympathy," in which "[w]e remember or anticipate our own pain and imagine the pain of the other" (Gaston 90) in an attempt to close an unfillable gap, which is only further exposed by the attempt.

By reading the lyrics of *The Holy Bible,* and some of those in *Everything Must Go,* you can intimate a sense of vulnerability and ambivalent exposure and exhibitionism in response to being the object of intense scopophilia by others, especially when they look at you as a suffering martyr. In a song like "Kevin Carter," this interrogation of looking in relation to suffering and conscience is applied to photographs of distant atrocities. In *Regarding the Pain of Others,* Susan Sontag asserts that such images "cannot be more than an invitation to pay attention, to reflect, to learn, to examine the rationalizations for mass suffering offered by established powers" (117); looking at images of suffering, as well as looking at suffering, are acts of distance, regardless of the immediacy implied by photography (118). Ultimately, in the act of all of this looking, we are often still left with the "Can't understand, can't imagine" (126), an acknowledgment of the unassimilable nature of difficult knowledge. All of this looking can also be read as the inability to witness, the imposition of surfaces and barriers that do not allow for direct signification, yet perpetuate the sense of a truer hidden meaning. In this second-degree witnessing, whether by fans, the media or the creative memory work of artists, the distance is necessary. As Felman and Laub observe,

> such second-degree testimony is complex and can no longer be direct. Because it seeks above all to preserve the distance necessary for the witnessing (the inner distance of the radical departure), it requires not the involved proximity of memory (that of the submersion of the witness) but the *distancing* of this submersion

through the reflectiveness of *theory*. (140)

In many ways, Gillen and McKelvie's Rue Britannia assumes such a posture of theorization in order to cope with and critique personal and cultural memories.

Not only are fans impossible witnesses to the Manics' trauma, but the band itself cannot be anything but belated witnesses. Moreover, this temporal dislocation is exacerbated by the fact Richey disappeared, but did not "die." As Nicky explains, this lack of knowledge leads to a sense of delay: "It's not like someone who's passed away who you can think of in a different context. Being selfish about it, at least if you knew it was final perhaps all the grief would come out, because I'm not sure it has really, which is a bit frightening" (qtd in Lynskey, "Redesign" 100). Once again, Richey is a signifier whose index is absence. Discussing the possibility of using the lyrics left behind by Richey in 1996, Nicky revealed the limits of engaging with the difficult knowledge of their recent past and the barriers to bearing witness to Richey's disappearance:

> Maybe one day we could use them and do an album of those manuscripts, but we need to come to terms with what's in there. There is some good stuff there ... I know you can't get much bleaker than *The Holy Bible* ... but after that we didn't think people were ready for songs about cutting the feet off ballerinas. There are no clues there as to what was going to happen. Let's face it, you don't need any clues for Richey. Ever since he carved "4 Real" on his arm, nothing would surprise you.
> (qtd in Maconie, "We Shall Overcome" 88)

This lack of clues puts the band in an ongoing position of unknowing, and in many ways silenced the Manics regarding this difficult knowledge for nearly a decade. Since past trauma is "regulated, controlled, manipulated, and managed by stories" (Ihanus 123), the Manics worked incessantly at the narratives they told and repeated. These stories acted as what Derrida termed a *récit,* which is a narrative that "begins *without* a present event"; "[t]he repetition of the *ré-cit* marks at once a double affirmation and an impossible mourning. [...] It is an affirmation – a re-citation – that is *open* to what remains to come," but also "refuses any synthesis or reconciliation, a *gaping opening*" (Gaston 104). And in an effort to move on and avoid misusing Richey's disappearance and memory, they often sublimated their difficult knowledge into other themes.

Following the unprecedented, almost surreal success of *Everything Must Go,* the Manics expressed anxiety over the band's identity and continued to interrogate themselves. In 1998, this process resulted in *This is My Truth, Tell Me Yours,* an album in which much of their soul searching and memory work was redirected at Welsh identity and history. The title itself, a quotation from Aneurin Bevan, signalled this transference. Their first number one single, "If You Tolerate This, Your Children Will Be Next," concerned the Welsh who volunteered to fight in the

Spanish Civil War, comparing their principles to the contemporary notions of a more inadequate, less principled Welshness, especially as felt by Nicky Wire personally. "Tsunami" told the story of the "silent twins," June and Jennifer Gibbons, Welsh sisters who only communicated with each other, possibly as a response to the racist abuse they received as the only black children in the community. They were eventually sent to Broadmoor Hospital after committing arson, and only after Jennifer died, did June begin to speak to others again, seeing her sister's death as a sacrifice for her release. This track could be interpreted as a certain kind of release in lyrical style post-*The Holy Bible;* however, besides "Ready for Drowning," which alludes to both Richey's possible drowning and the flooding of a Welsh village to provide water for Liverpool, the only song explicitly about Richey on the record is "Nobody Loved You."

After the softer melancholia and mournful rumination on Welshness that defined *This is My Truth,* the Manics appeared to need to reconstitute the band as a version closer to the one that produced *The Holy Bible.* In a *Q* feature story called "A Redesign for Life," Dorian Lynskey interviews the Manics in 2001 on the cusp of their release of *Know Your Enemy.* "'The enemy for us was what we had become,' says Wire. 'What we had *let* ourselves become'" (96). Significantly, Nicky says that Richey's memory "has informed the spirit of *Know Your Enemy*" (100). At the same time, Lynskey senses the dogged death drive inherent in the Manics' work and concludes his article with "there is a sense that the end is, if not nigh, then in sight" (100). Ultimately, *Know Your Enemy* was an overly eclectic record that felt incoherent and stylistically confused. The album embodied the struggle against themselves, the problematic, seemingly disorganized side of schizophrenic hyper-reflexivity. Sass interrogates this possible paradox of over-thinking and self-reflexivity:

> Could the disorganization in question be something more intricate, not a process of being overwhelmed by antagonistic forces but more of a self-undermining—like

something turning in upon itself until, finally, it collapses of its own accord? If so, we might find the peculiarities of schizophrenic experience less a matter of brute contradiction than a paradox: the paradoxes of the reflexive. (8)

As the Manics said, the enemy was only themselves.

In producing *Everything Must Go,* such an unexpected and unimaginable following act to *The Holy Bible,* the Manics put themselves in the position of trying to follow an impossible act for the rest of their career. Another way of explaining the process of dealing with their identity quandary could be "archive fever." Derrida delineates the terms under which archive fever is enacted: "It is to have a compulsive, repetitive, and nostalgic desire for the archive, an irrepressible desire to return to the origin, a homesickness, a nostalgia for the return to the most archaic place of absolute commencement" (*Archive Fever* 91). Dorian Lynskey describes this impulse in more concrete terms: "Manics albums follow a cycle of sorts. Twice now they have released an agenda-setting album followed by a compromised one, which then led to a turbulent, angry record" ("Redesign" 99). This pattern of recalibrating their identity to what they think Manic Street Preachers should mean, often predicated on the significance of *The Holy Bible,* is one of the most fascinating aspects of the band. In 2011, after ranking the top fifty of their own singles for *NME,* James speculated on the band's next steps: "I think we will, as a band, reinvestigate ourselves as a concept" ("We Sanctified" 27). More than most bands, Manic Street Preachers constantly take stock of themselves. This hyper-self-reflexivity and anxiety over identity proves that they are not entirely haunted by Richey, but by themselves as a band.

In the same year that the Manics released the tenth anniversary edition of *The Holy Bible,* they put out *Lifeblood,* an underrated album that is positively haunted. Its music is ironically bloodless, eschewing guitar solos for washes of synth, but this static translucence quietly declares the ghosts of the past to be alive and well and living within the Manics. "Emily," a track about suffragette Emmeline Pankhurst, reveals some of the most telling themes behind the album: "The relics the ghosts all down so many roads [...] It's what you forget [...] that kills you/It's what you remember [...] that makes you/We used to have answers/now we only have questions/but now have no direction." This rumination on memory and forgetting expresses the significance of memory for identity, but it also interrogates whether the Manics' artistic methods post-*The Holy Bible* were as effective and "true" as they should have been. The preponderance of unanswerable questions and lack of direction is a telling insight into the band's ongoing memory work. The last track of *Lifeblood,* "Cardiff Afterlife," is an apt tribute to this difficult work and the feelings of oscillating laterally rather than moving forward:

> The paralysed future
> The past sideways crawl
> I must give up on this
> It makes no sense at all
> Makes no sense at all

> In the Cardiff afterlife
> We sense the breaking of our lives
> [...]
>
> And yet I kept my silence
> Your memory is still mine
> No I will not share them
> Acquaintance through denial
>
> For I witnessed a splendour
> And evil that no one saw
> And I felt kindness
> And vanity for sure

This song reclaims the band's memories of Richey and the ambivalence this reclamation entails, especially as it recounts the more difficult knowledge about him as a real person and friend. "Cardiff Afterlife" also recoups some of their witnessing of the events surrounding and immediately following *The Holy Bible,* and the silence this witnessing required; however, the use of "afterlife" still reinforces the belatedness of witnessing their own trauma, and the breaking of lives suggests the unanswerable aporia of difficult knowledge. Speaking about

Lifeblood, James said, "we did find a different version of ourselves. Sometimes when you delineate and deconstruct, you find nothing, that's the scary process. But we did find something (even if) we confused ourselves and our audience in the process" (qtd in Power 266). *Lifeblood,* in many ways, paved the way for an epiphany and the beginning of a return, as well as a more direct confrontation with the past.

On the tenth anniversary of Richey's disappearance, *NME* asked Nicky, "Why do you think everybody hates the Manics' 05?" He replied:

> I think people forget that we're just completely aware. We don't expect to be on the cover of *NME,* we don't expect to be the band that we were ten years ago, we're really comfortable with that. I spent months putting *The Holy Bible* reissue together, and there it is, a tribute to Richey, it's a tribute to the band at the time. *Lifeblood* is *The Holy Bible* for 35-year-olds.
> ("Nothing" 31)

At the same time, he acknowledged that "surviving has become a curse." This survival becomes *sur-vivre,* the Derridean "living on," which is in excess of life and death, and hovering somewhere above, on, or in between the two. The Manics' *récit* of *The Holy Bible* and its attendant meaning for the band's identity became stronger around the time of *Lifeblood,* as afterlife and survival collided with archive and revival. In the video interview included with the tenth anniversary reissue of *The Holy Bible,* James describes the album as the band's "most definitive period," and says that the reissue special edition was made because "as an era, it deserves to be represented this way." By 2014, Nicky was saying "really Richey's in all our lyrics" (qtd in Barry).

After a three-year break during which James and Nicky released solo albums, the Manics produced *Send Away the Tigers,* a record heralded as their "comeback." They managed to blend the anthemic side of their identity with the more vigorous ambitions of their past. As described by Nicky Wire, the lead single "Your Love Alone" appeared to be a combination of apostrophe and prosopopoeia, a dialogue with the absent Richey Edwards. In one interview, he said, "I feel like Richey is my guiding light at the moment" (qtd in "Glastonbury" 20). The song "Indian Summer" contains the lines, "I guess we'll have to test, until there's nothing left/We said the truth was fixed, it's lost without a trace [...] Indian Summer, still hurt and broken/And leave all this material belief/Remember the reasons/The reasons that made us be." The questions and fragmentation of *Lifeblood* remain, but with a renewed commitment to remember in the face of an ongoing future that remains strange because a pre-emptive end was both eluded and interiorized. Perhaps even more significantly, the band took to wearing what appeared to be military-style clothing again, and the typeface on the cover for *Send Away the Tigers* was a return to the Cyrillic font and reversed "r's" of *The Holy Bible.* Then, on November 4, 2008, the Manics revealed that they would be releasing a new album featuring Richey's remaining lyrics: "[m]usically, in many ways it feels like a follow up to the Holy Bible" ("Note").

CHAPTER 4

Archive Retraced

"Derrida's figure of the trace ... offers further ways of looking at consumption: a perennial, future leftover inviting contingent readings of the past, the present, and of haunting figure presences that cannot be digested."
– Ruth Cruickshank, "Humans, Eating and Thinking Animals? Structuralism's Leftovers"

"The paper as the body of my friend, And every word in it a gaping wound, Issuing life blood."
– William Shakespeare, *The Merchant of Venice*

"Traditional art invites a look. Art that's silent engenders a stare."
– Susan Sontag, "The Aesthetics of Silence"

The open-mouthed, glassy-eyed stare demands that the viewer stares back.

The facial flesh mottled with crimson could be contusions, blood, skin disease, a birthmark or a trick of the light. The Manics' use of Jenny Saville's *Stare* for the cover art for *Journal for Plague Lovers* not only signals a direct visual correspondence with *The Holy Bible,* but it also serves as a comment on the ambiguity of the album that only uses the lyrics left behind in Richey Edwards' notebook. It is a record that demands hermeneutics; so far, so much like *The Holy Bible.* But *Journal for Plague Lovers* adds a layer of obfuscation that comes with the silence and absence of Richey and the complications of temporality. The process of making the album becomes a combination of mourning and translation, which requires engagement with how one interiorizes and separates from the other. Though Richey's lyrics infer that "journal for plague lovers" is his name for the Bible, there remain important differences between *Journal for Plague Lovers* and *The Holy Bible.* At the time that the Manics were touring *Everything Must Go,* James told Stuart Maconie, "I really enjoyed how *The Holy Bible* confronts the audience.

But that album confronts us too" (qtd in "We Shall Overcome" 90). With *Journal for Plague Lovers,* the Manics confront the difficult knowledge of their own past and archive.

A New Mourning, A New Translation: Making Journal for Plague Lovers

It is fitting that *Journal for Plague Lovers* begins with a sample from *The Machinist,* a film about the hallucinatory questioning of memory and reality induced by insomnia and starvation. Christian Bale's character says, "You don't even know me. What if I turn into a werewolf or somethin'?" This inability to know another or even one's self, and the accompanying dread and trepidation that comes with exploring it, is writ large in the Manics' process of creating *Journal for Plague Lovers.* In the 2009 documentary *Shadows & Words,* which focuses on the making of the album, James says that after the success of *Send Away the Tigers,* the band "didn't want to compete with [themselves]," and decided that it might finally be the time to attempt setting Richey's remaining lyrics to music. Presumably, a record returning to Richey's words would be a return to a version of the band that stands apart from the incarnation that created *Send Away the Tigers.* The decision did not come without more than a decade of thought. James relates his struggle with Richey's journal of lyrics:

> I kept getting it out over the years and then putting it back in the drawer because it was too scary. Like that scene in *Friends,* putting a copy of *The Shining* in the freezer because it's too scary. And I could feel the drawer going *(mimes violent shaking)* "Bam-bam-bam ... Let me out! Let me be!" (qtd in Mackay, "Richey's" 26)

The journal in the drawer represents the exteriority of the archive, which though suppressed, keeps returning.

Emily Mackay describes *Journal for Plague Lovers* as "bringing a strange sort of, if not resolution, conversation between past and present" ("Richey's"

25); perhaps even a dialectic image in Benjamin's terms. *Journal*, as an archive, can also be read as a belated promise, never really present, but existing in some premature time that remains out of joint. This temporal dislocation became evident in the ways the band deliberately made *Journal* appear as a successor to *The Holy Bible* in terms of cover art, typeface, and number of tracks, but also in the ways the band set the album apart from all of their others: by not releasing any singles from it; by producing a deluxe hardback book edition; by choosing to play *Journal* in full for three nights at The Roundhouse in London; and by deciding to take the tour for the album to North America (the last time they toured North America was in 1996). As an archive, *Journal* remains a Derridean injunction for an unrealized future, or a belated future, but also a self-repetition and a self-confirmation (*Archive Fever* 79). The death drive or pre-emptive strike that has been inherent in all of the Manics' work is present again in *Journal*; by recording *Journal*, the band is establishing an end of sorts, knowing that there are now no further potentialities for making another record with Richey's lyrical content. Moreover, *Journal* can be seen as a more visible way of consigning through remembrance, and the act of memorialization completed can serve as an archive to allow for some forgetting.

Though *Journal* is arguably an attempt at putting the band back together and reincorporating that which they consigned to the archive, the experience of this significant shift can be compared with Sass' understanding of a schizoidal break, "an experience in which the familiar has turned strange and the unfamiliar familiar, often giving the person the sense of *déjà vu* and *jamais vu,* either in quick succession or even simultaneously" (44). Sass' description of this psychic break bears a valuable resemblance to Gerhard Richter's analysis of the workings of memory in general:

> While memory requires time to become what it is [...] time also hinders memory, veiling its specificities, blurring its details, accentuating too selectively and, in

doing so, uncannily rendering the familiar strange while, at the same time, causing the estranged gradually to appear more and more familiar. (150–151)

These vicissitudes of memory, and the uncanniness they produce, are emphasized in the lyrics used and the music produced for *Journal*. There are many moments in which it recalls *The Holy Bible,* but there is also a strangeness to some of the familiarity, and a familiarity to the strange; what exactly is strange and what is familiar depends on which version of the band a listener is looking for. *Journal* and *The Holy Bible* enact on each other, linked by difficult knowledge and the traces it can produce. There is an oscillation between the two records that allows each to illuminate and complicate the other.

Additionally, this interaction and tension between one and "the other," is found in the work of mourning, which Derrida describes as "[m]emory and interiorization"; mourning "entails a movement in which an interiorizing idealization takes in itself or upon itself the body and voice of the other, the other's visage and person, ideally *and* quasi-literally devouring them" (*Memoires* 34). Derrida warns against this kind of consumption and assimilation of the other, but also acknowledges it as one of the impossibilities of mourning. Part of the problem with interiorization of the other being mourned stems from "the dangers involved in speaking of the dead in the wake of their death, the dangers of using the dead, and perhaps despite one's own best intentions, for one's own ends or purposes" (Brault and Naas 6). Though Richey's fate remains uncertain, his long absence, as well as the loss of the band's earlier identity, make *Journal* a work of mourning. In fact, the Manics also demonstrate what Freud would term melancholia, in addition to mourning, because of the sense of emptiness felt in their own identity as a band. Freud describes the difference between the two by writing: "in mourning it is the world which has become poor and empty; in melancholia, it is the ego itself" (254). Furthermore, this melancholia without a direct object can relate to the ambiguity around the supposed object of their mourning, in other words, the unresolved doubt surrounding Richey's disappearance. The instability of truth, which permeates the Manics' two preceding records, *Lifeblood* and *Send Away the Tigers,* begins this mourning process by acknowledging and accepting the uncertainty. Derrida maintains that mourning is a tendency to accept this inability to understand and make space for it (*Memoires* 31). He goes on to argue that the traces that deny any sense of truth are "of a past that has never been present, traces which themselves never occupy the form of presence and always remain, as it were, to come" (58). As with most of the work by the Manics, *Journal* is of an absent past, a time that always anticipated and imagined the future, or the potential future of their past, rather than dwelled in the present. The crucial difference between *Journal* and the work of the preceding decade is the use of Richey's words and the responsibility of mourning and bearing witness that accompanies it.

In his discussion of Derrida's conception of memory, Richter asserts that "[l]eaving the word to someone else [...] letting the other speak instead of oneself, and yet continuing to think and write with and for that other is the act of memory and mourning par excellence" (155). In these terms, *Journal for Plague Lovers* qualifies as such an act. The band's process of creating and curating the album is made more apparent in the deluxe CD version, in which pages from Richey's journal are reproduced in the liner notes. It is in these facsimiles of his typewritten lyrics that you see his own emendments registered by a series of typed "x"'s and can compare the original lyrics with what the band selected to use and revise on the actual record. Numerous traces of Richey's actual hand remain amongst these lyrics, including in the handwritten note that prefaces the journal ("these songs are in no particular order of preference although some lyrics are obviously better than others"), as well as additional handwritten notes, collages and drawings from other pages. The responsibility of mourning sometimes made the band's "archive fever"—the desire to return to the "archive of pure language" that was *The Holy Bible*—more apparent and restrained it. Nicky spoke of his initial aspiration to make *Journal* more like *The Holy Bible:*

> I always get carried away with an idea and I think I did push James too much. I was saying, y' know, we really need to follow through on that claustrophobic singing-in-a-telephone-box idea but I think it became pretty apparent with "This Joke Sport Severed" and stuff like that that it was gonna be much more a broad rock album. I'm glad he didn't listen to me cos I was almost trying to contrive a situation.
>
> (qtd in Doherty 22)

The recognition of the falseness in attempting to repeat an unrepeatable moment of artistic creation underscores both the temptation to the familiar and the estrangement embedded in the current temporal position. In light of allowing the other to speak, James' comments regarding the recording of *Journal* are fitting:

> We just had this rule to "let the words guide you," because Richey wasn't that involved in the musical part of being in the studio. You know, obviously he did have a general aesthetic in his mind or what he wanted things to sound like or what he liked. Obviously we didn't have that, not that he directed much in the studio, but, still, we all contributed in some kind of way in terms of direction in the studio and because he wasn't here for this, we just had to let the lyrics guide us. And, if you read a lyric like "Facing Page Top Left," if you don't have an air of resignation to it, if you don't kind of recognize the slightly sarcastic gentle soul that's writing these words, then you're just betraying the lyrics so that's why it's dealing with the fallout of 'The Holy Bible,' rather than being a follow-up.
>
> (qtd in Doherty 22)

This surrendering of the process to the other, as well as the respect and the knowing again—both meanings inherent in the word *recognize*—needed to be part of the responsibility in creating *Journal.* James' reading of this album as part of the effect that *The Holy Bible* had on the band instead of a sequel reiterates the unrepeatability that Nicky speaks about. The words become a stand-in for Richey himself, his corpus as body.

Despite these careful, thoughtful processes, the band continued to wrestle with the implications of this act of mourning. In *Shadows & Words,* Nicky admits the doubt that he experienced after recording *Journal,* describing the moment as one in which he went "Bill Drummond mad" and suggested that they either burn or bury the *Journal* recordings in true KLF fashion. Discussing his concerns over how to write the music for *Journal,* James said,

> Deep down I was thinking, I couldn't have changed that much, I couldn't have forgotten that much about Richey that I can't do this. If we couldn't reconnect with what

Richey wrote, even at the apex of what was happening with him ... [...] if we couldn't do that then we would have lost a part of ourselves that we hadn't even realised we had lost.

(qtd in Petridis)

These anxieties reveal the significance of the meaning behind this record and ongoing negotiation of the band's identity in relation to their archive. Nicky's suggestion of burning or burying *Journal* could be read as an attempt to rectify the missing time of grieving a certain death, again substituting Richey's words for his body; moreover, this admission points to the fact that this record is not just an act of mourning, but a translation. Felman and Laub explain that the "task of the translator [...] is to read the textuality of the original event *without disposing of the body,* without reducing the original event to a false transparency of sense" (158). In translating the remaining lyrics, the Manics undertook a complex arbitration between the sense of the original and their current interpretation, which includes a belated witnessing. Though Felman and Laub describe translation as reading the original event without disposing of it, they acknowledge that the "original is killed because there is no possible witnessing of the original event; and this impossibility of witnessing is, paradoxically, inherent in the very position of the translator, whose task is nonetheless to try to render—to bear witness to—the original" (159). This paradoxical demand to bear witness within the act of translation happens not through imitation but by creating something new that testifies to the original's afterlife (Felman and Laub 160). As James said, *Journal* becomes a representation of the aftermath of *The Holy Bible* rather than a sequel, and Nicky's realization that trying to repeat the latter would only be false displays the difficulty in producing a "true" translation.

Furthermore, the Manics had not only translated Richey's remaining texts, but curated them, or in other words, cared for them. Part of caring for them was courageously revealing the process of making *Journal,* including the original pages of Richey's lyrics, which testify to the verses not used in the final album. These unused verses are not only an invitation to a multiplicity of hermeneutics and eschatology, but also destabilize the meaning of the recorded versions of the songs. These remainders of lyrics become apocryphal, whilst at the same time demonstrating a lack of assimilability, a refusal to be consumed and digested by an interiorizing action of those who mourn and those who can never understand. Any potential interpretation of the album is and remains inherently fraught; however, in allowing these meanings to remain unresolved and even contradictory, the Manics showed the respect and care required for mourning and translating their friend and archive.

Repetition with Difference: Palimpsest and the Exhaustion of Language

On *The Holy Bible,* the track "Of Walking Abortion" begins with a soundbite from author Hubert Selby Jr: "I knew that someday I was gonna die. And I knew that before I died, two things would happen to me, that number one: I would regret my entire life; and number two: I would want to live my life over again." This citation is an apt description of the kind of life *The Holy Bible* lives through *Journal for Plague Lovers.* Though the impossibility of actual repetition stands, *Journal* bears traces, often difficult ones, of *The Holy Bible* in aspects of its content, whilst establishing differences that follow *The Holy Bible* like its aftermath or its logical conclusion. The music of *Journal* is markedly more metallic and post-punk than the Manics' previous five records; as Nicky explains in *Shadows & Words,* Richey's words bring out a different side to James' music composition that Nicky doesn't feel he can reach with his own lyrics. "Jackie Collins Existential Question Time" and "Me and Stephen Hawking" recall the sarcastic playfulness of "Ifwhiteamerica," as well as the comedic pauses of Buzzcocks' "Boredom," and "Doors Closing Slowly" shares its limping beat with "The Intense Humming of

Evil." There are also flashes of *Everything Must Go* in "Facing Page: Top Left," which bears some of the gentle sadness of "Small Black Flowers That Grow in the Sky," and in "She Bathed Herself in a Bath of Bleach," which lumbers with the same grunge as "Removables." Though much of *Journal* returns to the sharper post-punk of *The Holy Bible,* the bonus track "Bag Lady" is its true musical heir with its sub-aquatic, dubby bass and serrated guitar, and perhaps this is the reason it is kept apart from the record proper. Overall, the most marked musical difference between *Journal* and *The Holy Bible* is the pace; in *Journal,* there is less frenzy and the extreme discipline has relaxed. It dissolves rather than implodes. The final track on the album proper, "William's Last Words" stands out with particular poignancy, with Nicky taking over the lead vocals and the music becoming more oneiric and acoustic. After the intensity of the previous twelve tracks, there is a slow drift into oblivion. The musical repetitions and recitations with distinct differences speak to the strange temporal situation of the album.

Sitting somewhere between *The Holy Bible* and *Everything Must Go,* but in actuality created roughly thirteen years later, *Journal* has odd continuities and distances. The "riderless horses on Chomsky's Camelot" in *Journal* opener "Peeled Apples" carry on from "Zapruder the first to masturbate" from "Ifwhiteamerica"; together they seem to allude to Noam Chomsky's 1992 article "Vain Hopes, False Dreams," an explanation of the then current revival of interest in John F. Kennedy, including the need for a messianic saviour figure and the unfulfilled futures he represented at a time of social disruption and anomie. In another temporal slip, "All is Vanity" and "Doors Closing Slowly" have their shadow text in "Picturesque," a track from the *God Save the Manics* EP from 2005. "Picturesque," which embodies the musical style used on *Lifeblood,* features lyrics from both songs unbeknownst to listeners until 2009. Listening to it after *Journal* is an uncanny experience, especially since the band has never addressed this earlier use of Richey's remaining lyrics. "Picturesque" is a foreshadowing, but remains a haunting, unstable source for these lyrics, which find their canonical place in separate tracks on *Journal*. In essence, *Journal* becomes a palimpsest that traces back and forth through time.

The palimpsestic nature of *Journal* can be read as part of the allegorical inheritance from *The Holy Bible*. Whilst the latter was an allegory of the impossibility of assimilating difficult knowledge, the former is an allegory of the first allegory. As Craig Owens asserts, in allegory "one text is *read through* another, however fragmentary, intermittent, or chaotic their relationship may be; the paradigm for the allegorical work is thus the palimpsest" (69). The nature of the palimpsest can also be regarded as temporally fluid in its dependence on memory. Referring to Hegel's concept of *Gedächtnis* as well as Derrida's thoughts on memory and anteriority, Gerhard Richter argues that memory is not mere restoration of the past, but instead it is a process of constant repetition and return, re-establishing its relationship to the thought process of remembering as well as to the future, "between the 'after' of something that never was present and a futurity that has not yet been thought" (158). In other words, memory as related to thinking and re-thinking does not assimilate and incorporate; rather, it anticipates and precedes itself, in addition to reflecting on itself in perpetuity. This form of memory is a constant oscillation in a dialectic at a standstill. As sung in "All is Vanity," "Haven't shaved for days/Gives me the appearance of delay." Or as articulated in "Die in the Summertime," "I have crawled so far sideways · I recognize dim traces of creation." These lateral movements of temporal dislocation are written on the body.

Like *The Holy Bible*, *Journal* uses the body and skin as texts of difficult knowledge and abjection. Throughout the album bodies are crucified, bruised, beautified, bleached, stitched, whipped and torn. In "Pretension/Repulsion," Richey writes, "shards [...] oh the androgyny fails/Odalisque by Ingres, extra bones for sale," echoing the preoccupation with bodily flesh found on *The Holy Bible*. The references to crucifixion that appear in "Of Walking Abortion" and "Ifwhiteamerica" proliferate on *Journal:* "bruises on my hand from digging my nails out" ("Peeled Apples"); "bruised and nailed and quit" ("This Joke Sport Severed"); and "that shadow is a cross okay [...] crucifixion is the easy life" ("Doors Closing Slowly"). In *Journal,* bodies are also rendered impotent, echoing "4st 7lb," "Die in the Summertime," and "P.C.P."; the purity preached on *The Holy Bible* has metastasized into sterility. Moreover, the eugenic sterilization practiced at the Virginia State Epileptic Colony, the subject of the song of the same name, becomes not only about preventing reproduction, but also implies extreme cleanliness and asceticism. The mind-over-body discipline of *The Holy Bible* ultimately does away with the material body altogether. "Peeled Apples" and "She Bathed Herself in a Bath of Bleach" imply a complete loss of the skin barrier between the inside and outside; the psychic envelope has fallen apart and dissolved. The visceral bodily feeling of *The Holy Bible* turns into a floating, out-of-body experience in *Journal,* and the distance between subject and difficult knowledge turns into a distance from the self that harbours its own difficult knowledge. In one of the unused lyrics from "Doors Closing Slowly," Richey uses the term heautoscopy, also known as autoscopy, which is defined as having "rare illusory visual experiences during which the subject has the impression of seeing a second own body in extrapersonal space" (Blanke and Mohr 184), or simply an "out-of-body experience." The disconnection between signifiers and the signified seem like the natural conclusion of walking in the snow and not leaving a footprint. The journal from which *Journal* was made becomes Richey's bodily signifier, a shed cocoon.

Nevertheless, the difficult knowledge of human atrocities does still circumscribe *Journal*'s content in the form of a Beckettian preoccupation with Dante and *The Divine Comedy.* Dante's circles of hell from *The Divine Comedy* appear in *The Holy Bible* in the form of "purgatory's circle" in "Yes," and they return in *Journal* explicitly and more obliquely. One of the reproduced pages from Richey's journal features four cut-out images of Dante's allegorical circles covered in Richey's doodles and handwritten notes referencing Nick Cave and the Bad Seeds' "A Box for Black Paul."[3] Also, one of the photos of Richey appended to the liner notes shows him at his typewriter, his left arm tattooed with the ninth circle, the circle of treachery. The track "Virginia State Epileptic Colony" includes the lyrics: "Draw a perfect circle, sleep foetus-like." These lines echo "my heart shrinks to barely a pulse · a tiny animal curled into a quarter circle" from "Die in the Summertime." These foetal images are disturbing evocations of retreating into a time before birth, or "dim traces of creation," but, furthermore, the concentricity suggests the hellishness of imprisonment. The audio clip sampled

---

[3] Interestingly, "A Box for Black Paul" could also be an inspiration for "Small Black Flowers That Grow in the Sky," as Cave's lyrics use the same trope of black flowers.

in "Virginia State Epileptic Colony" is from Alexander Sokurov's 1998 documentary *The Dialogues with Solzhenitsyn* and describes the author's fate from the gulag to exile: "The obtuse regime, his fatal disease, the silence of millions of witnesses, the envy of the guild, his exile, his perseverance. The photo for the other world in a suit, lent by the prison. [...] Just think over these words: 'For eternal residence.'" This citation draws parallels between the incarceration of pathologized individuals for reasons of mental and political difference. Felman and Laub discuss Camus' *The Fall,* including its symbolism of hell in Amsterdam's circular canals, in relation to his conflict with Sartre over the resemblance between Russian totalitarianism and Nazi fascism. They argue that

> [i]n addition to its geometrical or geographical significance, (as well as to the literary, allegorical allusion to the circularity of hell in Dante), "concentric" in effect is pregnant with another meaning which derives its resonance from the debate with

Sartre, and, referring quite specifically to the political context and to the history evoked by the debate, connotes Camus' allusion to—and insistence on—the historically indubitable *fait concentrationnaire,* the fact of a concentration-camp universe. (187)

This concentration-camp universe attempts to reach a centre that doesn't exist; there is no closure, no cure, no meaning.

The round bullet points dividing lyrics in *The Holy Bible* are replaced with the full-stop of periods in Richey's source material for *Journal.* The concentration of black dots appears to be faltering into a stuttering, slowly disintegrating language. For example, in "Facing Page: Top Left," the lyrics are a series of sentence fragments: "Skin care tones. Clean. Sharp fashion lines sharpened. Monopolised. Tinted UV protection. Unnaturalised antiseptic white. Nutrition. Moisture content. Meaning. Focusing." In "Pretension/Repulsion," language is broken down even further with the absences provided by asyndeton and contracted adjectives: "Sicken'd, howl'd, streak'd, spurn'd/Pluck'd, liv'd, compell'd, call'd/Clos'd, swallow'd, form'd, regain'd/Lock'd, curs'd, glow'd, discern'd." It is through this fragmentation and obscurity that the lyrics also recall Beckett's paratactical prose, undoing, disconnecting and deconstructing language in an ultimately frustrated obligation towards witnessing and alterity (Ziarek). On the other hand, the polysyndeton in "This Joke Sport Severed" overwhelms meaning whilst sounding biblical in its rhythm: "Loose and guilty and whipped/Sterility persecutes and I have plenty/Bruised and nailed and quit/Merciful and mourned and meek." Though *The Holy Bible* utilized parataxis, odd breakages and excess in its lyrics, *Journal*'s language appears less concentrated, as though struggling against a slow stifling, or a descent into silence. In "Doors Closing Slowly," "silence is not sacrifice"; the martyr figure of "Marlon J.D." stands like a statue "as he was beaten across the face"; "Virginia State Epileptic Colony" renders its patients silent ("tomorrow the necks split, there is no voice"); and "Peeled Apples" states, "the more I see, the less I scream." The wish in "All is Vanity," "I would prefer no choice/One bread one milk one food that's all/I'm confused I only want one truth/I really don't mind if I'm being lied to," can be interpreted as the necessity of rhetoric to create borders and delineate meaning in the face of an overwhelming glut of possible meaning and representation.

The extreme deconstruction of Nietzschean nihilism, a philosophy that the Manics have referenced in their music since *Generation Terrorists,* reaches its logical conclusion of silence and meaninglessness in *Journal.* The eventual falling into silence perhaps parallels a similar descent made by Nietzsche. "Judge Yr'self," a song recorded in 1995 for the *Judge Dredd* film soundtrack but which didn't see release until it was included on the *Lipstick Traces* compilation from 2003, features the Nietzsche-referencing lines, "Blessed be the blades/Blessed be the sighs/Dionysus against The Crucified." The music video, comprised largely of old video clips of the Manics, begins with a Nietzsche quote: "The devotion of the greatest is to encounter risk and danger and play dice for death." The chorus, with its commands of "Heal yr'self/Hurt yr'self/Judge yr'self," is Übermenschian, but also finds its refraction in the titular track of *Journal:* "Only a god can bruise/Only a god can soothe/Only a god reserves the right to forgive those who revile him." There is a possibility here of the conflation of the Übermensch and a traditional sense of a deity; if you yourself have become god, you must contend with the implications of your own meaninglessness. "Judge Yr'self" and "Journal for Plague Lovers" taken together imply an ultimate failure of nihilism: its own self-negation. The confusion and madness produced by this fatal flaw perhaps led to Nietzsche signing his last delusional letters as both "Dionysus" and "The Crucified" (Wolin 29). "This Joke Sport Severed" seems to express a similar loss of mooring in the lines "I endeavoured/To find the place where I became untethered." The incommensurability in both nihilism and the Judeo-Christian religions produces a vacuum, especially in the face of human cruelty and loss, and the difficult knowledge that defies witnessing and testimony. The confining concentricity of *Journal*'s universe and the full stops and ellipses permeating its language converge in a black hole as the silent scream of Munch, or Jenny Saville's *Stare*. The ultimate fall into silence of Richey Edwards produces yet another gap in *Journal for Plague Lovers*, but as Sean Gaston says of the impossible mourning for Derrida, you must begin with the gaps and "gaps move."

"This Joke Sport Severed": Journal for Plague Lovers as Missing Punchline

Though *Journal for Plague Lovers* contains dark material, it differs from *The Holy Bible* in its periods of levity, and even humour. Tracks such as "Jackie Collins Existential Question Time" and "Me and Stephen Hawking" play with the absurd, the former using an old badge slogan "Oh mummy, what's a sex pistol?" as a taunt, and the latter describing the sharing of a laugh with the famous physicist and even ending with "hahahaha (Joke)" in Richey's original journal. The idea of the joke can be related to the productive ambiguity of the archive. Jaimie Baron argues that

> the affinity between the historical archive and the joke has to do with the fundamental ambiguity of the meaning of the archival fragment as both figurative (it stands for something else as a sign of history) and literal (it gains its evidentiary power from its specificity and particularity), which lends itself not only to factual assertion but also to "misuse" and play. (112)

The resulting "glut of signification" prevents any certainty of meaning (Baron 115), even as the gaps produced by archival fragments reinforce the sense of loss (121). Works of art can be made to reproduce this ambiguity. Referencing Lacan, Darian Leader explains the relationship between jokes, language, and art:

To speak, we have to use codes imposed on us by our care-givers and their language. In this process, part of what we "mean" to say is always lost, and jokes involve a privileging of this dimension of meaning "in between the lines" that is actually sanctioned, recognized by the code itself. The code scrambles our message, but at the same time gives a place to this scrambling in the form of jokes. A joke, in this sense, is a message about the code. In the context of [...] art, what a joke and a work of art have in common here lies in this fact of a system housing a special place for the presentation of what the effects of the system are. Civilization sanctions art as a kind of message about itself, about the loss that makes it all possible. And hence, as Martin Kippenberger once pointed out, art is like a running joke. (85–86)

The losses of meaning built into language itself are thus addressed by the ambiguity of jokes. Leader's reference to Kippenberger is apposite as his work appears in the singles of *The Holy Bible,* and as the style of his work is largely built around indecipherable jokes. Gregory Williams observes that "[m]any of his works possess an aesthetic residue left behind by verbal jokes that were partially recorded within the space of the image and in the appended title" (39). Furthermore, Williams could be describing *Journal* in his account of Kippenberger's artistic milieu and its effect on the audience:

> Kippenberger is the member of the group who most thoroughly pursued the alienating effects of a work of art that provides us with an abundance of clues but no clear answers. The negativity at the heart of much of his work is partially mitigated by the initial sense of freedom granted by his open narratives. One can enjoy getting lost in the cross-references of coming up with possible thematic threads. Yet for many members of his general audience, especially those not privy to his particular sense of humour or fluent in

German, the groups of paintings and drawings can represent an excess of options, a total lack of guidance that can finally seem overwhelming. The sense of freedom is short-lived; Kippenberger's observer is subsequently struck by the lack of a coherent conceptual framework, like a joke without a punch line. (41)

The extreme intertextuality provides both an excess and a dearth of meaning, a joke without a punchline, or in Peter Lunenfeld's terms "an aesthetic of unfinish," which is more often applied to the digital world. This lack of definitive meanings has been exacerbated by Kippenberger's premature death. The problematic negotiation of meaning also speaks to the aesthetic of an artist who saw the joke as flawed in its ambiguity, yet useful to "work through his issues of failure, compromised authenticity, second-order status, etc." (Williams 47). Issues of forgone failure and the impossibility of finding truth and authenticity can be seen within the incomplete jokes and punchlines, and the ambiguous gaps of *Journal.*

In "Doors Closing Slowly," the Manics acknowledge the fraught gaps in their understanding of both *Journal*'s lyrics and their absent friend himself by using a sample from the film *The Virgin Suicides,* in which the narrator-observer voiced by Giovanni Ribisi, says, "In the end we had pieces of the puzzle, but no matter how we put them together, gaps remained, oddly shaped emptinesses mapped by what surrounded them, like countries we couldn't name." As with most of the audio samples that the Manics use in their albums, this one was precisely fitting. It evokes the plight of helpless voyeurs and perpetually stymied searchers for an undiscoverable truth, or the lay of the land, as it were. There can be no closure and no mastery, just fragments curated into an archive that forgets as much as it remembers. Derrida refers to these gaps as aporia in relation to mourning and contends that those who mourn actually bear the one who is mourned within them "like an unborn child, like a future"; however, mourners must also engage in a respectful separation from and rejection of the other, keeping the object of mourning at a distance (*Memoires* 35). As mentioned earlier, Derrida's conception of mourning maintains an impossible position of both interiorization of and separation from the other. The Manics' schizoidal consignment of their older identity could be read in the terms of a "tender rejection" even as they do bear their losses inside their later identity and work. The ongoing struggle between the different versions of themselves can be encapsulated by Gaston's impossible mourning of Derrida: "This tracing of gaps (*ecarts*) is a preface to an impossible mourning, a mourning that one must *at once* avoid and affirm" (vii). The unbridgeable gap created by belated witnessing and difficult knowledge is made even more prominent in the unfinish of *Journal*.

Notably, the table of contents page for Richey's journal is reproduced in the liner notes, but with eighteen of the twenty-eight listings excised with black felt-tip. Furthermore, there are a limited number of pages from the journal replicated in the liner notes, leaving everyone outside of the Manics with even more gaps in their knowledge. At the same time, the aporia can also be described as openings, through which yet more connections and interpretations can be made. There is a positive quality to emptiness, especially in art, where often what is missing is just as important as what is present, and where absence interrogates the feeling of loss and otherwise hidden meaning. The Manics have been making productive use of the gaps in their history throughout their career. To some extent, the apertures of intertextuality and cross-references have always been a part of the band's art, encouraging listeners to make their own creative and generative links between the pieces of politics, history, culture and philosophy strewn liberally throughout the Manics' work. Jeremy Deller's work involving the Manics, including *The Uses of Literacy,* which included fans' artistic responses to the band, and *Unconvention,* which imagined the artistic tastes of fans of the band and curated accordingly, has aptly demonstrated this creative work of intertexts and proliferation of meanings, the possible misuse and play embodied in the joke, emerging from the gaps. In many ways, these kinds of missed punchlines produce moments ripe for a Greil Marcus *Lipstick Traces*-like odyssey of intertextuality and recurrence within disparate times and spaces.

Speaking at the time of *Journal*'s release, Nicky said, "The only thing I think we've just managed to do for all our ups and downs since Richey disappeared is never appear to be trying to be like we were when he was in the band. We might have fucked up, but we never did that" (qtd in Petridis). This comment points to the same anxiety about authenticity and contriving situations that emerged as part of the process of making *Journal*. The inability of returning to an origin within the archive is underlined. *Journal* does overwhelm hermeneutics just as *The Holy Bible* overwhelmed understanding. They both ask the listener to be immersed but apart from them, taking distances and gaps as interventions into her/his comfortable, habitual perspective. And as Pitt and Britzman say, "interpretation makes narrative, but there is also something within narrative that resists its own interpretation" (759).

CHAPTER 5
Rewind, Fast Forward, or Retro-Futurism

"One day we will return, no matter how much it hurts, and it hurts."
– Manic Street Preachers, "Futurology"

Following *Journal for Plague Lovers*, Manic Street Preachers produced what they described as their "last shot at mass communication," 2010's *Postcards from a Young Man,* which led up to a second greatest hits collection called *National Treasures* and a marathon gig at the O2 Arena, at which they performed all of their singles. Speaking of the *National Treasures* concert, Nicky Wire commented, "Doing that O2 show it did feel like perhaps we could leave a lot of ... not the memories but the fucking baggage behind. [...] There is a real power in those last words of

'P.C.P.' and everything. Just the desperation in that" (qtd in Martin, "Richey" 35). Memory and forgetting continued to inform the Manics' work and hyper-reflexivity. In 2014, Nicky said,

> We'd just done [...] *Send Away the Tigers,* it was fucking everywhere [...] and there was this nagging feeling that we've done all this; that people are *still* convinced we can't be the band we were. It's a fucking powerful entity, this band. It's a joy, but it's a weight. It feels like something you can never escape from sometimes. That's my own neurosis; I'm not blaming everyone else. I spend way too much time thinking about this band. (qtd in Martin, "Regeneration" 28)

Despite promising to take a long break after the O2 gig, Manic Street Preachers released two albums over 2013 and 2014: the subdued, melancholic *Rewind the Film,* and *Futurology,* a foray into the promise and past of modernism and post-punk, which paradoxically moved the band into the fastest forward motion of their last decade. Robert Barry describes *Futurology* as "shot through with a certain kind of melancholia, with mourning for a time when other futures remained available," and Nicky said, "[i]t's got the same ridiculous ambition as *Generation Terrorists,* but it's more cultured. It has that intent, though; it's got the post-punk jaggedness of *The Holy Bible,* but it merges that with the retro-futurism we've always been obsessed with" (qtd in Martin, "Regeneration" 29). James also refers to *The Holy Bible* in his comments on *Futurology:*

> It's the first time I've been given lyrics since *The Holy Bible,* where I'd think 'I never thought I'd be writing music to a lyric like this.' [...] With 'Misguided Missile' it felt like we were trying to cram as much narrative into the song as possible, like we did on *The Holy Bible* with 'IfWhiteAmerica....', 'Misguided Missile' has four different choruses, four different lyrics-no bands do that anymore.
> (qtd in Burrows)

These references to *The Holy Bible* coincide with the familiar Cyrillic font and reversed "r's" on the cover art for *Futurology.* Tellingly, Simon Price writes: "THAT version of the Manics was back, and *Futurology* was going to be one of THOSE albums" ("A Masterpiece"). The archive fever remains a powerful force.

The lead single from *Futurology,* "Walk Me to the Bridge," is a case in point of hermeneutics exploding. Not only does it allude to Nicky's renewed sense of belief in the band after crossing the Øresund Bridge and to the art of Die Brücke, but as Price notes in his review of the album, one can't help thinking of Richey's connection to the Severn Bridge, especially in the chorus: "So long, my fatal friend/I don't need this to end/I reimagine the steps you took/Still blinded by your intellect/Walk me to the bridge Walk me to the bridge/So long my faithful friend, I don't need this." Whilst the instrumental bridge to the song recalls the exhilarating soar of the middle eight in Echo & the Bunnymen's "The Cutter," the metaphor of the bridge that cannot be crossed due to the impossibility of witnessing is reiterated. Felman and Laub discuss this impasse in relation to Albert Camus' *The Fall* and the inability to witness difficult knowledge:

> when the woman is precisely *not seen* falling off the bridge, at the moment when her fall is being *missed,* when the body strikes the water—and when history strikes—with no seeing and no hearing, with the failure of the passerby—of the historical bystander—to be a witness, the scene of history is symbolically and radically transformed. Physically and metaphorically, the bridge no longer is a bridge: a safe passage from one bank of the Seine to the other. A bridge, from now on, can always lead nowhere, end in a dead end, or fall apart, lead to an abyss, not only for the woman but for her witness, whose own life also loses its continuity, its sense, its ground and its balance. (199)

The precarity of the belated witness continues to haunt the Manics' work even as it evokes the future, and their schizoidal split in identity still operates and is made manifest in the fact that the band felt the need to release two separate records instead of the intended one. In an interview with Dan Martin, James explains that the original "plan had been to record one sprawling opus, dubbed '70 Songs Of Hatred And Failure,'" but then they came to the conclusion that "'the tracks will harm each other; it'll turn into an even more incoherent version of [...] "Know Your Enemy"'" (qtd in "Regeneration" 28–29). The Manics' insight into the dichotomy of their identity, along with the use of "harm" to describe the result of both sides meeting, is revealing.

Though the Manics were originally quite hedgy and noncommittal about the possibility of doing twentieth anniversary shows for *The Holy Bible,* it didn't seem conceivable that a band so defined by the archive and committed to its own memory would miss such an opportunity. So we waited. And thus, I found myself awake at 4am on September 26, 2014, heart racing, to purchase tickets online for all three of the *Holy Bible* shows at the Roundhouse in London, located 6, 300 kilometres away and six hours of time zone apart from my home in Winnipeg, Canada. These three Roundhouse gigs before Christmas were pregnant with the meaning of the notorious 1994 Astoria gigs played before Christmas, as well as with the three-night residency in May 2009 at the Roundhouse for their *Journal for Plague Lovers* gigs (not to mention the fact they used the Roundhouse as the set for their "A Design for Life" music video). In my own, perhaps compulsive, journey into memory work and repetition with a difference, I not only attended all three Roundhouse gigs in December 2014, but also the *Holy Bible* show at the Danforth Music Hall in Toronto in April 2015. The multiple viewings of nearly the same gig in consecutive nights do beg the question of how they can be remembered. I suppose this question only intensifies for those fans who end up seeing dozens or hundreds of shows by the same band.

    The day after arriving in London, my accompanying friend, Laura, and I managed to see the Anselm Kiefer exhibit at the Royal Academy of Arts on its last day, and with its meditations on individual and cultural memory, especially the difficult knowledge of the Holocaust and Germany's response to it, it became a perfect overture to the triptych of *Holy Bible* shows we were about to see. Looking at *Winter Landscape,* I heard the chorus of "No birds, no birds" emanating from the silent, bloodied snow. I was also reminded of the quote from Kiefer, which Nicky cited in an interview, "Ruins, for me, are the beginning. With the debris, you can construct new ideas." The enforced ruins of the monumental *Holy Bible* find their traces straight through to *Futurology,* producing as much as they preserve.

Admittedly, there are gaps in my memory of the Roundhouse gigs despite my best efforts. There are elisions and indefinite shadows—likely even false recollections—that blur them together. Then there are moments, some significant and some more trivial, that remain. As Jane Blocker writes about attempting to capture the ephemerality of performance, "[t]o write a history of performance [...] is to experience and engage with desire, desire for that which is already lost" (xii). By trying to recreate what I saw, I feel increasingly belated and conscious of the narratives, the *récits,* that I'm telling myself. Besides my memory fragments, I have a handful of notes I made after I had already travelled home and the series of photos I took. Of course there is also the shaky footage captured by others on YouTube, but these supposedly mimetic recordings never seem to correspond with my own experiences and only leave me with an uncanny combination of *déjà vu* and *jamais vu.* So, these are the moments I think I know.

Each show was prefaced by a longer wait in the queue outside the venue in our attempt to make the best estimate of the ideal ratio of waiting time to desirable places in front of the stage. In spite of the relative balminess of the London December (at home it was more likely to be −20°C than +10°C), I spent much of the time contemplating the word "chilblains," and wondering whether sitting for hours on cold pavement caused them. I also read and re-read the awning across the street that advertised "hot dogs, liquor and vintage sounds 'til 3AM" when I wasn't answering curious passersby questions about why we were all sitting outside the Roundhouse for hours wearing military gear, sailor suits, leopard print coats and boiler suits (one particular boiler suit had the very Manics slogan of "Rimbaud was a cunt" scrawled on the back).

Due to a particularly strict security guard who made Laura check her camera before entering, I spent the first gig separated from her on the stage right side, listening to the pre-show Erol Alkan DJ set and the conversation between two fans discussing their favourite Manics records (incidentally, neither favoured *The Holy Bible,* but instead loved *Generation Terrorists* and *Send Away the Tigers).* The seamless DJ mix was an appropriate precursor, taking in the obvious post-punk influences on *The Holy Bible*—Public Image Ltd., Magazine, Joy Division, Wire—as well the less obvious ones like The Sound, Grauzone, Cabaret Voltaire, Siouxsie and the Banshees, and Killing

Joke. Alkan cleverly added tracks from motorik and post-punk artists that informed *Futurology,* the most current incarnation of THAT version of the band: Simple Minds' "I Travel," Kraftwerk's "Uranium," David Bowie's "V-2 Schneider," Neu's "Super," Orchestral Manoeuvres in the Dark's "Taking Sides Again," and Echo & the Bunnymen's "The Cutter." I should add that this mix was repeated on the third night, and on the first night it didn't make it to "I Travel" before the lights went out and the Chemical Brothers' remix of "Faster" began. The crowd chanted "it's so damn easy to cave in" just before the band made their way to the stage, which had been draped in *Apocalypse Now* red light and camouflage netting. James wore the dark navy sailor suit, Nicky wore the camouflage, and Sean wore the Russian beret behind a drum kit emblazoned with the CCCP logo used at the time of *The Holy Bible.* I know I remained overly conscious of the carrier bag holding my vinyl copies of *The Firstborn is Dead, Scott Walker Sings Songs from His TV Series,* and *To Bring You My Love,* which I had unthinkingly purchased a few hours earlier in the Camden Stables Market, and then spent the gig either clutching them to my body, or trying to wedge them between my numb feet. The first three songs flowed into one another, only punctuated by the appropriate audio samples as intros, with the audience swept up by the intensity and near surreality that this was actually happening live within metres of their faces. The fact that the Manics were performing without their regular accompanying musicians for this set was visually striking and affective; they seemed both strong and vulnerable. Notwithstanding James' battle with a "Christmas bug" that was supposedly affecting his vocals, the only indication he wasn't on full form was his allowing the audience to pick up any missed bits of chorus and his general lack of movement away from his microphone. In other words, there weren't any backward kick spins. To alleviate the seriousness and bleakness of the content, there were a few of the obligatory remarks of gallows humour from Nicky like "Here's 'Mausoleum' the feel-good hit of the winter" and "Richey wrote 'I T'd them' instead of 'tossed off' because he was such a polite boy."

Erol Alkan's remix of *Futurology*'s "Europa Geht Durch Mich" played through the intermission, indicating the break between sets and band identities, as the Manics changed out of their *Holy Bible* uniforms and regained their regular backing musicians. The first song of the second set was "Motorcycle Emptiness," and all I can remember is leaping up and down, occasionally belting the words into the air as I tilted my head back and caught a glimpse of the dizzying, concentric roof above and the singing fan in a sailor suit behind me. I also remember trying to time my jumping to coincide with the man next to me, so that I didn't keep colliding with his elbow. I remember nerdily singing along to the guitar parts of the brilliant instrumental "Dreaming a City (Hughesovka)," the *Futurology* track that manages to encapsulate the hope and failure of both industry and ideology in the present-day Ukrainian city of Donetsk, a city that represents the major upheavals of the twentieth century and beyond. I recall my excitement and disbelief in watching actress Nina Hoss sing her parts for "Europa Geht Durch Mich" directly in front of me as the electronic grind borrowed from Simple Minds' "70 Cities as Love Brings the Fall" pulsed in the background. I remember Nicky warning the audience that this was the last time he would ever be singing "Divine Youth," and that he was doing it to help out the ailing James. In a nod to the Astoria gigs, James sang Wham!'S "Last Christmas" and segued into "A Design for Life." Part way through the first half of "A Design for Life" I was hoisted into the air on the shoulders of a stranger behind me. I remember the heady mixture of looking around at the rest of the people packed onto the floor below me and the soaring music; unfortunately, security ensured that I had to come down soon after I had been lifted.

Even though I had made sure that I hadn't purchased any large items this time, the Tuesday gig was much more physically uncomfortable, my face often diving into the purple polyester-clad back of a fan in front of me, my head being punched by a female fan behind me who was vigorously pointing at Nicky whilst I was watching James, and my back being used as a tripod for the man filming the gig from behind me. This time the pre-show DJ mix was from Andrew Weatherall, and though appropriate in its mood, the music itself was unrecognizable to me. I remember Nicky complaining about having left his make-up behind at the hotel, wishing Simon Price was there to assist with this oversight, and making do with gold star stickers plastered to his face. I remember James saying his voice hadn't been great the night before, the audience shouting "No," and his resolute "Yes, it was." I remember Nicky making a comment about knowing *The Holy Bible* was good when it wasn't nominated for the Mercury Prize. I remember James requesting applause for Richey, and then requesting more. I remember Georgia Ruth appearing to sing on "Divine Youth," which she did again on the last night. I also recall James singing a soft acoustic version of "Anthem for a Lost Cause" before the rest of the band came back for the second half. And it rained that night as we exited the venue.

Before the last show, we visited the Kevin Cummins *Assassinated Beauty* photography exhibit of Manic Street Preachers at Proud Camden, a few blocks away from the Roundhouse. The majority of the photos were from before Richey's departure, and old Manics songs played in the one-room gallery space; it provided a strange nostalgic refuge to complement the memories being made down the street for the past two nights. It was also a reminder of the excessive visuality of the Manics, and the archive of images they amassed throughout their career, not only documented by Kevin Cummins in the book that accompanied the exhibit, but also in Mitch Ikeda's *Forever Delayed,* and Nicky Wire's *Death of a Polaroid.* By the third Roundhouse show, it felt like we were meant to prepare by singing "Let's Go to War," the Manics fan morale booster from *Futurology,* which can put you in the correct mindset of steely determination to endure through deadened limbs, the mental and vocal strain of screaming along to the difficult *Holy Bible* lyrics, the sad state of the uniform you wear every night in solidarity with the band and other fans, the jumps and punches that more often than not punish your knuckles and sternum with the bounce of the camera around your neck. When the drum kit came apart after the first few songs, Nicky was prompted to continue his goading of the rest of the band to destroy their instruments in Astoria fashion. I also remember a small moment in which James made an error at the point of "Hitler reprised in the worm of your soul" in "Archives of Pain," but as the crowd carried on correctly without him, he just shook his head slightly, made a small smile, and continued into the next line. This was the only gig of the three in which the band played "Walk Me to the Bridge," and I remember feeling a euphoric chill run through me as the chorus kicked in. For "You Love Us," James invited Therapy?'S Andy Cairns to the stage to add even more guitar power to the all-out chaos. There was a sense of relief and achievement that we had all made it through these shows, band and fans. James ended the show with "We've been the Manics, and you've been fucking mega," and as "A Design for Life" played out, golden confetti filled the air like a shimmering cloud, landing and sticking to the sweaty crowd like a celebratory anointment. I found pieces of confetti about my person well into the following day.

Much of the rest of these gigs are enfolded into each other in some sort of ritualized blur. I remain an unreliable witness in spite of, and perhaps because of, the repetition. The best I can recollect are the abstractions of how it felt—cathartic, galvanizing, maddening, utterly exhausting. It is not often that a live gig can drain you both mentally and physically, but the engagement between the Manics and their fans for these shows proved the mind and body dynamic continue to inform the band's work.

The Holy Bible experience didn't quite end with the final Roundhouse gig. We also opted to attend British Sea Power's Christmas Krankenhaus club night in Brighton on the Friday night.

Despite the numerous differences between British Sea Power and Manic Street Preachers, bands who toured with each other, there still seems to exist some strange affinity of cultishness, out-of-step, intertextual art, and the potential for dominating all facets of fans' lives. Surreal doesn't quite describe the organized chaos of the night. I do remember that an opening band sang a song featuring the lines "Release the ferrets"; that a man won a stalk of Brussels sprouts after playing a quiz guessing cover versions played by a marimba duo; that members of British Sea Power performed Krautrock Karaoke for an appropriately infinite time (it felt like a Damo Suzuki wormhole had opened up as band members were passed through the crowd, hanging vertically upside down). The British Sea Power set itself inspired a frenzy that I would think is unrivalled at a hardcore gig. Lead singer Yan Wilkinson stared with an almost catatonic madness out on the crowd of pushing, ecstatic bodies. I don't think I've ever quite felt like my femurs might break in half at a gig; if I hadn't been so numbed and high on adrenaline, I might have felt more concern about being right at the front of the stage, repeatedly sent sprawling over the monitor, half-full beer bottles, and a particularly enthusiastic fan in laddered tights who was now sitting on the stage shaking a tambourine. The entire night ended with a DJ set from Simon Price, and it was at this point that a Manics fan wearing cat ears approached us, clocking my *Holy Bible* t-shirt from the Roundhouse gigs. She had attended all of the Roundhouse shows as well, and wondered if we had requested that Simon play something from the Manics. To be honest, I was still attempting to collect pieces of my shattered brain and rest my sweaty ruined body, and couldn't even contemplate asking for anything, or the thought of having to leave the venue and walk back up the hill to the Brighton train station for the first train out in the morning. She eventually requested "Faster" and so we found ourselves mad on Baileys, cider and sheer bruised exhaustion, dancing in the aftershock and proving the strength of that chorus: your blazing mind can truly overtake your broken body in a transcending rush. The next day Laura and I discovered that we both had perverse souvenirs of bruises, six inches in diameter on each thigh. Bruised and soothed all in one night.

The April gig in Toronto came as a surprise since a Manics tour to North America is always a rarity. This time it was *Jean-Michel Basquiat: Now's the Time* at the Art Gallery of Ontario, rather than Anselm Kiefer at the Royal Academy, but the exhibition proved to be just as evocative and appropriate as a prelude to seeing *The Holy Bible* live. Basquiat's engagements with racial violence and inequality in the USA, perhaps most poignantly in the painting *Irony of a Negro Policeman,* was heightened by the recent unrest in Ferguson and the Black Lives Matter movement, as well as reinforcing the enduring power and tragedy of "Ifwhiteamerica" I also couldn't help but stop at the black void of *To Repel Ghosts* and reflect on *Lifeblood.*

The Toronto show itself felt more subdued than the run at the

Roundhouse. The band chose to speak in between the opening three songs this time, breaking some of the intensity, and the crowd seemed to stay quite reverently still through *The Holy Bible* set. Someone screamed Nicky's name, and he responded with a grin, a thumbs-up, and a small "Hello." In the interval, during which he never actually left the stage, James performed acoustic versions of "This Sullen Welsh Heart" and "Small Black Flowers That Grow in the Sky." I remember him making an analogy between Wales' relationship with England and Canada's relationship to the United States, and I also remember softly singing along with ragged breath to "Small Black Flowers," thankful that I was finally witnessing it live. I do remember that by the time the band played "You Love Us," the woman next to me had grabbed my shoulder in sheer excitement as we jumped in unison, and the second half overall seemed to free the audience to respond more physically. All in all, it was a shorter show than the ones at the Roundhouse; the Manics hadn't taken their back-up musicians with them for this tour, so it felt like they bore some extra weight into their second half. The compression of their time on this tour also forced them leave the venue more quickly than usual.

Surprising to me, only after this gig did I experience a sense of loss. The preclusion and finality of being unable to see *The Holy Bible* performed in full again was a bittersweet realization. Then again, so much of the way Manic Street Preachers' art functions is with this bittersweetness. They're always ending, and they're always becoming, a dialectic at a standstill.

In Emily Mackay's *NME* feature about the rehearsals for the twentieth anniversary *Holy Bible* gigs, she quotes James' description of the album, the "feeling of becoming," to depict the feeling of the rehearsals themselves ("Holy" 35). The idea of becoming speaks to the significance of *The Holy Bible* as an archive of identity for the band to return to, but it also explains the impossibility of closures and the persistence and productivity of gaps. After the extreme embodiment recorded in *The Holy Bible* and *Journal for Plague*

Lovers, it is the absence of a body that has created the strongest archival impression. *The Holy Bible* remains Manic Street Preachers' *Gesamtkunstwerk,* a promise to a future that never fully arrives and can never fully be witnessed. In the bonus material of the documentary *No Manifesto,* Sean and Nicky are shown having an amicable argument over what kind of musical art is truly memorable and will ultimately stand the test of time, Sean on the side of classical music, Nicky taking that of twentieth-century popular music. At one point, Nicky says, "There will always be *The Holy Bible.*" I couldn't agree more.

Works Cited

Ahmed, Sara, and Jackie Stacey, eds. *Thinking Through the Skin.* London: Routledge, 2001. Print.

Anzieu, Didier. *The Skin Ego.* Trans. Chris Turner. New Haven: Yale UP, 1989. Print.

Anzieu, Didier, et al. *Psychic Envelopes.* Trans. Daphne Briggs. London: Karnac, 1990. Print.

Baron, Jaimie. *The Archive Effect: Found Footage and the Audiovisual Experience of History.* Abingdon: Routledge, 2014. Print.

Barry, Robert. "Bleeding Edge: Nicky Wire on Futures, Futurism and Futurology." *The Quietus.* 27 May 2014. Web.

Benjamin, Walter. *The Origin of German Tragic Drama.* Trans. John Osborne. London: NLB, 1977. Print.

———. "Paralipomena to 'On the Concept of History.'" *Selected Writings Volume 4: 1938–1940.* Trans. Edmund Jephcott et al. Ed. Howard Eiland and Michael W. Jennings. Cambridge: The Belknapp P of Harvard UP, 2003. Print.

Benthien, Claudia. *Skin: On the Cultural Border Between Self and the World.* Trans. Thomas Dunlap. New York: Columbia UP, 2002. Print.

Birnbaum, Daniel, and Anders Olsson. "An Interview with Jacques Derrida on the Limits of Digestion." *e-flux journal* 2 (2009). Web.

Blanke, Olaf, and Christine Mohr. "Out-of-Body Experience, Heautoscopy, and Autoscopic Hallucination of Neurological Origin: Implications for Neurocognitive Mechanisms of Corporeal Awareness and Self-Consciousness." *Brain Research Reviews* 50 (2005): 184–99. Web.

Blocker, Jane. *What the Body Cost: Desire, History, and Performance.*

Minneapolis: U of Minnesota P, 2004. Print.

Bordo, Susan. "Anorexia Nervosa: Psychopathology as the Crystallization of Culture." *Cooking, Eating, Thinking: Transformative Philosophies of Food.* Ed. Deane W. Curtin and Lisa M. Heldke. Bloomington: Indiana UP, 1992. 28–55. Print.

Boswell, Matthew. *Holocaust Impiety in Literature, Popular Music and Film.* Basingstoke: Palgrave, 2012. Print.

Brault, Pascale-Anne, and Michael Naas. "To Reckon with the Dead: Jacques Derrida's Politics of Mourning." *The Work of Mourning.* Chicago: The U of Chicago P, 2001. Print.

Britt, Brian. *Walter Benjamin and the Bible.* New York: Continuum, 1996. Print.

Britzman, Deborah P. *Lost Subjects, Contested Objects: Toward a Psychoanalytic Inquiry of Learning.* Albany: SUNY Press, 1998. Print.

Burrows, Marc. "DiS Meets the Manic Street Preachers." *Drowned in Sound.* 13 Jul. 2014. Web.

Cameron, Keith. "Don't Give Up the Deity Job." *NME Originals: Manic Street Preachers* 1.4: 72–74. Originally published in *New Musical Express* (Aug. 27, 1994). Print.

Cave, Nick. "A Box for Black Paul." *From Her to Eternity.* Mute, 1984. CD.

Chomsky, Noam. "Vain Hopes, False Dreams." *Z Magazine* (September 1992). Web.

Cruickshank, Ruth. "Humans, Eating and Thinking Animals? Structuralism's Leftovers." *Contemporary French and Francophone Studies* 16.4 (2012): 543–51. *Taylor & Francis Online.* Web.

Cummins, Kevin. *Assassinated Beauty: Photographs of Manic Street Preachers.* London: Faber, 2014. Print.

Day, Gail. *Dialectical Passions: Negation in Postwar Art Theory.* New York: Columbia UP, 2011. Print.

De Bolle, Leen. "Preface: Desire and Schizophrenia." *Deleuze and Psychoanalysis: Philosophical Essays on Deleuze's Debate with Psychoanalysis.* Ed. Leen De Bolle. Leuven: Leuven UP, 2010. Ebook.

Deller, Jeremy. *The Uses of Literacy.* London: Book Works, 2004. Print.

de Man, Paul. "The Rhetoric of Temporality." *Blindness and Insight: Essays in the Rhetoric of Contemporary Criticism.* 2nd ed. Minneapolis: U of Minnesota P, 1983. Print.

Derrida, Jacques. *Archive Fever: A Freudian Impression.* Trans. Eric Prenowitz. Chicago: The U of Chicago P, 1996. Print.

―――. *Memoires for Paul de Man.* Trans. Cecile Lindsay, Jonathan Culler, and Eduardo Cadava. New York: Columbia UP, 1986. Print.

———. *The Work of Mourning*. Ed. Pascale-Anne Brault and Michael Naas. Chicago: The U of Chicago P, 2001. Print.

The Dialogues with Solzhenitsyn. Dir. Alexander Sokurov. Facets, 1998. DVD.

Doherty, Niall. "The Great Plague." *The Fly* (June 2009): 21–24. Print.

Ellmann, Maud. *The Hunger Artists: Starving, Writing, and Imprisonment.* Cambridge: Harvard UP, 1993. Print.

Failler, Angela. "Narrative Skin Repair: Bearing Witness to Mediatized Representations of Self-Harm." *Skin, Culture and Psychoanalysis*. Ed. Sheila L. Cavanagh, Angela Failler, and Rachel Alpha Johnston Hurst. Basingstoke: Palgrave, 2013. 167–87. Print.

Felman, Shoshana, and Dori Laub. *Testimony: Crisis of Witnessing in Literature, Psychoanalysis, and History*. New York: Routledge, 1992. Print.

Foster, Hal. "An Archival Impulse." *October* 110 (2004): 3–22. *JSTOR*. Web.

Gaston, Sean. *The Impossible Mourning of Jacques Derrida.* London: Continuum, 2006. Print.

Gillen, Kieron. *Phonogram: Rue Britannia.* Illus. Jamie McKelvie. Berkeley: Image Comics, 2007. Print.

"Glastonbury's the Big One, It's the Daddy." *New Musical Express* (June 232007):19–22. Print.

The Gospel of Us. Dir. Dave McKean. Perf. Michael Sheen, Matthew Aubrey, Nigel Barrett. Soda, 2012. DVD.

Gubar, Susan. *Poetry After Auschwitz: Remembering What One Never Knew.* Bloomington: Indiana UP, 2006. Print.

Harris, John. "Freed from the Century with Nothing But Memory: Everything Must Go in Its Time." Liner notes. Manic Street Preachers. *Everything Must*

Go: 10th Anniversary Deluxe Edition. Columbia Records, 2006. CD.

Herr, Cheryl. "The Erratics of Irishness: Schizophrenia, Racism, and *Finnegans Wake.*" *Cultural Studies of James Joyce.* Ed. R. Brandon Kershner. European Joyce Studies. Vol. 15. Amsterdam: Rodopi, 2003. 117–36. Print.

Hewitt, Kim. *Mutilating the Body: Identity in Blood and Ink.* Madison: U of Wisconsin P, 1997. Print.

Huyssen, Andreas. *Present Pasts: Urban Palimpsests and the Politics of Memory.* Redwood City: Stanford UP, 2003. Print.

———. *Twilight Memories: Marking Time in a Culture of Amnesia.* New York: Routledge, 1995. Print.

Ihanus, Juhani. "The Archive and Psychoanalysis: Memories and Histories Toward Futures." *International Forum of Psychoanalysis* 16 (2007): 119–31. *Taylor & Francis Online.* Web.

Ikeda, Mitch. *Forever Delayed, Photographs of the Manic Street Preachers.* London: Vision On, 2002. Print.

Jameson, Fredric. *The Political Unconscious: The Narrative as a Socially Symbolic Act.* Ithaca: Cornell UP, 1981. Print.

"'Journal for Plague Lovers,' Track by Track." *New Musical Express* (May 162009):30. Print.

Kilby, Jane. "Carved in Skin: Bearing Witness to Self-Harm." *Thinking Through the Skin.* Ed. Sara Ahmed and Jackie Stacey. London: Routledge, 2001. Print.

Kristeva, Julia. *Powers of Horror: An Essay on Abjection.* Trans. Leon S. Roudiez. New York: Columbia UP, 1982. Print.

Lafrance, Marc. "From the Skin Ego to the Psychic Envelope: An Introduction to the Work of Didier Anzieu." *Skin, Culture and Psychoanalysis.* Ed. Sheila

L. Cavanagh, Angela Failler, and Rachel Alpha Johnston Hurst. Basingstoke: Palgrave, 2013. 16–44. Print.

Leader, Darian. *Stealing the Mona Lisa: What Art Stops Us From Seeing*. New York: Counterpoint, 2002. Print.

Lehrer, Erica, Cynthia E. Milton, and Monica Eileen Patterson. *Curating Difficult Knowledge: Violent Pasts in Public Places*. Basingstoke: Palgrave, 2011. Print.

Lintott, Sheila. "Sublime Hunger: A Consideration of Eating Disorders Beyond Beauty." *Hypatia* 18.4 (2003): 65–86. *JSTOR*. Web.

Lunenfeld, Peter. "Unfinished Business." *The Digital Dialectic: New Essays on New Media*. Ed. Peter Lunenfeld. Cambridge: MIT Press, 1999. 6–23. Print.

Lynskey, Dorian. *33 Revolutions Per Minute: A History of Protest Songs, from Billie Holiday to Green Day*. New York: Ecco, 2011. Print.

―――. "A Redesign for Life." *Q Magazine* (March 2001): 93–100. Print.

Mackay, Emily. "The Holy Bible: Inside the Live Rehearsals." *New Musical Express* (December 2014): 34–37. Print.

―――. "Richey's Final Mystery." *New Musical Express* (May 162009):25–29. Print.

Maconie, Stuart. "Everything Must Grow Up." *Q Magazine* (October 1998): 98–101. Print.

―――. "We Shall Overcome." *Select* (July 1996): 82–91. Print.

Manic Street Preachers. *Everything Must Go: 10th Anniversary Edition.* Sony BMG, 2006. CD.

―――. *Forever Delayed: Manic Street Preachers Greatest Hits.* Sony, 2002. CD.

―――. *Futurology: Deluxe Book Edition.* Sony, 2014. CD.

———. *Generation Terrorists.* Columbia Records, 1992. CD.

———. *God Save the Manics.* Manic Street Preachers, 2005. CD.

———. *Gold Against the Soul.* Columbia Records, 1993. CD.

———. *The Holy Bible: 10th Anniversary Edition.* Columbia Records, 2004. CD.

———. *Journal for Plague Lovers: Deluxe Book Edition.* Sony, 2008. CD.

———. *Know Your Enemy.* Sony, 2001. CD.

———. *Lifeblood.* Sony, 2004. CD.

———. *Lipstick Traces: A Secret History of Manic Street Preachers.* Sony, 2003. CD

———. "A Note from the Band." 4N ov. 2008. Email.

———. *Postcards from a Young Man: Deluxe Book Edition.* Sony, 2010. CD.

_____. *Rewind the Film: Deluxe Book Edition*. Sony, 2013. CD.

_____. *Send Away the Tigers*. Sony, 2007. CD.

_____. *This is My Truth Tell Me Yours*. Sony, 1998. CD.

Manic Street Preachers: Shadows & Words. Dir. Douglas Hart. Channel 4. 17 May 2009. Television.

Marcus, Greil. *Lipstick Traces: A Secret History of the Twentieth Century*. 1989. Cambridge: Harvard UP, 2003. Print.

Martin, Dan. "' Richey Started Doubting Everything. From Feeling Indestructible, It All Started to Fade Away.'" *New Musical Express* (August 162014):30–35. Print.

_____. "Regeneration Terrorists." *New Musical Express* (July 262014):26–29. Print.

McLane, Janice. "The Voice on the Skin: Self-Mutilation and Merleau-Ponty's

Theory of Language." *Hypatia* 11.4 (1996): 107–119. *JSTOR.* Web.

Meagher, Michelle. "Jenny Saville and a Feminist Aesthetics of Disgust." *Hypatia* 18.4 (2003): 23–41. *JSTOR.* Web.

No Manifesto: A Film About Manic Street Preachers. Dir. Elizabeth Marcus. Wibbly Wobbly, 2014. DVD.

"Nothing's Ever Gonna Replace Richey." *New Musical Express* (Jan. 29, 2005): 31. Print.

Owens, Craig. "The Allegorical Impulse: Toward a Theory of Postmodernism." *October* 12 (1980): 67–86. *JSTOR.* Web.

Petridis, Alexis. "This Album Could Seriously Damage Us." *Guardian.* Guardian News and Media Limited, 8 May 2009. Web.

Pitt, Alice, and Deborah Britzman. "Speculations on Qualities of Difficult Knowledge in Teaching and Learning: An Experiment in Psychoanalytic

Research." *Qualitative Studies in Education* 16.6 (2003): 755–76. *Taylor & Francis Online.* Web.

Power, Martin. *Nailed to History: The Story of Manic Street Preachers.* London: Omnibus, 2012. Print.

Price, Simon. *Everything: A Book About Manic Street Preachers.* London: Virgin, 1999. Print.

———. "A Masterpiece: Simon Price on Manic Street Preachers' Futurology." *The Quietus.* 3 July 2014. Web.

Reynolds, Simon. *Rip It Up and Start Again: Postpunk 1978–1984.* New York: Penguin, 2005. Print.

Richter, Gerhard. "Acts of Memory and Mourning: Derrida and the Fictions of Anteriority." *Memory: Histories, Theories, Debates.* Ed. Susannah Radstone and Bill Schwarz. New York: Fordham UP, 2010. Print.

Sass, Louis A. *Madness and Modernism: Insanity in Light of Modern Art,*

Literature, and Thought. Cambridge: Harvard UP, 1992. Print.

Shaw, William. "The Long Goodbye." *Q Magazine* (December 2006): 76–84. Print.

Sontag, Susan. "The Aesthetics of Silence." *Styles of Radical Will.* New York: Picador, 2002. Print.

_____. *Regarding the Pain of Others.* New York: Picador, 2003. Print.

Tambling, Jeremy. *Allegory.* The New Critical Idiom. London: Routledge, 2009. Print.

"'We Sanctified the Single as a Holy Phenomenon.'" *New Musical Express* (Oct. 82011):24–27. Print.

Williams, Gregory. "Jokes Interrupted: Martin Kippenberger's Receding Punch Line." *Martin Kippenberger.* Ed. Doris Krystof and Jessica Morgan. London: Tate, 2006. Print.

Williams, Simon. "Revelation Terrorists." Rev. of *The Holy Bible* by Manic Street Preachers. *NME Originals: Manic Street Preachers* 1.4: 76. Originally published in *New Musical Express* (August 27, 1994): 37. Print.

Wire, Nicky. *Death of the Polaroid: A Manics Family Album.* London: Faber, 2001. Print.

Wolin, Richard. *The Seduction of Unreason: The Intellectual Romance with Fascism from Nietzsche to Postmodernism.* Princeton: Princeton UP, 2004. Print.

Ziarek, Ewa Płonowska. *The Rhetoric of Failure: Deconstruction of Skepticism, Reinvention of Modernism.* Albany: State University of New York Press, 1996. Print.

Selected Bibliography

Ahmed, Sara, and Jackie Stacey, eds. *Thinking Through the Skin.* London: Routledge, 2001. Print.

Anzieu, Didier, et al. *Psychic Envelopes.* Trans. Daphne Briggs. London: Karnac, 1990. Print.

Baron, Jaimie. *The Archive Effect: Found Footage and the Audiovisual Experience of History.* Abingdon: Routledge, 2014. Print.

Benjamin, Walter. *The Origin of German Tragic Drama.* Trans. John Osborne. London: NLB, 1977. Print.

Blanchot, Maurice. *The Writing of the Disaster.* Trans. Ann Smock. Lincoln: U of Nebraska P, 1995. Print.

Britzman, Deborah P. *Lost Subjects, Contested Objects: Toward a Psychoanalytic Inquiry of Learning.* Albany: SUNY Press, 1998. Print.

Boswell, Matthew. *Holocaust Impiety in Literature, Popular Music and Film.* Basingstoke: Palgrave, 2012. Print.

Crawford, Anwen. *Hole's Live Through This.* New York: Continuum, 2014. Print. 331/3.

Cummins, Kevin. *Assassinated Beauty: Photographs of Manic Street Preachers.* London: Faber, 2014. Print.

de Man, Paul. "The Rhetoric of Temporality." *Blindness and Insight: Essays in the Rhetoric of Contemporary Criticism.* 2nd ed. Minneapolis: U of Minnesota P, 1983. Print.

Derrida, Jacques. *Archive Fever: A Freudian Impression.* Trans. Eric Prenowitz. Chicago: The U of Chicago P, 1996. Print.

Dyhouse, Carol. *Girl Trouble: Panic and Progress in the History of Young Women.* London: Zed, 2013. Print.

Felman, Shoshana, and Dori Laub. *Testimony: Crisis of Witnessing in*

Literature, Psychoanalysis, and History. New York: Routledge, 1992. Print.

Foster, Dawn. *Lean Out.* London: Repeater, 2016. Print.

Gilroy, Paul. *Ain't No Black in the Union Jack: The Cultural Politics of Race and Nation.* London: Hutchinson, 1987. Print.

Hoggart, Richard. *The Uses of Literacy: Aspects of Working Class Life.* London: Transaction, 1958. Print.

Jones, Rhian E. *Clampdown: Pop-Cultural Wars on Class and Gender.* Winchester: Zer0, 2013. Print.

Kelman, James. *How Late It Was, How Late.* London: Secker & Warburg, 1994. Print.

Kristeva, Julia. *Powers of Horror: An Essay on Abjection.* Trans. Leon S. Roudiez. New York: Columbia UP, 1982. Print.

Lynskey, Dorian. *33 Revolutions Per Minute: A History of Protest Songs, from Billie Holiday to Green Day.* New York: Ecco, 2011. Print.

Meštrović, Stjepan Gabriel. *The Balkanisation of the West: The Confluence of Postmodernism and Postcommunism.* London: Routledge, 1994. Print.

Middles, Mick. *Manic Street Preachers.* London: Omnibus, 1999. Print.

Milne, Seumas. *The Enemy Within: The Secret War Against the Miners.* London: Verso, 1994. Print.

Niven, Alex. *Oasis' Definitely Maybe.* London: Continuum, 2014. Print. 331/3.

Noyes, Benjamin. *Malign Velocities: Accelerationism and Capitalism.* Winchester: Zer0, 2014. Print.

Nuttall, Jeff. *Bomb Culture.* London: Paladin, 1968. Print.

Owens, Craig. "The Allegorical Impulse: Toward a Theory of Postmodernism." *October* 12 (1980): 67–86. *JSTOR.* Web.

Power, Nina. *One Dimensional Woman.* Winchester: Zer0, 2009. Print.

Price, Simon. *Everything (A Book About Manic Street Preachers).* London: Virgin Books, 1999. Print.

Pyzik, Agata. *Poor but Sexy: Culture Clashes in Europe East and West.* Winchester: Zer0, 2014. Print.

Sass, Louis A. *Madness and Modernism: Insanity in Light of Modern Art, Literature, and Thought.* Cambridge: Harvard UP, 1992. Print.

Savage, Jon. *Teenage: The Creation of Youth: 1875–1945.* London: Chatto & Windus, 2008. Print.

Sontag, Susan. *Regarding the Pain of Others.* New York: Picador, 2003. Print.

Turner, Alwyn. *A Classless Society: Britain in the 1990s.* London: Aurum, 2013. Print.

Welsh, Irvine. *Trainspotting.* London: Secker & Warburg, 1993. Print.

Wolin, Richard. *The Seduction of Unreason: The Intellectual Romance with Fascism from Nietzsche to Postmodernism.* Princeton: Princeton UP, 2004. Print.

Repeater Books

is dedicated to the creation of a new reality. The landscape of twenty-first-century arts and letters is faded and inert, riven by fashionable cynicism, egotistical self-reference and a nostalgia for the recent past. Repeater intends to add its voice to those movements that wish to enter history and assert control over its currents, gathering together scattered and isolated voices with those who have already called for an escape from Capitalist Realism. Our desire is to publish in every sphere and genre, combining vigorous dissent and a pragmatic willingness to succeed where messianic abstraction and quiescent co-option have stalled: abstention is not an option: we are alive and we don't agree.

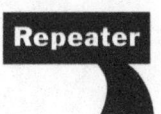

Index

A

Abjection, *222, 250, 293, 312, 324, 327, 396, 398, 461, 492, 495, 496, 499, 500, 502, 521, 530, 575*

Adam and the Ants, *472*

Adolescence, *10, 13, 14, 16, 18, 19, 21, 24, 25, 27, 29, 30, 46, 55, 56, 66, 68, 70, 73, 74, 76, 78, 80, 81, 84, 85, 87, 89, 98, 146, 148, 184, 186, 187, 189, 191, 193, 195, 197, 199, 202, 203, 205, 207, 222, 225, 227, 229, 242, 260, 324, 341, 365, 393, 419*

Adorno, Theodor, *233*

Agamben, Giorgio, *285*

Ageyev, M., *354, 370*

Anohni, *430*

Alice in Chains, *222*

Alice (Lewis Carroll), *117, 404*

Alighieri, Dante, *168, 239, 307, 346, 354, 412, 577, 580*

Alkan, Erol, *604, 605*

Allegory, *468, 471, 472, 474, 476, 478, 481, 483, 485, 487, 489, 517, 527, 573*

Allitt, Beverley, *476*

Alzheimer's, *523*

Améry, Jean, *275*

Amin, Idi, *476*

Amis, Martin, *384, 407*

Amos, Tori, *187*

Androgyny, *191, 193, 195, 197, 199, 202, 391, 575*

Anorexia, *37, 48, 56, 58, 73, 181, 184, 186, 187, 189, 312, 327, 346, 404, 415, 449, 466, 472, 495, 496, 499, 500, 502, 505*

Antoinette, Marie, *115*

Antony and the Johnsons, *291*

Apocalypse Now, *604*

Aragon, Louis, *290*

Archive, *250, 443, 446, 449, 450, 452, 453, 456, 457, 460, 461, 463, 466, 468, 471, 472, 474, 476, 478, 481, 483, 485, 487, 489, 492, 495, 496, 499, 500, 502, 505, 506, 509, 510, 512, 513, 516, 517, 520, 521, 523, 527, 530, 532, 534, 536, 538, 540, 542, 543, 546, 547, 549, 552, 555, 556, 558, 561, 564, 565, 567, 571, 572, 573, 575, 577, 580, 582, 583, 584, 587, 588, 590, 591, 594, 596, 597, 599, 601, 604, 605, 607, 609, 612, 615*

Arendt, Hannah, *151, 266*

Aristotle, *391*

Army of Lovers, *199*

Aronofsky, Darren, *315*

Athey, Ron, *334, 335*

Atwood, Margaret, *132*

Austin, Craig, *199, 202*

B

Bailie, Stuart, *48, 55, 56, 58, 63, 113, 161, 166, 236, 329, 386*

Bale, Christian, *346, 556*

Ballard, J. G., *153, 238, 239, 250, 277, 337, 349, 351, 371, 393, 396, 398, 399, 400, 496*

Banks, Iain, *229*

Barbie, Klaus, *285*

Barker, Clive, *220*

Baron, Jaimie, *474, 584*

Baroque, *478, 481, 483*

Basquiat, Jean-Michel, *612*

Bataille, Georges, *487*

Battle of the Boyne, *245*

Baudelaire, Charles, *229, 348, 381*

Baudrillard, Jean, *163, 304*

Bauhaus, *53*

BBC (British Broadcasting Corporation), *16, 408*

Beackon, Derek, *161*
Beckett, Andy, *163*
Beckett, Samuel, *577, 582*
Beat Generation, *53, 80, 348*
Beatles, The, *335*
Beautiful South, The, *516*
Bedaux, Charles, *157, 158*
Belsen, *293*
　See also Holocaust,
Benjamin, Walter, *456, 474, 476, 478, 481, 483, 558*
Bevan, Aneurin, *543*
Bible, The, *130, 315, 407, 408, 411, 412, 456, 556*
Bin Laden, Osama, *430*
Bird, Phil, *16*
Birdland, *364*
Birthday Party, The, *460, 461*
Black Lives Matter, *113, 612*
Blackwood, *4, 197*

Blair, Tony, *21, 37, 64, 102, 104, 136, 430*
Bloc Party, *393*
Blocker, Jane, *601*
Blues, *108*
Blur, *40, 222, 415, 426*
Bon Jovi, *43*
Boo Radleys, The, *425*
Boss, Hugo, *157*
Boswell, Matthew, *150, 259, 260, 262, 412, 487*
Bowie, David, *332, 334, 335, 337, 460, 604*
Bradfield, James Dean, *7, 18, 19, 36, 39, 40, 44, 46, 48, 51, 89, 96, 104, 109, 115, 120, 126, 134, 136, 138, 140, 142, 151, 153, 161, 168, 178, 197, 246, 274, 281, 289, 340, 343, 352, 388, 404, 421, 449, 466, 468, 471, 472, 476, 478, 483, 485, 505, 506, 509, 510, 517, 520, 521, 523, 532, 547, 549, 552, 555, 556, 558, 561, 564, 565, 567, 571, 572, 596, 597, 599, 601, 604, 605, 607, 609, 612, 615*

Brady Handgun Violence Prevention Act, The, *113, 430, 471*
Brady, Ian, *146, 476*
Branden, Nathaniel, *125*
Brennan, Claire, *268*
Brezhnev, Leonid, *492*
Brit Awards, The, *21*
Britain, *7, 21, 24, 25, 27, 29, 30, 40, 43, 44, 74, 84, 101, 108, 109, 112, 115, 126, 130, 140, 146, 157, 158, 161, 171, 181, 184, 186, 187, 193, 222, 241, 367, 399, 407, 415, 430, 453, 460, 471, 534, 536, 538, 540, 542, 543*
British National Party, *161*
British Sea Power, *612*
Britpop, *37, 40, 64, 117, 158, 349, 370, 430, 534*
Britt, Brian, *456, 481*
Britton, Amy, *404*
Britzman, Deborah, *468, 471, 472, 474, 476, 478, 481, 483, 496, 520, 591*
Brontë, Emily, *238*
Brooks, Mel, *403*
Bruce, Lenny, *101, 112*
Bukowski, Charles, *229, 365*
Bulgakov, Mikhail, *370*
Bulger, James, *140*
Burgess, Anthony, *315, 317*
Burn, Gordon, *367*
Burroughs, William S., *19, 53, 98, 109, 229, 277, 334, 365*
Bush, George W., *408*
Bush, Kate, *238*
Butler, Octavia, *351*
Buzzcocks, *572*
Byron, George Gordon, *346*

C

Cabaret Voltaire, *460, 604*
Cairns, Andy, See Therapy? Cameron, Keith, *403, 517*

Camus, Albert, *140, 236, 359, 365, 492, 580, 597*
Cardiff, *24, 25, 44, 49, 549*
  Millennium Stadium, *24, 25*
Carter, Angela, *407*
Céline, Louis-Ferdinand, *348, 371*
Chapman, Dinos and Jake, *260*
Chatterton, Thomas, *348*
Chemical Brothers, The, *604*
Chilcot, John, *430*
Childhood, *10, 84, 96, 98, 106, 125, 140, 171, 174, 191, 227, 239, 266, 275, 304, 327, 329, 349, 351, 381, 407, 452, 466, 468, 499, 527, 530, 543, 588*
Childish, Billy, *370*
Chomsky, Noam, *572*
Christie, Agatha, *352*
Churchill, Winston, *157, 158*
Clash, The, *40, 46, 68, 76, 85, 102, 109, 241, 341, 364*
Clinton, Bill, *64, 104, 115, 136*
Clock DVA, *460*
Cobain, Kurt, *14, 48, 56, 58, 66, 84, 222, 238, 332, 334, 348, 349, 373, 386, 425, 426*
  See also Nirvana,
Cold War, *37, 136, 155, 271*
Colt, Sam, *471*
Communism, *37, 63, 74, 106, 108, 117, 119, 120, 123, 161, 163, 164, 492*
Conrad, Joseph, *348*
Conservative Party, The, *21, 24, 84, 112, 113, 115, 117, 119, 120, 123, 125, 126, 128, 130, 367*
Cool Britannia, *25, 130, 430*
  See also Britpop,
Cope, Julian, *370*
Cort, Lorna, *34*
Costa-Gavras, Constantin, *290*
Courtenay, Tom, *418*
Cows, *227*
Crawford, Anwen, *10, 61, 202*

Cronenberg, David, *391, 393*
Cruickshank, Ruth, *555*
Cummins, Kevin, *46, 51, 197, 609*
Curtis, Ian, *55, 348, 373*

D

Dachau, *155, 293*
  See also Holocaust,
Dahmer, Jeffrey, *140, 142, 143, 146, 158, 476*
Daiches, David, *249, 250, 253, 255*
Daily Mail, The, *140, 142*
Daily Mirror, The, *14*
Damiens, Robert-François, *295, 297*
Darwin, Charles, *408*
Day, Gail, *492*
de Man, Paul, *474, 476, 478, 487, 489, 492*
Dean, James, *81, 450*
Death In June, *284, 285*
Deller, Jeremy, *27, 70, 73, 238, 239, 453, 590*
Depression, *186, 205, 238, 245, 265, 266, 268, 271, 272, 289, 340, 341, 367, 376*
Derrida, Jacques, *461, 463, 483, 487, 496, 502, 506, 516, 517, 527, 543, 546, 555, 561, 564, 573, 583, 588, 590*
Devo, *487*
Dialogues with Solzhenitsyn, The, *577*
Diana, Princess of Wales, *58, 187*
DiCaprio, Leonardo, *352*
Dick, Philip K., *351*
Didion, Joan, *346*
Die Brücke, *596*
Difficult knowledge, *453, 456, 457, 460, 461, 463, 466, 468, 471, 472, 474, 476, 478, 481, 483, 485, 487, 489, 492, 495, 496, 499, 500, 502, 505, 506, 509, 510, 512, 513, 516, 517, 520, 521, 523, 527, 530, 532, 534, 536, 538, 540, 542, 543, 546, 547, 549, 552,*

555, 556, 558, 561, 564, 565, 567, 571, 572, 573, 575, 577, 580, 582, 583, 584, 587, 588, 590, 591, 594, 596, 597, 599

Disraeli, Benjamin, *96*

Dostoevsky, Fyodor, *174, 371*

Drummond, Bill, *565*

Dresser, The, *418, 419, 421*

Drowned in Sound, *346*

Dunst, Kirsten, *341*

Durutti Column, The, *460*

Dworkin, Andrea, *365*

E

Eastern Bloc, *460*

Easton Ellis, Bret, *143, 365, 370*

Echo & the Bunnymen, *597, 604*

Edwards, Richey, *4, 14, 36, 37, 39, 40, 43, 44, 46, 48, 49, 51, 53, 55, 56, 58, 61, 63, 64, 66, 73, 80, 81, 87, 89, 90, 93, 95,* *96, 98, 101, 102, 104, 113, 120, 123, 125, 126, 128, 130, 132, 134, 136, 138, 140, 148, 161, 166, 168, 171, 172, 174, 176, 178, 179, 181, 184, 186, 187, 189, 191, 193, 195, 197, 199, 202, 203, 205, 207, 231, 236, 238, 249, 255, 268, 275, 277, 293, 300, 308, 324, 329, 334, 343, 346, 348, 349, 351, 352, 354, 355, 357, 359, 362, 364, 365, 367, 370, 371, 373, 376, 377, 381, 383, 384, 386, 388, 393, 411, 415, 430, 449, 456, 471, 505, 510, 512, 513, 516, 517, 523, 527, 530, 532, 534, 536, 538, 540, 542, 543, 546, 547, 549, 552, 555, 556, 558, 561, 564, 565, 567, 571, 572, 573, 575, 577, 580, 582, 583, 584, 590, 591, 594, 596, 605, 607, 609*

disappearance of, *49, 56, 61, 66, 89, 231, 354, 357, 373, 381, 384, 386, 430, 449, 452, 512, 513, 516, 517, 527, 530, 532, 534, 536, 542, 543, 552, 561, 591*

Eichmann, Adolf, *151*

Einstürzende Neubauten, *461*
Eliot, T.S., *236, 249, 250, 253, 255, 348, 349, 354, 404, 419, 421*
Ellen, Barbara, *171, 512*
Ellington, Duke, *108, 128*
Ellmann, Maud, *499, 500*
Eugenides, Jeffrey, *70*
Everything But the Girl, *516*
Ewing, Tom, *4*

F
Fabulous, *199*
Falwell, Jerry, *407*
Farm, The, *199*
Fascism, *36, 37, 74, 136, 148, 150, 157, 158, 161, 163, 164, 271, 275, 279, 281, 284, 285, 289, 290, 291, 293, 295, 297, 299, 300, 399, 457, 487, 489, 492, 580*

Felman, Shoshana, *468, 481, 492, 510, 512, 540, 567, 580, 597*
Femininity, *53, 55, 56, 58, 61, 174, 176, 178, 179, 181, 184, 186, 187, 189, 191, 193, 195, 197, 199, 202, 203, 205, 207, 281, 284, 312, 315, 317, 319, 322, 323, 324, 327, 335, 351, 388, 391, 393, 396, 472, 495*
Feminism, *61, 63, 64, 138, 140, 142, 178, 179, 312, 365, 407*
Finney, Albert, *418, 468*
Fitzgerald, F. Scott, *348*
Flaubert, Gustave, *348*
Foo Fighters, *426*
Food, *84, 125, 181, 186, 495, 496, 499, 500, 502, 505, 506, 582*
Ford, Henry, *157*
foreverdelayed.org.uk, *218*
Foster, Hal, *492*

Foucault, Michel, *140, 142, 241, 289, 290, 291, 293, 295, 297, 299, 300, 307, 337*
Francisco, Franco, *290*
Franklin, Aretha, *516*
freakytrigger.co.uk, *4*
Freud, Sigmund, *398, 463, 561*
Friends, *558*

G

Gadda, Carlo Emilio, *348*
Gang of Four, *40, 241, 460*
Gallagher, Liam, *236* See also Oasis,
Gallagher, Noel, *19* See also Oasis,
Garfield, Leon, *227*
Gaston, Sean, *540, 542, 543, 583, 590*
Genet, Jean, *148, 370, 371*
Gillen, Kieron, *453, 534, 542*
Gilroy, Paul, *112, 415*
Ginsberg, Allen, *55, 348, 412*
Glam, *178, 195, 197, 199, 202, 203, 238, 241, 281, 391*
Glamour, *81, 84, 85, 148, 195, 197, 199, 202, 203, 315, 335, 450*
Glassjaw, *308*
Glastonbury, *49, 552*
Gloeckner, Phoebe, *393*
GLR (Greater London Radio), *16*
Goa, *352*
Goebbels, Joseph, *18*
Gorbachev, Mikhail, *492*
Gore, Tipper, *106, 130, 403, 471*
Gore, Vidal, *106*
Gothic, *53, 55, 56, 58, 61, 76, 78, 80, 81, 96, 150, 281, 334*
Grauzone, *604*
Gray, John, *396*
Gubar, Susan, *487*
Guns, *37, 109, 112, 113, 281, 471*

Guns N' Roses, *102, 293, 364, 415*

H

Haines, Luke, *370, 534*
Hall, Philip, *357, 530*
Hamlet, *346, 359*
Hamsun, Knut, *348, 359, 370, 371*
Hanoi Rocks, *364*
Happy Mondays, The, *199, 236, 408*
Harvey, Marcus, *146, 148*
Harwood, Ronald, *418*
Haunting, *53, 166, 271, 312, 343, 346, 348, 349, 351, 415, 426, 453, 463, 495, 527, 530, 547, 555, 573, 597*
Hawking, Stephen, *260, 404, 572, 584*
Hedges, Mike, *516*
Hegarty, Antony,
 See also Anohni, and Antony and the Johnsons,
Hegel, Georg Wilhelm Friedrich, *418, 573*
Hemingway, Ernest, *348*
Hepburn, Kathryn, *197*
Hesse, Hermann, *18*
Hewitt, Kim, *456*
Hindley, Myra, *140, 142, 143, 146, 148, 297, 476*
 See also Brady, Ian,
Hiroshima Peace Memorial Museum, *155*
Hirst, Damien, *334, 335*
Hitler, Adolf, *136, 157, 285, 291, 293, 295, 391, 485, 609*
Hoban, Russell, *412*
Hoggart, Richard, *108, 212, 239*
Hole, *43, 56, 58, 61*
 See also Love, Courtney,
Holocaust, *36, 146, 148, 150, 151, 153, 155, 157, 158, 161, 163, 164, 231, 259, 260,*

262, 265, 266, 268, 271, 272, 274, 275, 277, 279, 281, 284, 285, 411, 415, 468, 471, 487, 510, 512, 599
Horthy, Miklós, *136, 164, 255*
Hoss, Nina, *605*
Houellebecq, Michel, *351*
Howard, Rowland S., *461*
Howe, Geoffrey, *112*
Humour, *229, 239, 364, 398, 403, 404, 583, 584, 587, 588, 590, 605*
Hunter, Ian, *370*
Hurt, John, *174, 352*
Huyssen, Andreas, *446, 449, 450, 452, 453, 456, 457*

I

Idle, Eric, *403*
Ikeda, Mitch, *609*
Ingres, Jean-Auguste-Dominique, *575*
Innocence, *73, 96, 136, 138, 140, 232, 239, 262, 304, 322, 452, 468, 527*

IRA (Irish Republican Army), *16*
Ireland, *245*
Ireland, Colin, *476*
Irony, *21, 64, 119, 151, 246, 249, 275, 277, 279, 289, 381, 384, 396, 400, 412, 449, 468, 471, 472, 474, 476, 487, 489, 492, 517, 523, 532, 547, 612*
ISIS (Islamic State of Iraq and Syria), *300*
Israel, *275*
Ivor Novello Award, *343*

J

Jazz, *108, 460*
Jeffery, Ben, *340*
Johnson, Andy, *281*
Jokes, *58, 205, 255, 349, 377, 383, 398, 399, 403, 404, 583, 584, 587, 588, 590*
Jones, Emily, *30*
Jordan, Berry, *25, 202*
Jovanovic, Rob, *354*
Joy Division, *232, 238, 239, 241, 259, 408, 461, 487, 604*

Joy, Eileen, *383*
Joyce, James, *245, 246, 348*

K

Kaeff, Scot, *34*
Kant, Immanuel, *246, 502*
Kaysen, Susanna, *187*
Keats, John, *346*
Keenan, Maynard James, *229, 304*
Kelman, James, *128, 130*
Kenickie, *178, 203*
Kennedy, John F., *572*
Kerouac, Jack, *348*
Kerrang!, *46, 63, 362*
Khrushchev, Nikita, *492*
Kiefer, Anselm, *599, 601, 612*
Killing Joke, *241, 604*
King, Richard, *80*
King, Rodney, *113*
King, Stephen, *377*
Kippenberger, Martin, *492, 584, 587, 588*
KLF, The, *565*
Korn, *236*
Kraftwerk, *604*
Kristeva, Julia, *495, 496, 499, 500, 502, 521*
Kulkarni, Neil, *112, 113*
Kundera, Milan, *157*

L

Labour Party, The, *16, 21, 119, 163*
Lacan, Jacques, *584*
Laibach, *277, 279*
Lamacq, Steve, *505*
Laub, Dori, *468, 481, 492, 512, 540, 567, 580, 597*
Lawnmower Man, The, *337*
Le Pen, Jean-Marie, *142, 476*
Leader, Darian, *532, 584, 587*
Led Zeppelin, *238*
Leigh, Mike, *232*
Lenin, Vladimir, *492*
Lennon, John, *291, 425*
Letwin, Oliver, *112*

Levi, Primo, *231, 236, 239, 262, 384, 411, 412*
Levin, Ira, *227*
Lewis, C.S., *236*
Limp Bizkit, *308*
London, *14, 24, 25, 27, 29, 70, 112, 337, 357, 365, 376, 377, 512, 558, 599, 601, 609*
  O2 Arena, *594*
  Camden Stables Market, *604*
  London Astoria, *512*
  Millennium Dome, *24*
  The Roundhouse, *558, 599, 601*
  The Royal Academy of Arts, *599*
Lords, Traci, *176, 178, 179*
Los Angeles, *16, 113*
Love, Courtney, *56, 58, 178, 203*
  See also Hole,
Lunenfeld, Peter, *587*
Luther, Martin, *412*
Lyngstad, Sverre, *370*
Lynskey, Dorian, *291, 293, 485, 542, 543, 546, 547*

M

Macey, David, *289, 290, 291*
Machinist, The, *346, 556*
Mackay, Emily, *558, 615*
Maconie, Stuart, *161, 195, 274, 520, 530, 532, 542, 556*
Madonna, *58*
Magazine, *40, 120, 241, 461, 604*
Mailer, Norman, *85, 106, 227, 231, 343, 367, 474, 513*
Major, John, *21*
Malraux, André, *290*
Manchester, *19, 408*
Manic Street Preachers '4-REAL', *58, 87, 505*
  Everything Must Go, *176, 197, 349, 425, 426, 446, 452, 516, 517, 520, 521, 523, 527, 530, 532, 534,*

536, 538, 540, 542, 543, 546, 547, 549, 552, 555, 556, 572

'A Design for Life', *21, 61, 63, 68, 95, 246, 426, 427, 521, 523, 530, 546, 599, 607, 612*

'Australia', *523, 530*

'Elvis Impersonator: Blackpool Promenade', *527*

'Everything Must Go', *516, 521, 523, 530*

'Further Away', *527*

'The Girl Who Wanted to Be God', *530*

'Interiors (Song for Willem De Kooning)', *523*

'Kevin Carter', *530, 540*

'No Surface All Feeling', *527*

'Removables', *426, 530, 572*

'Small Black Flowers That Grow in the Sky', *530, 572, 577, 615*

Futurology, *594, 596, 597, 599, 601, 604, 605, 607, 609*

'Anthem for a Lost Cause', *607*

'Divine Youth', *607*

'Dreaming a City (Hughesovka)', *605*

'Europa Geht Durch Mich', *605*

'Misguided Missile', *596*

'Walk Me to the Bridge', *352, 596, 597, 609*

Generation Terrorists, *39, 40, 43, 44, 81, 178, 357, 386, 446, 582, 596, 604*

'Little Baby Nothing', *55, 176*

'Motorcycle Emptiness', 530, 538, 605
'You Love Us', 68, 202, 609, 615
Gold Against the Soul, 13, 40, 43, 44, 46, 176, 241, 262, 453, 463
 'La Tristesse Durera (Scream to a Sigh)', 419
 'Life Becoming a Landslide', 176, 452, 468
 'Roses in the Hospital', 128, 453
God Save the Manics, 573
 'Picturesque', 573
Holy Bible, The,
'4st 7lb', 37, 49, 55, 61, 73, 115, 153, 166, 168, 171, 172, 174, 176, 178, 179, 181, 184, 186, 187, 189, 281, 312, 327, 388, 391, 415, 425, 466, 468, 471, 472, 474, 492, 495, 496, 499, 500, 502, 505, 575
 'Archives of Pain', 34, 113, 115, 120, 123, 132, 138, 140, 142, 143, 146, 148, 150, 151, 164, 281, 297, 299, 300, 303, 304, 307, 412, 466, 476, 485, 487, 609
artwork, 63, 238, 415, 492
See also Saville, Jenny,
'Die in the Summertime', 34, 49, 70, 73, 84, 90, 93, 95, 96, 98, 153, 168, 174, 284, 329, 381, 384, 466, 505, 506, 530, 575, 577
'Faster', 16, 18, 37, 48, 55, 61, 70, 81, 84, 85, 87, 89, 90, 93, 95, 96, 98, 120, 148, 168, 174, 184, 186, 225, 227, 229, 284, 343, 367, 400, 403, 404, 457, 471, 472, 474, 485, 487, 489, 492, 495, 496, 499, 500, 502, 505, 534, 604, 612
'The Intense Humming of Evil', 34, 132, 148, 150, 151, 153, 161, 163,

259, 260, 262, 274, 461, 468, 485, 487, 489, 492, 495, 496, 499, 572

'Mausoleum', 132, 148, 150, 151, 153, 155, 161, 163, 164, 239, 259, 262, 274, 284, 415, 466, 476, 495, 496, 505, 510, 605

'Of Walking Abortion', 63, 132, 134, 136, 138, 146, 148, 163, 164, 172, 275, 290, 291, 293, 303, 329, 485, 571, 575

'P.C.P.', 19, 36, 61, 85, 95, 101, 120, 123, 125, 126, 128, 130, 176, 404, 419, 468, 487, 495, 499, 505, 575, 594

'Revol', 19, 36, 101, 115, 117, 120, 138, 140, 151, 398, 403, 492, 530

'She Is Suffering', 96, 138, 140, 142, 166, 174, 179, 181, 312, 388, 466, 483, 485, 487, 489, 492, 505

'This Is Yesterday', 36, 70, 90, 95, 96, 98, 115, 174, 419, 466

'Yes', 89, 109, 132, 134, 166, 168, 171, 172, 174, 176, 178, 179, 181, 281, 312, 324, 386, 388, 391, 481, 485, 487, 489, 492, 495, 505, 506, 530, 577

Journal for Plague Lovers, 184, 393, 404, 426, 452, 555, 556, 558, 561, 564, 565, 567, 571, 572, 573, 575, 577, 580, 582, 583, 584, 587, 588, 590, 591, 594, 596, 597, 599, 601, 604, 605, 607, 609, 612, 615

'All is Vanity', 573, 582

'Bag Lady', 572

'Doors Closing Slowly', *572, 573, 575, 582, 588*

'Facing Page: Top Left', *565, 572, 580*

'Jackie Collins Existential Question Time', *572, 584*

'Marlon J.D.', *582*

'Me and Stephen Hawking', *404, 572, 584*

'Peeled Apples', *572, 575, 582*

'Pretension/Repulsion', *575, 580, 582*

'She Bathed Herself in a Bath of Bleach', *572, 575*

'This Joke Sport Severed', *404, 564, 575, 582, 583*

'Virginia State Epileptic Colony', *575, 577, 582*

'William's Last Words', *572*

Know Your Enemy, *76, 546, 597*

Lifeblood, *547, 549, 552, 561, 573, 615*

'Cardiff Afterlife', *549*

'Emily', *547*

Lipstick Traces, *453, 582, 590*

'4 Ever Delayed', *453*

'Judge Yr'self', *582, 583*

National Treasures, *594*

Postcards from a Young Man, *349, 594*

Rewind the Film, *95, 126, 594*

'30-Year War', *158*

'This Sullen Welsh Heart', *615*

Send Away the Tigers, *426, 552, 556, 561, 594, 604*
  'Indian Summer', *552*
  'Your Love Alone', *552*
Shadows & Words, *556, 565, 572*
This Is My Truth, Tell Me Yours, *126, 543, 546*
  'If You Tolerate This, Your Children Will Be Next', *543*
  'Tsunami', *543*
manics.nl, *349*
Mankowski, Guy, *299, 357*
Manson, Charles, *106, 140*
Manson, Marilyn, *335*
Marcus, Greil, *590*
Marks, Howard, *357*
Martin, Dan, *597*
Marx, Karl, *93, 95, 112, 120*
Masculinity, *55, 56, 58, 138, 140, 142, 143, 146, 195, 197, 250, 281, 284, 308, 312, 315, 317, 319, 322, 323, 324, 335, 348, 351, 367, 371, 384, 386, 388, 391, 404, 425*
Massive Attack, *430*
Mauriac, Claude, *290*
McAlmont & Butler, *516*
McCarthy, Cormac, *229, 322, 370*
McCarthy, Joseph, *271*
McCartney, Paul, *419*
McCormick, Rebecca, *207*
McEwan, Ian, *229*
McInerney, Jay, *359*
McKelvie, James, *453, 534, 536, 538, 540, 542*
Meagher, Michelle, *500, 502*
Melancholia, *95, 426, 430, 546, 561, 596*
Melancholia (von Trier), *340, 341*
Melody Maker, *14, 49, 66, 112, 191, 205, 222*

Melvins, 222
Memory, 157, 161, 249, 250, 268, 443, 446, 449, 450, 452, 453, 456, 457, 460, 461, 463, 466, 468, 487, 489, 492, 509, 510, 512, 513, 516, 517, 520, 521, 523, 527, 530, 532, 534, 536, 538, 540, 542, 543, 546, 547, 549, 552, 555, 556, 558, 561, 564, 565, 567, 571, 572, 573, 594, 596, 597, 599, 601
Mencken, H.L., 101
Mensa, 85, 227, 343, 474, 513
Meštrović, Stjepan G., 163, 164
Middles, Mick, 236, 246, 291, 430
Miller, Henry, 85, 106, 227, 239, 343, 348, 365, 367, 381, 474, 513
Milošević, Slobodan, 142, 476, 485
Milton, John, 412
Milton Keynes, 43
Miners' Strike, 7, 8, 128
Ministry, 279
Minogue, Kylie, 176, 178, 179, 195, 197
Mirbeau, Octave, 150, 151, 241, 307, 308, 312, 400
Mishima, Yukio, 284, 348, 354, 359, 365, 370, 373, 381, 383, 384
Moers, Ellen, 53
Monroe, Alexei, 279
Monroe, Marilyn, 81, 450
Montand, Yves, 290
Monty Python's Life of Brian, 403
Moore, Sean, 18, 40, 104, 134, 352, 523, 604, 615
Morens, David M., 166
Morissette, Alanis, 187
Morley, Paul, 408
Morrissey, 364
Morrison, Jim, 348
Moss, Kate, 178
Mourning, 58, 95, 155, 222, 274, 523, 543, 546, 555, 556, 558, 561, 564, 565, 567, 571, 572, 573, 575, 577, 580,

582, 583, 584, 587, 588, 590, 591, 594, 596
Murder, *37, 68, 106, 132, 134, 136, 138, 140, 142, 143, 146, 148, 150, 151, 153, 155, 297, 299, 300, 303, 304, 307, 308, 327, 334, 335, 337, 399, 430, 474, 476*
  See also serial killers,
Myers, Ben, *348, 357, 359, 362, 364, 365, 367, 370, 371, 373, 376, 377*

N
Nabokov, Vladimir, *246*
Naked, *232*
Nazism, *146, 155, 157, 158, 161, 163, 164, 259, 260, 262, 265, 266, 268, 271, 272, 274, 275, 277, 279, 281, 284, 285, 289, 290, 291, 293, 295, 419, 580*
Neu, *604*
New Order, *232*
New York Dolls, The, *199*

NHS (National Health Service), *125*
Nick Cave and the Bad Seeds, *577*
Nietzsche, Friedrich, *93, 95, 148, 236, 408, 487, 582, 583*
Nilsen, Dennis, *476*
9/11,, *66, 136*
Nine Inch Nails, *222, 229, 236, 281, 308, 426*
Nirvana, *14, 43, 222, 236, 426*
  See also Cobain, Kurt,
Nitsch, Hermann, *334, 335*
NME (New Musical Express), *14, 48, 56, 171, 222, 547, 552, 615*
Nostalgia, *73, 74, 76, 430, 450, 452, 453, 478, 534, 547*
Nuttall, Jeff, *98, 155*

O
Oasis, *24*
Obama, Barack, *430*
Oberg, Arthur, *268*
Oedipus, *346*

Ogata, Ken, *383*
Orchestral Manoeuvres in the Dark, *604*
Orton, Joe, *348, 365*
Orwell, George, *18, 117, 120, 132, 236, 335, 351*
Outhwaite, Paul, *357*
Owens, Craig, *474, 492, 573*
Øresund Bridge, *352, 596*

P

Paglia, Camille, *365*
Pankhurst, Emeline, *547*
Parker, Dorothy, *197*
Parkes, Taylor, *49, 205, 259*
Patience, Mark, *18*
Peace, David, *370*
Pearce, Douglas See Death in June
Pearl Jam, *332*
Pere Ubu, *460*
Pessoa, Fernando, *245*
Petrarch, *346*
Picasso, Pablo, *51*
Pickles, James, *142, 476*
Pinter, Harold, *227, 229, 232, 367, 474*
Pitt, Alice, *468, 471, 472, 474, 476, 478, 481, 483, 496, 591*
Pitt, Brad, *359*
Phonogram: Rue Britannia, *453, 534, 536, 538, 540, 542*
Pixies, The, *43*
Placebo, *222*
Plath, Sylvia, *55, 90, 227, 229, 231, 238, 265, 266, 268, 271, 272, 274, 308, 365, 367, 370, 371, 373, 399, 474, 530*
PMRC (Parents Music Resource Center), *106, 108, 130, 174*
  See also Gore, Tipper,
Political correctness, *37, 120, 123, 125, 126, 176, 487, 502, 505*
Politics Pop Art, *450*
Pop, Iggy, *51, 364*
Porter, Gillian, *308*

Post-Punk, *40, 43, 58, 241, 289, 357, 446, 460, 461, 487, 516, 571, 572, 596, 604*
Pound, Ezra, *348, 430*
Power, Nina, *166*
Price, Simon, *51, 289, 300, 352, 370, 388, 452, 456, 461, 513, 596, 607, 612*
Producers, The, *403*
Prosser, Jay, *506*
Prostitution, *37, 55, 166, 172, 176, 312, 324, 327, 391, 408, 449, 485, 489, 505, 530*
Prozac, *125, 187, 468*
Public Enemy, *102, 109, 277, 364, 415, 450*
Public Image Ltd., *40, 241, 461, 604*
Pulitzer Prize, *108, 128, 343, 530*
Punk, *40, 43, 58, 74, 80, 238, 241, 259, 289, 460, 461*

Q
Q, *63, 274, 352, 546*

R
Radiohead, *430*
Ramones, The, *259*
Rand, Ayn, *125*

Reading Festival, *49, 532*
Reagan, Ronald, *64, 104, 143, 398, 407*
Rechy, John, *370*
Reed, S. Alexander, *279, 281*
Reni, Guido, *381*
RE/Search, *393, 400*
Reynolds, Simon, *460, 487*
Reznor, Trent, *229, 281, 303, 304, 334, 346*
   See also Nine Inch Nails,
Ribisi, Giovanni, *588*
richeyedwards.net, *218*
Richter, Gerhard, *561, 564, 573*
Right Said Fred, *199*
Rimbaud, Arthur, *55, 348, 601*
Riots, *16, 108, 112, 113, 126*
   Los Angeles riots, *16, 113*
   Tonypandy riots, *158*
Riot Grrl, *58, 178*

Robb, John, *370*
Romanticism Rose, Gillian, *259, 274, 275*
Roth, Tim, *349*
Ruth, Georgia, *607*

S

See also Antony and the Johnsons
Al-Turabi, Hassan, *300*
Sachs, Tom, *157*
Sade, Marquis de, *146, 334*
Sarajevo, *262*
Sartre, Jean-Paul, *290, 359, 370, 580*
Sass, Louis A., *512, 513, 520, 527, 546, 561*
Savage, Jon, *70, 78, 85, 115, 158, 191*
Saville, Jenny, *189, 241, 335, 388, 396, 446, 492, 500, 502, 505, 555, 583*
Scargill, Arthur, *128*
Schrader, Paul, *383*
Schizophrenia, *513, 516, 517, 520, 521, 523, 527, 530, 538, 546, 561, 588, 597*
Scott, Walter, *58*
Scritti Politti, *460, 516*
Selby, Hubert Jr., *134, 136, 138, 229, 315, 317, 319, 322, 323, 324, 327, 329, 571*
Select, *199*
Self, Will, *349, 412*
Self-harm, *39, 48, 49, 51, 53, 55, 56, 58, 61, 63, 64, 66, 68, 87, 98, 126, 168, 186, 187, 189, 191, 193, 341, 449, 474, 495, 496, 499, 500, 502, 505, 506, 509, 510, 512, 513*
Serial killers, *143, 146, 239, 245, 299, 322, 334, 335, 337, 449, 476*
Sex Pistols, The, *150, 259, 408, 584*
Shakespeare, William, *126, 418, 419, 468, 499, 555*
Shaw, William, *517*
Sheen, Michael, *453*
Shelley, Percy Bysshe, *96, 346*
Shining, The, *558*
Simple Minds, *460, 604, 605*

Siouxsie and the Banshees, *604*
Sisters of Mercy, The, *53*
Situationism, *64, 123, 398*
Skin, *14, 18, 89, 166, 225, 349, 412, 466, 505, 506, 509, 530, 555, 575, 577, 580, 582, 583*
Smash Hits, *13, 73*
Smith, David, *146*
See also Brady, Ian
Smith, Richard, *40, 81, 199*
Smiths, The, *362, 371*
Sokurov, Alexander, *577*
Solanas, Valerie, *138, 250, 312, 357, 386, 388, 391, 403*
Solheim, Kasper, *207*
Solzhenitsyn, Alexander, *370*
Sontag, Susan, *540, 555*
Sorrows of Young Werther, The, *348*
Sotos, Peter, *299, 300*
Sound, The, *604*
Spanish Civil War, *161, 543*
Spillane, Mickey, *108, 109*
Stone Temple Pilots, *222*
Street, Adrian, *195*
Strummer, Joe, *109*
See also Clash, The
Stalin, Joseph, *119, 492*
Strategy (South Face/Front Face/North Face), *189, 335, 337, 396, 415, 446, 492, 500*
    See also Saville, Jenny,
Suede, *40, 199, 222, 371, 512*
Suicide, *14, 48, 49, 66, 70, 84, 231, 266, 271, 274, 300, 354, 373, 381, 383, 384, 386, 452, 530, 536*
Sun, The, *299*
Super Furry Animals, *7*
Sutcliffe, Peter, *142, 143, 312, 476*

Suzuki, Damo, *612*
Svevo, Italo, *348*
Swartz, Aaron, *383*

T
Take That, *222*
Tanizaki, Jun'ichirō, *359, 370*
Taxi Driver, *109*
Temporality, *474, 476, 478, 481, 496, 527*
Terre'Blanche, Eugène, *476*
Testimony, *468, 509, 510, 540, 583*
Thailand, *48, 171, 505, 512*
Thatcher, Margaret, *7, 64, 104, 112, 357*
Therapy?, *146, 236, 245, 246, 609*
Third Man, The, *303, 304*
thisisyesterday.com, *218*
Thomas, Dylan, *370*
Thomas, R.S., *370*
Thomson, Ian, *384*

Throbbing Gristle, *232, 241, 277, 284, 289, 461, 487*
Tiso, Jozef, *136*
Tocqueville, Alexis de, *407*
Tolkien, J.R.R., *238*
Tool, *43, 222, 229, 236, 304*
Toploader, *427*
Top of the Pops, *16, 29, 191*
Toronto: Danforth Music Hall, *599, 612, 615*
Tosches, Nick, *367*
Tower Records, *426*
Tozzi, Federigo, *348*
Trade Union Congress, *157*
Trainspotting, *84, 85*
Trauma, *98, 268, 271, 275, 446, 468, 481, 483, 485, 487, 496, 499, 500, 502, 505, 506, 509, 517, 520, 521, 523, 527, 542, 543, 546, 547, 549, 552*
Trier, Lars von, *340*
Trump, Donald, *430*

U
Ueda, Yoshinori, *476*

United States of America, *46, 78, 101, 102, 104, 106, 108, 109, 112, 113, 130, 132, 134, 271, 359, 365, 407, 408, 427, 430, 471, 575*

Union of Soviet Socialist Republics, *63, 74, 117, 119, 123*

V

Vidal, Gore, *106*
Videomusic, *225*
Virgin Suicides, The, *70, 184, 346, 588*
Virilio, Paul, *341*
Vonnegut, Mark, *370*

W

Wagner, Richard, *450*
Wales, *4, 7, 8, 10, 13, 14, 16, 18, 19, 21, 24, 25, 39, 80, 113, 123, 125, 126, 161, 189, 271, 357, 359, 453, 536, 543, 546, 615*
    Rhondda, *158*
    Severn Bridge, *334, 536, 596*
See also Blackwood, Cardiff,

Walker, Scott, *461, 604*
Warhol, Andy, *138*
Watkins-Isnardi, Jenny, *357*
Wells, Steven, *10*
Welsh, Irvine, *84*
West Side Story, *104, 471*
Wham!, *607*
Wharton, William, *238*
Whiteread, Rachel, *449*
Wilde, Oscar, *115*
Wildhearts, The, *425*
Wilkinson, Yan, *612*
Williams, Gregory, *587*
Williams, Robbie, *430*
Wire, *241, 461, 604*
Wire, Nicky, *4, 18, 21, 36, 37, 39, 40, 43, 44, 46, 48, 49, 63, 64, 87, 90, 93, 95, 119, 120, 128, 142, 143, 146, 148, 157, 178, 186, 195, 197, 199, 202, 203, 205, 236, 238, 255, 293, 343, 346, 348, 349, 351, 352, 354, 355, 357, 388, 512, 521, 527, 530, 532, 542, 543, 546,*

552, 564, 565, 567, 571, 572, 591, 594, 596, 597, 599, 601, 604, 605, 607, 609, 612, 615
   Death of a Polaroid, *609*
Witnessing, *163, 238, 291, 304, 449, 456, 468, 481, 487, 495, 505, 506, 509, 510, 512, 527, 530, 532, 534, 536, 538, 540, 542, 543, 546, 547, 549, 561, 567, 577, 580, 582, 583, 584, 587, 588, 590, 591, 594, 596, 597, 612, 615*
Wittig, Monique, *386, 388*
Woolworths, *4, 16, 191*
Working class, *4, 7, 8, 21, 37, 44, 64, 73, 108, 109, 112, 128, 130, 161, 197, 203, 239, 246, 250, 404, 453, 471, 521*
World War II, *153, 155, 303, 418, 471*
Wurtzel, Elizabeth, *187*

X
X, Malcolm, *112, 136*

Y
Yeats, William Butler, *85, 174*
Yeltsin, Boris, *117, 476, 492*
Young, James E., *268*
Young, Neil, *84, 373*
Youth, *40, 55, 70, 78, 80, 96, 108, 184, 186, 187, 189, 239, 250, 329, 341, 421, 452, 466, 472, 527*
Yugoslavia, *16, 153, 164*

Z
Zapruder, Abraham, *400, 572*
Zhirinovsky, Vladimir, *476*
Zola, Émile, *365*

www.ingramcontent.com/pod-product-compliance
Lightning Source LLC
Chambersburg PA
CBHW010717300426
44114CB00022B/2881